AVATAR AND INCARNATION

by the same author

WORSHIP IN THE WORLD'S RELIGIONS

WITCHCRAFT: European and African

UPANISHADS, GĪTĀ AND BIBLE:
A Comparative Study of Hindu and Christian Scriptures

JESUS IN THE QUR'ĀN

AVATAR AND INCARNATION

The Wilde Lectures in Natural and
Comparative Religion in the
University of Oxford

by
GEOFFREY PARRINDER

FABER AND FABER
LONDON

First published in 1970
by Faber and Faber Limited
24 Russell Square London WC1
Printed in Great Britain by
Western Printing Services Ltd Bristol

SBN: 571 09319 1

Preface

The appointment to deliver the Wilde Lectures in Natural and Comparative Religion in the University of Oxford provided an opportunity for intensive reading and research upon a subject that had long interested me. Very little critical study had been undertaken previously of the Avatar beliefs of India, and comparison that is commonly made between them and Christian doctrines of the Incarnation is based upon weak foundations. The source literature is immense, in Indian and Christian scriptures and commentaries, and nobody could hope to read it all. I have discussed some of the principal texts, outlined the main features of beliefs, and examined the possibilities of fair comparisons not only between Hinduism and Christianity but also between other religions which have comparable elements of this kind.

The Sanskrit word *avatāra* has entered English usage and dictionaries as Avatar, and the English form is used in this book for the convenience of general readers. Most Sanskrit, Pāli and Arabic words quoted have been put in their Latinized forms in brackets, but diacritical marks have been omitted altogether in common names such as Vishnu, Krishna, Rig Veda, Muhammad and Islam, and dots have also been omitted in words such as Śankara, Purāna and Sūfī according to modern practice.

I am indebted to many scholars, but some must be mentioned with special gratitude. Professor E. O. James has been for many years a kindly helper and guide, and Professor R. C. Zaehner was constantly generous with hospitality, as were also Professor H. Chadwick and Dr. I. Ramsey, the Bishop of Durham. My colleague Professor M. F. Wiles read through one chapter, and parts of others were used for addresses which were followed by valuable discussions at the London Society for the Study of Religions, the Modern Churchmen's Conference at Oxford, the Friends of Dr. Williams's Library, and the theological discussion group at King's College, London. I am very grateful to the Warden and Fellows for granting me membership of the Common Room at All Souls College during the three years of my lectures, and I am deeply appreciative of the honour which the University of Oxford conferred in selecting me as its Wilde Lecturer from 1966 to 1969.

Contents

I. AVATARS IN HINDUISM

II. BUDDHAS, JINAS AND SŪFĪS

Contents

PART I

AVATARS IN HINDUISM

1

Introduction

Some years ago Aldous Huxley said that 'the doctrine that God can be incarnated in human form is found in most of the principal historic expositions of the Perennial Philosophy – in Hinduism, in Mahayana Buddhism, in Christianity and in the Mohammadanism of the Sufis'. He added that 'every human being can thus become an Avatar by adoption', and finally declared that 'because Christians believed that there had been only one Avatar, Christian history has been disgraced by more and bloodier crusades', and so on, 'than has the history of Hinduism and Buddhism'.[1]

These assertions, in a book which the publishers call 'a mine of curious and erudite learning', can be criticized on grounds of theology and history. But Huxley was an influential writer and other people have said much the same. The approximation, or identification, of Indian and Christian beliefs in Avatar and Incarnation seems to be acceptable today, and it might be claimed that the idea of an Avatar is more comprehensible than some of the classical expositions of the doctrine of Incarnation.

Few theologians have discussed this problem, and there is need for a comparative study to discover how much or little ground exists between beliefs in Avatar and Incarnation.[2] It is remarkable that little has been written in European languages on Avatars and their meaning. This is perhaps an advantage, since recourse must be made to the classical Indian texts and commentaries, but it

[1] *The Perennial Philosophy*, 1946, pp. 60–2.
[2] In my book, *Upanishads, Gītā and Bible*, 1962, p. 13, it was said that 'some of the cardinal Biblical doctrines will be mentioned but not fully treated, for example, the incarnation and the atonement. That may be attempted some other time.'

13

suggests that modern assertions about the nature of Avatars can be made on too slender evidence. It is important also to consider Buddhist, and to some degree even Muslim, ideas to see to what extent the parallels which Huxley suggested exist, if at all.

An Avatar is a 'down-coming', a descent, a manifestation of the divine in human form. But is it a real Incarnation, in the flesh? Is it, to use an ugly theological term, an 'inhistorization' of the Deity? In Indian belief there have been numerous Avatars; is this an advantage or not? Christian theology speaks of the Incarnation 'once for all'; does this make it entirely different and incomparable?

If the Avatar is a human being, or appears to be so, does he 'become an Avatar by adoption'? If not, what is the difference between a divine descent and a revelation, and between an Avatar of God and a divinized or beatified human being? If the Avatar is divine in origin, is the Deity regarded as properly dwelling beyond the world, and descending into it only occasionally?

Such questions, and others that will be considered, are of more than narrow interest. In view of modern attempts to 'demythologize' or 'depersonalize' the idea of God, the presence and recurrence of such a vital belief as Incarnation in the history of the world's religions is of great significance. The effort to think of divinity without qualities, to rid the concept of all form, so that it could only be spoken about as 'not this, not this' (*neti, neti*), was nowhere carried so far as in the classical Hindu texts. Yet it was against this background, accepting but reacting against it, that belief in some of the most personal Avatars of the divine appeared.

So powerful was this trend that it can be paralleled in Buddhism and Jainism, which are often loosely called atheistic systems, but are more properly 'transtheistic' or 'transpolytheistic'. The cycles of Buddhas and Jinas have similarities to the Hindu cycles of Avatars, and they may have preceded them to some extent. The importance of this for the development of these religions must be considered.

The oldest and clearest expressions of faith in divine appearances among men were made in India, and it is the great body of texts on the subject in Hinduism that merits careful examination.

VEDIC THEISM

The Vedas are the most sacred compositions of India, the oldest literary record in the Indo-European languages. Their authority is unquestioned by Hindus, and they provide a background to later religion. But the importance also of the religions of other inhabitants of India before the arrival of the Vedic Aryans, especially those of the Indus Valley cultures, is being increasingly realized. These were of great influence in popular Hinduism, and it is possible that the idea of Avatars came from this popular level. But the evidence is fragmentary on Indus Valley religion, and on this point absent; it is a mere guess. Whereas there is a great body of Vedic and later literature that expresses Hindu beliefs in the relationships of the divine and the human.

The Vedas are hymns in praise of the gods of the Aryan pantheon. They incorporate myths, and make slight allusions to human affairs, but they are songs to the gods and not messages from gods to men. Indra, the national and storm god, is the favourite of all and he wanders about in many forms. He assumed various forms for his manifestation, and was multiform by his illusions.[1] Indra assumed the form of a ram and a bull, and some of the other Vedic gods appeared in similar transformations.

The nearest of all the Vedic gods was Agni, the sacrificial fire. With him occurs the image, popular in later religion, of conveying men in a ship across the sea, away from sin. And there are striking verses in which Agni is spoken of 'as father to his son, as kinsman to kinsman, as friend to friend'. Such language was used later of the great vision of God in the Bhagavad- Gītā, where it is added that God should be also 'as lover to beloved'.[2] Further, with Agni is seen the merging of the gods into one: 'You, O Agni, are Indra... you are wide-striding Vishnu... you are king Varuna... you are Rudra ... you are Savitri', and so on. It would be natural to identify the mediating fire with other divinities, but a 'tentative monism' appears here and there. In the first book of the Rig Veda an unidentified neuter One is called by the names of various gods:

[1] Rig Veda (R.V.), 6, 47, 18. See J. Gonda, *Aspects of Early Viṣṇuism*, 1954, pp. 124f.
[2] R.V. 1, 26, 3; 1, 97; 1, 1; Gītā 11, 44.; Indra also is called father and mother, R.V. 4, 17, 17.

> *They call it Indra, Mitra, Varuna, Agni . . .*
> *That which is One the seers speaks of in*
> *various terms.*[1]

For our purpose Vishnu is of particular significance, though he has only half a dozen hymns in the Rig Veda, for later he became the god of the Avatars. Vishnu is little anthropomorphic, and his chief activity in the Vedas consisted in taking three giant strides across the universe, the three realms of earth, air and heaven. Originally Vishnu may have personified the sun, passing through the three realms. He is compared to a dread beast haunting the mountains, or a wide-pacing bull. But all beings dwell in Vishnu's three wide strides, and his worshippers seek to attain to his 'dear domain', which is a 'well of mead' (*madhu*), the 'highest step (*pada*) of Vishnu'. This is the loftiest abode, where men and gods rejoice.[2]

Vishnu is often associated with Indra and helps him in fighting the demon Vritra. Curiously enough in the later Purānas Krishna, Vishnu's Avatar, opposes Indra and humbles him. But in the Vedas and Upanishads Vishnu holds a small place, and only in the Epic does he become pre-eminent. Thereafter with his Avatars, perhaps incorporating Indus Valley or forest divinities, Vishnu emerges as the deity who is to this day the greatest or sole God to millions of Hindus.

Towards the end of the Rig Veda there come more sophisticated hymns, mythological and speculative. Of special significance is the Hymn of Man (Purusha). This cosmic giant was sacrificed by the gods, and from him came all things; animals and the four castes of men, the gods Indra and Agni and others, and the cosmic powers. Yet Purusha is lord (*īśāna*) of all.

> *Purusha is all this, that has been and will be . . .*
> *A quarter* (pāda) *of him is all beings,*
> *Three quarters are the immortal in heaven . . .*
> *With three quarters Purusha rose upwards,*
> *One quarter came to be here again.*[3]

[1] R.V. I, 164, 46; 2.1, etc.
[2] R.V. I, 154; Sāma Veda 2, 8, 2.
[3] R.V. 10, 90; S. Dasgupta, *A History of Indian Philosophy*, ii, 1961, p. 523f.

Some writers have seen in this verse the germ of the doctrine of the Avatar; three quarters are in heaven, one quarter comes into being here below. Dasgupta, in his great critical history of Indian philosophy, says that here there is the starting-point of the theism of the Bhagavad-Gītā, the idea of God as not only immanent but transcendent, a universe which is no illusion, and the doctrine of Incarnation. Certainly this hymn is important, and it is quoted in the theistic Śvetāśvatara Upanishad and in the Gītā, but not the lines that place three parts of Purusha in heaven and the fourth part on earth.[1]

UPANISHADIC MONISM AND REACTION

After other priestly texts the Vedas were followed by the Vedānta, the 'Veda's end', or Upanishads. This speculative religious philosophy probed into the nature of the neuter divinity, Brahman, and its relationship to the gods and the human soul. It arrived at the non-dualism (*advaita*), or monism, which later Vedāntic philosophers like Śankara cherished as the quintessence of Upanishadic thought. The key verse, THAT THOU ART (*tat tvam asi*) identified the divine and the soul, and appeared to abolish any dualism or subject-object relationship between God and man.[2]

For religious life, however, some kind of objective relationship with a deity seems to be necessary, and even the Upanishads began to show that, whatever might pass for philosophy, a monistic or a godless religion was not enough. There are hints of grace in the Kaṭha Upanishad, and the Mundaka says that bliss is only gained by the one to whom the supreme Soul reveals his own person or nature (*tanum svam*). But the Śvetāśvatara is the most theologically significant of the classical Upanishads, insisting on the greatness of God (*deva*) as creator of all things. This God is identified with other deities, but especially he is called Rudra, who is 'kindly' (*śiva*). He is the adorable God who creates and rules all, standing opposite creatures, yet he is called upon to appear to men in his kindly form (*tanu*).[3]

---

[1] Śvetāśvatara Upanishad 3, 12ff.; Bhagavad Gītā 13, 13.
[2] Chāndogya Upanishad, 6, 1–16.
[3] Mundaka Upanishad 3, 2, 3; Śvetāśvatara Upanishad, 4, 4; 3, 1–7; 6, 18; 6, 23.

At the close of the Śvetāśvatara Upanishad the seer seeking liberation goes to God for 'refuge' (*śarana*), a technical term in later Hinduism and Buddhism. And in the very last verse the key word of 'devotion' (*bhakti*) appears, though it is shared between God and the spiritual teacher (*guru*). So with a personal and kindly God, grace, refuge and devotion, the way was prepared for the Bhagavad-Gītā.

Popular Hinduism knew little of the monistic speculations of the Upanishads and later philosophers. Yet not only the uneducated masses, but many learned men held to belief in a transcendent deity and sought closer contact with the One who 'stands opposite creatures'. The monism of many Upanishads, and the non-theism of Sāṁkhya, Yoga, Jainism and Buddhism, made an unpromising background. Yet partly from the popular level, but also by a religious reaction of the thoughtful, arose the powerful doctrines of divine speech to man and Incarnation. Men appealed to God and he came to them. It is in the Great Epic, the Mahābhārata, that the divine revelation and Avatar appear. So it is also claimed as scripture, truly 'heard', a fifth Veda.

2

Avatars in the Great Epic

VISHNU AND OTHERS

The epic poetry of India developed alongside the later Upanishads and the Great Epic, the Mahābhārata, Great Indian story, is the longest poem in the world. About a hundred thousand verses, compiled over centuries, it was formed mostly before the Christian era, with a core of secular story overlaid by masses of mythology, ethics and law. The basic narrative of heroic battles, culminating in a great fight for control of the plain of Kurukshetra, near modern Delhi, was probably preserved by the ruling classes and used in royal rituals. Priests and poets transmitting the texts included endless myths and moralizings, to make the Epic an encyclopaedia of Indian religion. In this religion the most prominent gods are Brahmā the creator, Vishnu and Śiva. Indra is still important but other deities appear that are popular today, such as Gaṇeśa the god of learning, Śrī or Lakshmī the spouse of Vishnu and goddess of fortune, and Pārvatī or Durgā the dread consort of Śiva.

The manifestations of the gods, especially Vishnu, as Avatars first appear clearly in the Epic. An *avatāra* is a descent, a 'downcoming' (from a verb *tṛī*, to cross over, attain, save, with the prefix *ava*, down; and so *ava-tṛī*, descend into, appear, become incarnate). The Avatar is an appearance of any deity on earth, or descent from heaven, but it is applied especially to the descents or appearances of Vishnu. However there are some Avatars of other gods; Varuna appeared out of the point of an arrow, and in later texts both the wives of Krishna and Rāma were Avatars of the goddess of the Earth.

The term Avatar is relatively late, and an older word for the phenomenon is 'manifestation' (*prādurbhāva*).[1] The word *avatāra* does not occur in the classical Upanishads, though there are a few references in later Upanishads.[2] It is listed in Pānini's great Sanskrit grammar of the fourth century B.C. and occurs in many standard writings after the Epic, for example in Purāna tales and the stories of Rāma. In the fifth-century A.D. poem, Raghuvaṃśa, Lakshmī sends an Avatar of herself to an ancestor of Rāma.[3] In later usage any unusual appearance or distinguished person could be called an Avatar, and often is today in the language of respect, though this diminishes the original theological purpose of the term.

Some of the early Avatars of Vishnu are traditionally said to have been in animal form, no doubt incorporating popular myths, and these will be considered below. In the first book of the Epic there are references to the Tortoise, on whose back the gods placed a mountain when they were churning the ocean for the nectar of immortality (*amrita*). But a whole section of the first book of the Epic is called 'partial Avatar' (*aṃśāvatarana*), and it gives the first exposition of the purpose and nature of Avatars. In a comment on the 'partial Avatar' H. Zimmer expounds the theory as 'the sending forth of a minute particle (*aṃśa*) of the infinite supramundane essence of the Godhead – that essence itself suffering thereby no diminution; for the putting forth of a saviour, the putting forth even of the mirage of the universe, no more diminishes the plenitude of the transcendent and finally unmanifested Brahman than the putting forth of a dream diminishes the substance of our own Unconscious.'[4] It seems that the Indian writers, though they oscillated between speaking of a 'full Avatar' (*pūrnāvatāra*) and 'partial' Avatars, did not want to suggest that the Avatar exhausted the divinity. This is apparent in the Bhagavad Gītā, where the Unmanifest is said to be beyond the

---

[1] See E. Abegg, *Der Messiasglaube in Indien und Iran*, 1928, p. 39n.

[2] See G. A. Jacob, *Concordance to the Principal Upanishads and Bhagavadgītā*, 1963 edn., p. 117.

[3] Pānini 3, 3, 120; 6, 2, 144; Raghuvaṃśa 3, 36.

[4] H. Zimmer, *Philosophies of India*, 1951, p. 390. J. Gonda in *Die Religionen Indiens*, 1960, i, p. 269, says that an Avatar is not a clear Incarnation but an 'appearance' (Erscheinung) of God as a man or an animal; but E. Abegg calls it an 'embodiment' (Verkörperung), *Der Messiasglaube*, p. 39.

Manifest, and it recalls Christian discussion on the relationship between the Incarnate Lord and the full Godhead, and the theory of Kenosis or self-emptying.

In the Epic the most important Avatar of Vishnu is that in Krishna and this is given in some detail in the first book. 'Vishnu himself, who is worshipped by all the worlds, was born of Devakī and Vasudeva [his human mother and father], for the sake of the three worlds. He who is without birth and death, the splendid creator of the universe, the Lord and invisible cause of all, the unchanging and all-pervading soul, the centre round which everything moves . . . that originator of all beings "appeared" (*prādur-bhūta*) in the family of the Andhaka-Vrishnis for the increase of right.'[1] This is the family of Krishna, of whom more will be said later. But the superlative divine attributes should be noted; it is the supreme deity who descends to a particular family on earth.

The same passage gives the divine origins of the human heroes of the Epic. Yudhishthira, eldest of the five Pāndava brothers who eventually won their struggle, was born from the god of Right (Dharma), who also took form (*rūpa*) in the womb of a Śūdra 'for the increase of virtue'. Arjuna, the third brother and questioner in the Bhagavad Gītā, was born of the god Indra.

A further reason for the Avatar is then said to be that the Earth, being oppressed by demons, and also by increasing population, those already born and those being born, sought the help of the god Brahmā. He told all the gods to have births on earth, to ease her burden and destroy demons. Indra and the gods accepted this, but in particular they went to Vishnu (Nārāyana), who holds discus and mace in his hands, and they said to him, 'incarnate a part of thyself' (*aṁśenāvatara*). And Vishnu (Hari) replied, 'So be it.'

TEN OR MORE AVATARS

Many times in the Mahābhārata various Avatars and manifestations of the gods are mentioned. The ten Avatars later ascribed to Vishnu are included by some editions in the twelfth book of the Epic, Śānti Parva, but these are not listed as such in the standard text though some Avatars appear. The twelfth book relates a

[1] Mahābhārata (MBH), Adi Parva, 58, 51, etc.; 59, 83.

popular cosmic myth of Vishnu in which he sleeps in the primeval ocean, resting on and sheltered by the hoods of the thousand-headed snake, Śesha or Ananta, the endless. While Vishnu sleeps a lotus appears from his navel, out of which the god Brahmā is born, who then creates the world. This continues for thousands of ages and finally everything dissolves again into Vishnu. The process of creation and dissolution goes on eternally, in great cycles. Within each cycle there are four great ages (*yugas*): Krita, Tretā, Dvāpara and Kali. These ages are respectively white, red, yellow and black. The Kali age, in which we live, is the last and of course the worst, and it is also called the Iron Age, in which only a quarter of virtue remains. The Avatars are distributed between the ages, in their respective colours; they are Yuga Avatars. In the Tretā age Vishnu appeared as Rāma, and as Krishna at the end of the Dvāpara and beginning of the Kali age.

Some editions of the Epic then insert here ten Avatars of Vishnu. Monier-Williams, in his great Sanskrit dictionary, gave this place as reference for ten Avatars, and included the Buddha which can hardly be right for the Epic. Other versions of the text give ten Avatars as: swan, fish, tortoise, boar, man-lion, dwarf, Rāma with the axe, Rāma, Krishna, and Kalkin. In other lists the swan drops out and yet another Rāma is inserted. In later books the number of Avatars is expanded to twenty-two, or even more, as will be seen.[1]

The standard critical text of the Epic speaks here simply of two 'manifestations' (*prādurbhāvā*) of Vishnu, as swan and horse-headed. But since other Avatars of Vishnu are often mentioned elsewhere in the Epic, even if not arranged together, it will be convenient to say something about each of them. It seems that in the Epic period the Avatar theory was still growing and so there is no systematic list of them in the Mahābhārata. A 'classic' list of ten Avatars came to be established later, but there are variations on this in the appendix to the Epic called the Harivaṁśa, and in the Purāna tales. There are also references to 'embodiments' (*tanus*) of the god.

---

[1] MBH, Poona edn., 12, 326, 71, says that the Kumbhakonom edition inserts ten Avatars here, with three Rāmas. After 12, 326, 94 two other editions give lists, quoted in Appendix I, 30. For twenty-two Avatars see later on the Bhāgavata Purāna.

The Horse-head (*hayaśira* or *hayaśīrsha*, or horse-necked, *hayagrīva*) is a form of Vishnu which he assumed to recover the Vedas when they were stolen. According to one story two demons had carried off the Vedas during the sleep of Brahmā at the dissolution of the universe, and Vishnu as Swan and Horse-head ranged through the oceans till the Vedas were recovered and recreated in the Krita age. The horse is a common figure in mythology and being particularly associated with the sun would symbolize Vishnu as a solar deity. In the Vishnu Purāna the horse is placed in the list of Vishnu's Avatars, in the place usually occupied by the dwarf Avatar; it is the Horse-avatar (*aśvāvatāra*).[1]

Although the Swan leads some lists of the Avatars in the Epic little is said about it. The Swan (*hamsa*), or Goose, or Flamingo, may also have been associated with the sun, like some other celestial birds and Garuda, the mythical bird who was the vehicle of Vishnu. In the Vedas the Swan was the vehicle of the Aśvins, divine horsemen, and later it was associated with the gods Brahmā and Indra. From the casual mention in the Epic it is assumed that the Swan was chiefly concerned with the recovery of the Vedas. But both the Horse-head and the Swan disappear from later lists of Avatars of Vishnu, and the first place is taken by the Fish, linking the Avatars with ancient and popular mythology.

The Fish (*matsya*) Avatar comes from an earlier myth which is akin to some other ancient eastern tales of a flood and the deliverance of man in a ship. In the Śatapatha Brāhmana it is said that a primeval man, Manu, was bathing when a fish came into his hands and said, 'I will save you, for a flood will carry away all these creatures.' Manu reared the fish and took it to the sea. He made a ship and entered it when the flood rose. The fish swam to Manu and he tied a rope from the ship to its horn, and so passed swiftly to the northern mountain. There is no reference to Vishnu.[2]

This story is enlarged considerably in the Epic, being told to encourage Yudhishthira. The fish was very small and Manu in pity gave it protection from big fishes. He reared it in a pot, then a tank, but it grew so big that it had to be put in the river Ganges and finally in the ocean. Then the dissolution of the world came,

---

[1] Vishnu Purāna 5, 17, 11.   [2] Śatapatha Brāhmana 1, 8, 1.

and the fish told Manu to build a ship and take with him seven sages and all the different seeds from earth. The fish towed the ark for many years to the highest peak of the Himalayas, and then told Manu, 'I am Brahmā, the lord of creatures' (Prajāpati). Later the fish is identified with Vishnu.[1]

The Tortoise (*kūrma*) Avatar has equally mixed beginnings. In the Śatapatha Brāhmana the tortoise is called the life-sap of the worlds and the same as the sun; the lower shell is the earth and the upper the sky. The god Prajāpati assumed the tortoise form and created living beings. In the Epic the tortoise helped the gods at the churning of the ocean, but only later was it formally identified with Vishnu. Neither the fish nor the tortoise Avatars were much worshipped, though they figure in sculpture.[2]

The Boar (*varāha*) Avatar is much more popular and is mentioned a number of times in the Epic. First of all, in the Śatapatha Brāhmana, the earth was very small, the size of a span, but it was torn up by a boar called Emūsha, who was her lord Prajāpati. In the Taittirīya Samhitā Prajāpati became a boar and seized the wind or the ocean. In the Epic it is first said that after the primeval flood Vishnu flew over the waters like a fire-fly and saw the need of raising the submerged earth. So he took the shape of a wild boar of great length, as huge as a mountain, and plunging into the waters it lifted up the earth on one of its tusks and restored it to its proper place. A further development blames a demon, Hiranyaksha (Golden-eyed), for casting the earth into the ocean. Vishnu as a boar killed the demon and raised the earth for the benefit of all creatures. The boar Avatar was regarded by some writers as the most important of all. Perhaps it included non-Aryan cults of a sacred animal. It is a common theme in sculpture.[3]

The fish, boar and tortoise Avatars, and perhaps the swan also, adapt to the service of Vishnu myths that were related to other creators, Prajāpati and Brahmā, and serve to relate Vishnu also to cosmology. The human Avatars are connected more directly with

---

[1] MBH 3, 186, references and chapter numbers from P. C. Roy's translation here and in future.

[2] Śatapatha Brāhmana 7, 5, 1.

[3] Śatapatha Brāhmana 14, 1, 2; Taittirīya Samhitā 7, 1, 5; MBH 3, 270; 12, 240. See H. Zimmer, *Myths and Symbols in Indian Art and Civilization*, 1946, pp. 77ff.

Vishnu, but continue to assist the purpose of deliverance from demonic oppression. The Man-lion (*Nara-siṁha*) Avatar was assumed to destroy a demon-king, Golden Garment, Hiranya-kaśipu. This monarch could not be killed by god or man or animal and so was all-powerful. But Vishnu appeared with a body half lion, half man, and rent the king in two with his sharp claws. Though not widely worshipped this Avatar is often seen in imagery.[1]

Vishnu appears as a Dwarf (*vāmana*) in the Śatapatha Brāhmana, though hardly yet as an Avatar. Vishnu is connected with the sacrifice at Kurukshetra. In one story the ants gnawed his bow-string, and the ends of the bow sprang up and cut off Vishnu's head. The gods rushed on the prostrate divinity and divided him among themselves (like Purusha), Indra arriving first and gaining glory. Earlier it was said that 'Vishnu was a dwarf', but the gods laid him down and encompassed him on all sides. Vishnu got tired of being a sacrifice and hid himself among the roots of plants, but the gods dug down and found him. The prosaic conclusion was reached that therefore the altar must be dug to the same depth. In the Taittirīya Saṁhitā it is said that when the gods and demons were struggling for the world, Vishnu sacrificed to himself in the shape of a dwarf and so conquered; therefore those who desire victory should offer a dwarf beast to Vishnu.[2]

In the Epic Vishnu is born in one Avatar as a dwarf, a Brahmin with matted locks, sacrificial thread, ascetic's staff and water pot. He came to the demon Bali who had gained control of the world and threatened even the gods by his ascetic and magical powers. Vishnu requested a boon of three paces of ground. Bali granted this, and Vishnu as dwarf then took three huge strides across the universe, so gaining it all from the demon. It will be remembered that in the Vedas the chief characteristic act of Vishnu was taking three paces across the world, like the sun. No doubt along with this goes a belief in the magical power of dwarfs. The Epic adds that from him all the gods had their being and the world is pervaded by Vishnu.[3] The demon Bali's capital was later said to be the great south Indian coastal temple of Mahā-bali-puram.

[1] MBH 3, 270.
[2] Śatapatha Brāhmana 14, 1, 1; 1, 2, 5; Taittirīya Saṁhitā 2, 1, 3.
[3] MBH 3, 270; 5, 10.

There are two Rāmas who are regularly called Avatars of Vishnu. The first is Paraśu-Rāma, Rāma with the axe. He is said to have been a Brahmin of the race of Bhrigu. At his father's command Rāma killed his mother, when she was possessed with unlawful desires, but at his prayer she was restored to life. Rāma destroyed the entire warrior (*kshatriya*) caste several times, and the stories reveal some of the rivalries of Brahmins and Kshatriyas. Paraśu-Rāma was present at the war council of the Kaurava princes before the great central battle of the Epic. He comes in later story, sometimes in conflict with the other Rāma Avatar. He seems to have been little worshipped.[1]

The greater Rāma Avatar is Rāma-chandra (Rāma-moon, though he was of the solar race). His story became one of the most popular of all, though apparently at a fairly late date, being earlier overshadowed by Krishna. He is mentioned several times in the Mahābhārata, but his story is the principal subject of the second great epic, the Rāmāyana. It will be considered under that heading later.

Krishna is the greatest human Avatar of Vishnu in the Mahābhārata and many later works. Before discussing him a word may be said of the last Avatar, according to the great epic. This is Kalkin, the Avatar yet to come. This figure when first mentioned is predicted for the end of the terrible times at the destruction of the world. Then in the cycle of ages, sent by Time, Kalkin will be born a Brahmin and will glorify Vishnu. Destroying all things he will bring in a new age. As king of kings he will exterminate foreigners, and restore order and peace to the world. At a great horse-sacrifice he will give away the earth to the Brahmins, and retire to the forest, where people will imitate his conduct. Kalkin will also roam over the earth and destroy thieves and robbers. Eventually he is identified as an Avatar of Vishnu. Kalkin was perhaps first Vishnu as a Horse and later Kalkin appears riding a white horse and holding a flaming sword. It has been suggested that the idea of a future deliverer, at least in later forms, owes something to the Buddhist belief in the coming Maitreya Buddha, or to Zoroastrian faith in the future Saviour Soshyans, if not to Jewish or Christian Messianic eschatology. But the Epic descrip-

[1] MBH 3, 115; 5, 96.

26

tions are probably earlier than some of this, and the hope of a mighty Vaishnavite Brahmin to inaugurate a new age is not out of place.[1]

It may have seemed tedious to pass in review the various animal and human Avatars of Vishnu, but it is useful to give a summary of what the Epic says about them, since this is not easily accessible, and it is important for the development of the worship of Vishnu. Now with Krishna develops the dominant Avatar of the Mahābhārata.

THE ORIGINS OF KRISHNA

The name Krishna means black, dark or dark-blue, and it is used in opposition to white and red, or the dark half of the lunar months, and of the last dark age. Rāma the Avatar also often appears dark-blue in pictures, and the God Śiva is blue or blue-throated, said to have come from drinking a poison and saving the other gods. It is maintained that this darkness comes from their being celestial deities and so the colour of heaven, but their heavenly consorts usually appear as white. The most notorious dark deity is the Great Goddess, whose name Kālī means 'black'. It is therefore possible that these popular Hindu deities came from the darker section of the population whose cities were overthrown by the light-skinned Aryans, but whose religion remained and finally mingled with that of the Aryans to form the amalgam of Hinduism. However, these names are Sanskrit and must have been applied fairly early.

The name Krishna is not uncommon. It occurs in the Vedas and Upanishads, though not as a divine title. A Krishna of the family of Angirasa composed Rig Veda 8, 84, addressed to the Aśvins: 'Krishna invokes you, hear the invocation of Krishna the hymner.' A short passage in the Chāndogya Upanishad shows a teacher, Ghora Angirasa, expounding the nature of the life of man as a sacrifice to Krishna, the son of Devakī, who has become free from desire.[2] His teaching can be paralleled in the Epic: that

---

[1] MBH 3, 139. For long discussions of Kalkin and eschatological hopes, see E. Abegg, *Der Messiasglaube in Indien und Iran*, pp. 40ff., 138ff. Kalkin is described at length in the Kalkin Purāna, which is not among the eighteen great Purānas.   [2] Chāndogya 3, 17, 6.

life is a sacrifice, that almsgiving, austerity and non-violence are virtues, and that in the hour of death one should hold to the thought that one is the unshaken and indestructible. But then almost anything can be paralleled in the vastness of the Epic.

In the Mahābhārata Krishna is both man and God. The early parts of the Epic may date from about 400 B.C. when the cult of Krishna begins to be attested, though it was probably much older. Pānini, the grammarian of the fourth century, spoke of Krishna under his name Vāsudeva as being worshipped. Megasthenes, the Greek writer in India about the same period, said that Heralkes was worshipped at Methora, which is usually taken to be the Krishna hero-cult at his sacred city of Mathurā. Inscriptions in the third and second centuries speak of Vāsudeva as God of gods (*deva-deva*).[1]

The origins of the divine Krishna have been much debated. To some he is a solar deity, though why he should then be called 'dark' is not clear. To others he was a vegetation spirit. His struggles with demons, and his death, are compared with vegetation myths of a dying god. But these, though popular in the ancient Near East, are not found in India. Krishna's death, comparatively, is a small incident which receives little attention.

No doubt the background of the cult is complex. A popular name for Krishna is Govinda, 'herdsman', and he is often associated with cowherds. It is noteworthy that in the Epic there are signs of opposition to Krishna. Śiśupāla, king of the Chedi tribe, objected to primary reverence being given to Krishna as if he were king, for his father was there and how could Krishna be greater? Śiśupāla called him 'that cowboy', whom even dull men could insult. Krishna had previously carried off Śiśupāla's intended wife, and now he struck off his head with his discus. But the outspoken opposition to the Krishna cult is significant.[2]

More serious criticism is refuted in the Bhagavad-Gītā. It refers to 'those who speak against me', and calls them 'fools' who only look at the human manifestation of the deity:

> *They ignore my higher being*
> *Which is both supreme and changeless.*

[1] See W. D. P. Hill, *The Bhagavadgītā*, 1928, pp. 2ff.   [2] MBH 2, 37ff.

Here the reference is to the debate between those who preferred the formless Brahman and those who believed in a personal God and Avatar.[1]

How Krishna came to be identified with Vishnu is not clear. It has been suggested that Vāsudeva, one of Krishna's chief names, comes from Vishnu. The meaning of Vishnu is not sure; it may mean 'active' or 'pervading'. If it is the latter then the all-pervading God could easily be linked with Avatars. The Avatar idea, once conceived, was an excellent method of incorporating various popular personal gods with a transcendent celestial deity. Vishnu in Vedic times was a solar god striding over the universe, but still a minor deity. In the Epic he is often called supreme, and his worship is reinforced by his diverse manifestations. It seems that the marriage of Aryan and native Indian religions produced this powerful and many-sided theology.

Krishna appears from the beginning of the Mahābhārata and plays a leading role throughout. In the summaries of the first book he is already the helper of the Pāndavas in their struggle for the throne. His birth of Devakī and Vasudeva in the Vrishni tribe is declared to be Vishnu himself being born. Later he is described as the ancient and supreme Lord Hari (Vishnu), who has taken birth as Krishna, and seems to sport in this world. He is dressed in yellow silk robes, has a curl of hair (*śrī-vatsa*) on the breast, and has four arms, holding conch-shell, discus and mace in his hands. This is his normal embodied form, distinct from his transfigured forms.[2]

There is no doubt that Krishna has a human body, and some human limitations. Occasionally he seems to admit his ignorance. He eats, drinks, plays, sleeps, and finally dies. So it has been said that he is first of all a teacher in the Epic and a hero, especially giving the long instruction in the Gītā. But along with this there are many divine traits. Even if the Gītā is later than much of the Epic, in its present form at least, Krishna is a divine teacher throughout its dialogues.

The Mahābhārata gives no details of the birth and says little of the childhood of Krishna, which were such favourite topics of the later Purānas. The Epic says that as a child with his bare hands he

---

[1] Gītā 7, 24–5; 18, 67.   [2] MBH 2, 188 and 270; Gītā 11, 46.

killed a giant (a Dānava) in the form of a bull, and while being brought up by cowherds he killed other demons. He was sent as an Avatar to human parents, as the response of Vishnu to the appeal of the earth for deliverance from oppression. Krishna killed Kaṁsa, king of Mathurā, and other demons. At a self-choice ceremony (*svayaṁ-vara*) Krishna bore away the daughter of the Gandhāra king. Later it is said that he had sixteen thousand wives.[1]

The death of Krishna is related fairly simply. After the battles were over, and most of his friends had died, Krishna, who knew the end of all things, and remembered premonitions that had been given, wandered in a forest practising Yoga. He had once entertained a sage, Durvāsas, but omitted to wipe fragments of food from his feet. The sage, known for his irascibility, thereupon declared that all Krishna's body would be inviolable except his feet. Krishna knew this, and although he was the Supreme Being he wished to die, to dispel all doubts and fulfil the sage's word. As he was sitting in Yoga a hunter called Jaras mistook Krishna for a deer and shot him in the heel. As Jaras came up to get his prey he saw a man with many arms, dressed in a yellow robe, rapt in meditation. Jaras fell at his feet in contrition, but Krishna comforted him. Then the great soul ascended to the heavens, filling the world with his glory. As he reached heaven all the gods and saints, including Indra and Rudra, came to greet and worship him. And so Nārāyana (Vishnu), creator and destroyer of all, reached his own inconceivable abode. It may be noted that Jaras means 'old age'. Having a vulnerable spot is characteristic of other ancient heroes, like Achilles.[2]

In the central episodes of the Epic, the struggle of the Pāndava brothers for their rights, Krishna is their ally. He is the particular friend of the third brother, Arjuna. They play together by rivers and Krishna advises Arjuna to seize his own sister by capture. Before the battle of Kurukshetra the leaders of the opposing sides both claimed Krishna's help. Duryodhana, prince of the Kauravas, pressed his petition, and Krishna promised to send an army of cowherds to his assistance. But he himself went to the other side, on the grounds that when the two claimants came to him he had been asleep. On awaking Krishna had looked at Arjuna first and

[1] MBH 3, 270; 7, 6; 12, 340.   [2] MBH 16, 4.

so chose his side. But Krishna was a non-combatant. He laid down his invincible arms and became a passive counsellor, and charioteer of Arjuna. This, however, was enough and the Pāndavas finally won. It is as charioteer of Arjuna that Krishna appears and speaks as the Avatar God in the Bhagavad-Gītā.[1]

[1] MBH 1, 221; 5, 7.

3

Krishna in the Bhagavad-Gītā

KRISHNA AND VISHNU

The Bhagavad-Gītā, the Song of the Lord (Bhagavat) Krishna, is the most popular of all Indian scriptures. It is also the best known outside India and there are said to be over fifty English translations. Whether the Gītā, as we have it now, formed an original part of the Epic has been much disputed. It is attested in good texts, but critical scholars have taken the many different strands of its teaching to indicate various recensions, on behalf of this or that school of thought. Rudolf Otto traced out at least eight editions, but even he did not deny that there was an original Gītā (an Ur-Gītā) which in some shape formed part of the Epic (notably chapters 1–2, 10–11, and 18). Long discourses are not uncommon in the Epic, and other dialogues besides the Gītā can be taken as works in their own right. This is only to say that the Epic is a great compilation, of many different elements and dates.[1]

Some writers say that the Avatar doctrine appears for the first time in the Gītā, since it was made necessary by the identification of Krishna with the supreme deity.[2] But we have seen that Avatars are mentioned earlier in the Epic. Moreover, it is a curious fact that the word *avatāra* does not occur at all in the Gītā. However the doctrine is there, and that is what matters.

Then there is the question whether Krishna really is an Avatar of Vishnu in the Gītā. There is no mention of Vishnu in the Avatar passages. Vishnu is named just three times in the eighteen chapters of the Gītā. One mention is in a list of many other celestial spirits and is of no importance for our subject. It is only in the great

[1] R. Otto, *The Original Gītā*, E.T. 1939, pp. 162ff.
[2] W. D. P. Hill, *The Bhagavadgītā*, p. 24.

Vision of chapter eleven that the transfigured Krishna is twice hailed 'O Vishnu'. This is clear and significant. But the Vision is in a different metre from most of the Gītā and could be by another hand. Most of the Gītā is in the simple eight-syllable line (*anushtubh* or *śloka*) used in much of the Epic. Only a few verses here and there are in a longer eleven-syllable line (*trishtubh*). It could be argued that the longer line is used for heightened description rather than simple narrative, or that it represents attempts at improvement (as at the beginning of chapter two), fuller explanation or greater polish. Be that as it may, the fact remains that only in chapter eleven is the name Vishnu used as a great title. The name Hari, also for Vishnu, similarly occurs only twice, again in chapter eleven, and in the epilogue of chapter eighteen.[1]

If Krishna is not an Avatar of Vishnu in most of the Gītā then what is he? Rudolf Otto said that the great God of the Vision is not Vishnu, but a deity who is 'Wholly Other'. He is not an 'Ultimate Reality' but an 'Almighty Will'. The only God who would fit this description, Otto suggests, is Rudra, the 'austere and magnificent' yet terrible storm deity of the Vedas and some Upanishads. It is strange that he does not refer to the Śvetāśvatara Upanishad, where Rudra is the named supreme deity. Yet Otto seems to be reading too much into the Gītā. This 'Wholly Other' is too Hebrew, or Barthian. And the fact is that Rudra is never named singly in the Gītā, only three times in a class of storm gods, in chapters ten and eleven. Śiva also is only mentioned once indirectly, by the title Śankara.[2]

Some writers, like Gonda and Hill, say that Krishna in the Bhagavad Gītā is not an Avatar of Vishnu but of Brahman. And K. Sharma has recently denied that the Gītā is a product of a Vaishnavite school, as has been commonly assumed, and declares that its teaching is not devotion to a personal God but pure non-dualistic monism.[3] This will be discussed later, but the first answer is that such considerations remove the Gītā completely from the Epic. For if there was an original Gītā in the Epic, and if the Avatar

[1] Gītā 10, 21; 11, 9; 18, 77.
[2] R. Otto, *The Original Gītā*, pp. 154ff.; Gītā 10, 23.
[3] Hill, *The Bhagavadgītā*, p. 25; J. Gonda, *Die Religionen Indiens*, 1960, i, p. 269; K. Sharma, unpublished thesis.

doctrine came into it, then Vishnu is the god of this Avatar. It has been seen that Avatars are early and frequently mentioned in the Epic; they are especially Avatars of Vishnu. The identity of Vishnu and Krishna Vāsudeva is stated a number of times: 'Krishna . . . even Nārāyana himself'; 'Vāsudeva . . . is called Vishnu because of his all-pervading nature'; 'O God, O Vishnu . . . O God of gods . . . O Krishna'. Several times later in the Epic there are requests for a repetition of the teaching of the Gītā, and in book fourteen there is a further transfiguration of Krishna to a Brahmin: 'the holy one showed that high and wonderful form of Vishnu, the supreme Lord'.[1]

Further, although it is true that in the Gītā, in isolation, there is little direct mention of Vishnu, this hardly affects the doctrine of Avatar. Whatever the deity, he reveals himself to men, and shows grace and compassion. Otto said that this god cannot be the ancient Brahman, for he has no attributes in common with him (if Brahman has any attributes). Nor is he the universal World-soul. He is no doubt a God beyond and greater than all these, and the complexity and subtlety of the Gītā's doctrines of the divine are not the least of its attractions.[2]

To understand the Gītā some knowledge of the background of the Epic is necessary. This must usually be acquired from a good introduction and commentary, and it is a pity that some English versions spend more time looking for parallels in Wordsworth, Keats, Meister Eckhart, St. Paul, St. Teresa – in fact anywhere – rather than explaining the names, terms and doctrines that demand some exposition, as clear and accurate as possible. The Epic itself is so long and unwieldy that acquaintance with it is difficult to obtain. There are a few summaries in English, but they concentrate upon the stories of people and battles, and omit most of the important religious doctrines. The theme of divine manifestation runs through the Epic. God never spoke to man in the Vedas, and in the Upanishads man was merged into divinity. 'Thou art that' precludes conversation, which demands some measure of subject-object relationship.

In the Epic not only is there objective deity, but there are teachings of grace which, once hinted at in the more theistic

[1] MBH 5, 7; 5, 70; 6, 65; 14, 55.   [2] Otto, *The Original Gītā*, p. 155.

34

Upanishads, now begin to flower. Vishnu is the Supreme Being, without attributes, consuming the whole universe and then creating it again. Indeed the Supreme Spirit has three conditions; as Brahmā he is creator, as Vishnu preserver, and as Rudra destroyer. Vishnu becomes an Avatar in every age, entering into diverse wombs, for the sake of Right (*dharma*). When he is born in the order of humanity, he must act as a human being. For the destruction of evil and the preservation of Right he takes birth in the Yadu race and Vishnu is called Krishna. So the god Nārāyana becomes the friend of the hero Arjuna.[1] The Gītā is fitted into this context of the Epic.

The Gītā might be called the Hindu answer to Buddhism, the first of many. Its use of the term *nirvāna* may be derived from Jains or Buddhists, and in the Gītā this word is not used in the sense of mere extinction of desire or calm, but in a more positive or theistic sense as Brahman-nirvāna. Similarly its brief description of meditation in chapter six could be Buddhist, or Yogic, except for the final goal which is more nearly theistic, 'put your thoughts on Me,' and 'be absorbed in Me.' The Gītā's great stress on devotion (*bhakti*) may have affected Buddhism in return. The Lotus Sūtra could be called Mahāyāna Buddhism's answer back, but if so that is a tribute to the importance of the teaching of devotion.

The Gītā is also addressed to Arjuna and others of the Kshatriya caste, from which Buddhist and Jain leaders came. If there is Buddhist influence, and counter-action, then the date of the Gītā would be before the Christian era. Dasgupta, however, suggests that the Gītā is pre-Buddhist, though he admits that this view is 'unfashionable'. This would make it even farther pre-Christian, a point that is important in view of some theories of parallels and borrowings.[2]

It is possible that part of the Avatar ideas may owe something to Jain and Buddhist beliefs in recurrent Jinas and Buddhas. This will be discussed later, but it can be noted here that theories of recurrent cycles of world existence, and divine manifestation, are found in many parts of the Epic.

---

[1] MBH 14, 54; 3, 270.
[2] *A History of Indian Philosophy*, ii, p. 551. But R. C. Zaehner in *The Bhagavad-Gītā* (1969) shows the considerable Buddhist influence on the early chapters of the Gītā, which is later displaced by personal theism.

AVATAR APPEARANCE

The first word of the Gītā is Field of Right (*dharma-kshetra*) and
the battle of Kurukshetra is symbolical of the struggle to maintain
right and destroy evil. Before the fight Arjuna hesitates in despon-
dency at the prospect of killing his enemies, who are also kinsmen,
since this would upset the balance of caste and family and bring
destruction of right order.

In his reply Krishna utters a long series of teachings, the first
divine messages of Hinduism; 'the blessed Lord said' resembles
'thus saith the Lord' of the Bible. The first answer uses two verses
of the Kaṭha Upanishad to show that the soul is indestructible, so
that the real nature of men is not killed in battle. This is the
Sāṁkhya philosophical theory of knowledge, of the eternity of
the soul. Krishna follows this by Yoga, the teaching of disciplined
and unattached activity. This is one of the most important themes
of the Gītā, constantly recurring, and showing the importance of
action against idle asceticism. Detached work frees man from the
entail of Karma, so that he will not be reborn on earth through the
power of Karma ('deeds'). Later a further note is added, in which
action is made more positive and religious by setting the mind not
on results, but on the Lord in devotion. This love to God ensures
speedy and complete salvation from rebirth.

Several times the Upanishadic teachers declared that their words
had been revealed by Brahmā to the ancient sages. Krishna in the
Gītā asserts that it was he himself who had told these truths to
past sages; the doctrines had lapsed in the course of time but they
are now revealed again. Arjuna objected that these wise men had
lived before him, so how could Krishna have taught them?
Krishna replied that he had had many births, so had Arjuna also, but
the difference is that Krishna knows his births and Arjuna does not.

Then come the famous words which express the Avatar belief.
Although Krishna is unborn, although his self is eternal, yet by
means of his own mysterious power (*māyā*) he comes into being.

> *Whenever there appears*
> *A languishing of Righteousness* (dharma)
> *When Unrighteousness* (adharma) *arises*
> *Then I send forth* (generate) *Myself.*

36

And the purpose of this coming is to maintain the Right by births in successive ages.

> *For protection of the virtuous,*
> *For destruction of the wicked*
> *For the establishment of Right,*
> *Age after age I come into being.*[1]

This is the clearest statement of the Avatar doctrine in the Gītā (there are others at 7, 24 and 9, 11), and although the word does not occur the doctrine is evident.

In the previous chapter, exhorting Arjuna to action, Krishna had cited his own example, for what noble men will do others will follow. For himself, there if nothing to be done in any world, nothing unattained to be grasped, 'yet I still keep on in action'. For if he were not to act 'all these worlds would perish', as the deity, such as Vishnu, always sustains the world. One is reminded of the Gospel: 'My Father worketh hitherto and I work,' and Rabbinic debates over whether God really did cease from his sustaining work on the Sabbath.[2]

So the Avatar doctrine shows that God is at work, and it justifies Arjuna's proper activity. It provides a religious rule for warriors and rulers. More, it proclaims the rightness and necessity of a man's own natural action, in the material world, rather than the rejection of work and the world by extreme ascetisicm.

IMMANENCE

Dasgupta says that 'the earliest and most recondite treatment regarding the nature and existence of God and His relation to man is to be found in the Gītā.'[3] After the declaration of the Avatar of the Lord, 'whenever Right languishes and Unright arises', it is said that whoever knows Krishna's divine birth and actions as they are truly, when he leaves the body at death he is not reborn but he goes to the Lord. Deliverance from the round of rebirth, the quest of Indian teachers since the doctrine of transmigration became articulate, is constantly said throughout the Gītā to be the sure result

---

[1] Gītā 4, 7–8.　　[2] Gītā 3, 24; John 5, 17.
[3] *A History of Indian Philosophy*, ii, p. 523.

of devotion to Krishna. 'Intent on Me', 'fixed on Me', 'coming to Me', 'attaining to Me', these often repeated phrases show the goal of work and worship.[1]

The knowledge of the Lord begins to be more fully expounded from chapter seven. By practical knowledge and experience (*vijñāna*), deeper than theory, perhaps one in a thousand may come to know the Lord in very truth. His lower nature is seen in the elements of the visible world, but his higher nature is the Life (*jīva-bhūta*) by which the universe is sustained. All beings spring from this, for he is both the origin and the dissolution of the cosmos. All the universe is strung on him like jewels on a thread, and there exists no higher thing whatever than the Lord. The wise man knows that 'Vāsudeva is everything', though such a great soul (*mahātma*) is hard to find.[2] These developments show clearly that Krishna is no mere teacher of ethics, as some interpreters have pretended, but he is the very God of gods.

The cyclic creation and dissolution, taught elsewhere in the Epic, is made plain here. At the beginning of a world-eon beings are sent out, and at the end of an eon they pass back into the Lord's material nature.

> *By applying my own nature*
> *I send out again and again*
> *All this helpless host of beings.*[3]

But these creative actions do not bind the Lord, for he sits as indifferent, 'sitting in as sitting out', unattached to all these actions. In the final chapter it is said that the Lord abides in the heart of all beings, and he causes them all to turn round like puppets fixed in a machine by his power.

The Avatar doctrine is stated again in this context. Critics of the incarnation of Krishna are ignorant of the divine nature that is behind it.

> *Foolish people despise me*
> *When taking a human body* (tanu),
> *They ignore my higher being*
> *As the great Lord of beings.*[4]

[1] Gītā 2, 61; 4, 9, etc. [2] 7, 19. [3] 9, 8. [4] 9, 11.

Then the Gītā proceeds to identify Krishna with everything, with sacrifice and sacred formula, with the origin and dissolution of the world, with being and non-being. His manifestation (*vibhūti*) in every class of being and with the head of every class shows that the Lord is present everywhere and identical with all beings and gods, and paves the way for his exaltation as supreme and sole God.

This is detailed in chapter ten as the highest message of the pervading power or supernal manifestation. First Arjuna calls Krishna the supreme Brahman, eternal divine Person (*Purusha*), unborn Lord, and primal Deity (*ādi-deva*). This is the only place in the Gītā where Krishna is directly called Brahman. But elsewhere he is called 'foundation of Brahman', and it is also said that 'those who trust in me know that Brahman altogether'. There seems no doubt that Krishna is Brahman, Vāsudeva is all, like the pervading divinity of the Upanishads but even greater.

It follows that, as in the Upanishads Brahman is *ātman* (soul), so is Krishna. He is called the essential life or individual soul upholding the universe; this is just a part of him which comes into the world. And now, having been hailed as Brahman by Arjuna, Krishna replies that he is the soul (*ātman*) which dwells in the heart of all beings. He has already been called Essential Self or Over Soul, in a series of high-sounding titles. And later he is the Supreme Soul (Paramātman) and Supreme Person (Purushottama).[1]

Arjuna continues by declaring that Krishna is God of gods (*deva-deva*). But his manifestation is not known by gods or demons, for he alone knows his self by his own self. Krishna replies by giving a long list of his presence in all great forms. He is Vishnu of the solar spirits, Indra (Vāsava) of the gods, Śiva (Śankara) of the Rudras, the letter A of the alphabet, immortal Time and Death. He is not only strength of the strong, but also gambling of deceivers. He is Vyāsa, the author of the Gītā. He is Vāsudeva, his manifest form. He is his very hearer Arjuna (Dhanamjaya). He is the seed of all beings, for no moving or unmoving being could exist without him. Every manifestation that shows power is sprung from a fragment of his glory. The entire world is supported with a single fragment of himself and he still remains.[2]

[1] Gītā 7, 5; 15, 7; 8, 1–4; 15, 17–19.   [2] 10, 15; 10, 20–42.

Such thoroughgoing pantheism, apparently complete non-dualism, would seem to leave no room for a God who 'stands opposite creatures'. Yet it is just to this that the Gītā passes immediately, giving pictures of immanence and transcendence face to face.

THE VISION OF TRANSCENDENCE

Chapter eleven is called in the colophon 'the Yoga of the Vision (*darśana*) of the Universal Form'. For Arjuna, having listened to the highest message of the origin and dissolution of all beings in Krishna, expresses his desire to see Krishna's form (*rūpa*) as the Lord, that is, transcendent. Krishna replies that his forms are to be seen in their thousands in the gods and heavenly spirits; the whole world of moving and unmoving things is in his body. But since Arjuna cannot see him with his mortal eye, Krishna by mystic power gives him a supernatural eye.

So Hari (Vishnu) revealed his supreme form. He appeared with many mouths and eyes, carrying the symbols of all the gods, facing in all directions. The light was like a thousand suns in heaven, and the whole world was united in the body of the God of gods.

Arjuna was filled with amazement, his hair stood on end, and folding his hands in reverence and bowing his head to God, he burst into the chant of astonished description that forms the central part of the chapter of vision. These are the verses in long metre (*trishtubh*), where Vishnu is at last hailed by name.

Some western critics have dissected the Vision and declared that certain verses are inconsistent interpolations. Richard Garbe cut out those verses (15–16, 18–19, 37–40) which speak of the All-God in infinite form, on the grounds that this was too much like Vedāntic non-dualism, whereas he thought that the Gītā was originally a manual of bhakti devotion to a personal God. Garbe was followed in the main by Otto, but with the justification that the Vision was not meant to display the 'all-forms' of God, a cosmic and universal divinity, but to reveal an 'Awful and Majestic Being' who, 'according to his own decree' when the time is fulfilled, 'carries out his deed of wrath—directs his judgement upon the people', and destroys them. This may be Semitic, but it is not Hindu.[1]

[1] *The Original Gītā*, pp. 148f.

There is no objective evidence for these excisions. They spring from theory, not from textual defect. Against them it must be stressed that the Gītā is syncretistic, constantly striving to include different points of view. Further, there are parallels to the Vision of the Gītā in other parts of the Epic. Not long before the sixth book, Krishna impressed his power on the opposing leader, Duryodhana. From his body, which was like a blazing fire, issued thousands of gods; on his forehead was Brahmā and on his breast Rudra, on his arms world-rulers and from his mouth came fire. His body was like the rays of the sun; all the assembled kings were frightened and the earth trembled. Then Krishna withdrew that wonderful form, and went out arm in arm with his friends.[1]

Much later, to the sage Utanka, Krishna revealed his universal form, blazing like a thousand suns. That great form of Vishnu had faces on all sides, its head filled the sky, its belly the air, and its feet covered the earth. At this vision Utanka said, 'Thou art all this, but now withdraw this supreme form, and show me thine own (human) form, which also is eternal'.[2]

In the Vision of the Gītā (11, 15) Arjuna cries out at once that all the gods are to be seen in the divine form, Brahmā seated on a lotus, and all the seers and heavenly serpents. The All-Lord and All-form has many arms, bellies, mouths and eyes, extending without beginning, middle or end. These recall the giant Purusha of Rig Veda 10, 90, and indicate the all-pervading greatness and the inclusiveness in one of all gods and attributes, as in the many-armed Indian sculptures. Otto says that these express the 'numi-nously terrible', not a 'universal unity'. But this unity was already present in the Purusha hymn, in many later references, and in the Gītā itself.

When the throngs of gods are seen to be entering into the divine body, the Vision takes an eschatological turn, and the Supreme Being becomes terrible. He shows yawning mouths, huge fiery eyes, and awful tusks, all blazing like the fire of world dissolution. Into these grim jaws the warriors on both sides are being drawn, and some are stuck between the teeth with their heads crushed. Both because of this fearful apparition, and because it is called 'teacher' (*guru*), Otto said that it was Rudra. But it is just here that

[1] MBH 5, 131.   [2] MBH 14, 55.

Arjuna twice cried, 'O Vishnu'. And Krishna is teacher throughout
the Gītā.

Arjuna was terrified at this appearance, and yet curious. It was
both *tremendum et fascinans*. 'Have mercy', he cried, yet 'tell me
who thou art, for I do not understand what thy coming to action
means'. The Blessed Lord explained:

> *I am Time, the cause of world-destruction,*
> *And now matured will gather in the worlds.*

He exhorts Arjuna to fight, because his foes are killed already by
divine action. Arjuna accepts, and bows low in homage, saying
that all the world should praise the Primal God.

This is the climax of the Vision, but important themes are still to
come. The divine majesty that has been revealed makes Arjuna
suddenly aware that he has been too familiar with Krishna in his
human form as Avatar.

> *Whatever I said rashly, thinking thee my friend,*
> *Saying Krishna, Yādava, Comrade . . .*

It was a real incarnation:

> *Or held thee disrespectfully, in jest,*
> *At play or sitting, eating or at rest.*

So Arjuna asks pardon of the one who is the father of the world,
the one of matchless greatness. He implores mercy, grace, and
human kindness:

> *As father to his son, as friend to friend,*
> *As lover to beloved, have mercy, O God.*

He goes on to appeal for the end of the terrifying vision, and the
return of Krishna's human four-armed shape.[1]

There are some traces of grace (*prasāda*) in the later classical
Upanishads; slightly in the Kaṭha and clearly in the Rudra-praising
Śvetāśvatara. This was a change from the early Upanishads. For it
could not be supposed that the formless Brahman, who could only
be described by the negative 'not this, not this', could show any
grace. Brahman has no interest in mankind, apart from absorption.
The Gītā acknowledges this background of Upanishads, and tries

[1] Gītā 11, 41–6.

to do justice to its pervading monism. It does not break away from Vedānta as do the later Purānas. Yet its theism emerges strongly. Not only is God interested in man, to the extent of declaring his teaching and giving guidance on moral problems, but he responds to the plea of his follower. Arjuna calls for grace, and Krishna responds.

> *The Mighty One consoled him in his fright*
> *By showing once again his gracious form.*

Finally Krishna declares that the Vision cannot be seen by use of scriptural texts, austerity, or sacrifice, but only by unswerving devotion. This is repeated in both metres, at the end of the Vision and after, and is emphasized.

> *Not by Vedas or by penance,*
> *Not by gifts or acts of worship,*
> *Am I seen in such a manner*
> *As you have seen me.*[1]

DEVOTION

Following on naturally from the Vision, chapter twelve is called the Yoga of Bhakti. Devotion (*bhakti*) to a personal God is particularly appropriate to a doctrine of Avatars. The gods of the Vedas called forth many hymns of praise, they were often represented with human characteristics, and their presence was sometimes sought as fathers and friends. But they inspired reverence and submission, rather than passionate devotion and love. In the Upanishads, when the gods are mentioned, there may be reverent praise but that is all. Only in the last verse of the Śvetāśvatara Upanishad is the word *bhakti* found, and then for the teacher as well as for God.

Like the Avatar, then, *bhakti* appears first clearly in the Epic and the Gītā.[2] Arjuna is called 'My devotee (*bhakta*) and friend (*sakha*)' from 4, 3. There is constant emphasis on turning thoughts and

---

[1] 11, 50 and 53.

[2] Elsewhere in the Epic Krishna is said to love his devotees (*bhaktavatsala*; 7, 83, 12), Śiva is said to be kind to his bhaktas, Lakshmī loves him who was *bhakti*, and Sūrya tells Karna that he is inspired by *bhakti* for him. Even Vishnu seeing Śiva becomes full of love (*bhaktimat*; 7, 201, 77). Yet in the main, *bhakti* in the rest of the Epic is not so intense or lofty as in the Gītā.

worship 'towards me', and this is the great means of overcoming karmic entail, by making the Lord the motive and object of all actions.

Krishna, in the Gītā, is a worthy object of devotion. There is no indication how he was depicted in imagery in the early centuries of the Epic, for the many statues and pictures now available are all later. But it would be without that erotic symbolism that later permeated the Krishna cult. This will be considered below, but it is important to stress the picture given by the Gītā. Here Krishna is the Charioteer, friend, moral teacher and counsellor. He is also the revealed God, Primal Deity, terrible cause of doom, of dissolution but also of creation. Then he is merciful, and shows affection for his follower.

The Gītā often shows respect for knowledge; 'nothing purifies like knowledge', and the true knower finds the way to salvation. Yet it has been seen that it exalts the way of disinterested action above ascetic renunciation, and finally it exalts devotion over everything else.

In chapter twelve Arjuna asks which are the best followers of Yoga: those who revere Krishna with devotion, or those who seek the unmanifested deity, the 'not this, not this', by the way of knowledge? Krishna replies that 'those who fix their thoughts on me' are the best. He does not deny that men who seek the unknown divinity, the unmanifested, indefinable, and inconceivable, can reach him also. But this is a much harder way, for 'the unmanifested goal is hard to reach for embodied beings'. Whereas those who fix their thoughts on the manifested God are quickly saved from the ocean of transmigration, and they come to dwell in him. The ways of knowledge, works and devotion are all valid, but the first two are hard and liable to bring rebirth, whereas devotion is speedy, open to all, and brings complete salvation.

This had been suggested before. The simplest devotion is acceptable, rather than complex sacrifices.

> *If one gives me with devotion*
> *Leaf or flower, fruit or water,*
> *From that earnest soul I relish*
> *Such an offering of devotion.*

Moreover this way of devotion is open to all, to both sexes and to all castes.

> *Women, artisans and servants,*
> *These attain the highest goal.*[1]

It was noted earlier that Krishna declared that his devotees are 'dear' to him. In chapter twelve this is repeated six times, in a picture of the unattached and disinterested Yogi. 'One who is devoted to me, is dear (*priya*) to me.' And in the last verse such devotees are 'beyond measure dear to me'.

The love of God in the Gītā is first of all devotion directed towards God by his adoring follower. But signs begin to appear of the concern of the deity for his follower. This is taken up most fully in the closing verses of the last chapter of the Gītā. Krishna offers deliverance and says, 'I promise you this truly, for you are dear to me'. But he uses a still more loving word, his highest secret, that the devotee is 'greatly loved' (*ishta*) by him.

> *Further, hear the greatest secret*
> *Of them all, my highest message,*
> *Since by me you're much belovèd*
> *I will speak to your advantage.*

And so the favourite final verse (*charama śloka*) appears to go beyond duty, the earlier concern of the Gītā, a suggestion which has troubled commentators, and it demands that man go to the Lord alone for refuge.

> *Abandoning all duties*
> *Come to me alone for refuge;*
> *From every evil*
> *I will save you, do not sorrow.*[2]

IMPLICATIONS

Although the word *avatāra* does not occur in the Gītā, as it does elsewhere in the Epic, and the expression of the idea is fairly short, yet the theme of the divine appearance on earth recurs in a number of passages.

---

[1] Gītā 9, 26; 9 32.   [2] 18, 64; 18, 66.

In 7, 24 there is a reference to criticisms of the cult of Krishna incarnate. Previous verses had spoken of the worship of other gods, saying that it was really Krishna who ordained these acts of worship and answered all prayers, whereas those who criticized his own worship looked only on his manifested aspect and knew nothing of his higher nature.

> *Fools think of me, the unmanifest*
> *As having come to manifestation,*
> *They do not know my higher essence*
> *As the supreme and unchangeable.*

The meaning seems to be that whether foolish people think that the bodily appearance of Krishna is all there is of him, or even if they think of him as a god, they are mistaken, for he is really the supreme of all. The conclusion is that critics of the Avatar are vain and ignorant, deluded by nature. Further, 'I am not revealed to all men', for the world is deluded and does not recognize the imperishable. Krishna, on the contrary, knows all beings, past, present and future, and nobody knows him. Nobody, that is, except his devotees, for they adore him with resolution and at the hour of death they will find deliverance in the knowledge of Brahman.

Right at the beginning of Krishna's answers, in 2, 20 ,which Otto accepted as part of the basic Gītā, there is an important variant. The Kaṭha Upanishad is quoted which says of the soul that it has not come from anywhere, 'has not become anyone' (*na babhūva kaścit*). Some modern critics of Avatar doctrine have taken this verse as proof from the ancient scriptures that God never becomes incarnate.[1] But the Gītā, in quoting this verse, changes the words to alter the whole sense by saying that the soul having come to be 'nor will evermore come not to be' (*vā na bhūyah*). This emendation averts any denial of the incarnation, of God or soul, which would be against the whole teaching of the Gītā.

A further possible reference to the Avatar is in 18, 5 where it says 'when the Lord acquires a body' (*śarīra*). The Lord here probably refers to the soul, however, although the previous verse had said that it is 'a part of me'. Yet the involvement of the soul

---

[1] Kaṭha Upanishad 2, 18; see the criticism by Devendranath Tagore quoted in a later chapter (p. 100).

and God in the material world is real, and this interpretation is strengthened by the Avatar doctrine. See also 9, 11 (above p. 38).

The Gītā stands out from the mass of the Epic, having many links with it, yet surpassing much of its teaching, notably in theology and ethics. It is partly repeated in a further section of the Mahābhārata called the Anugītā, but without the Avatar teaching of the transcendental Vision.[1] The differences are significant, and partly for this reason these other discourses have never attained the popular appeal of the Gītā. The supreme and transcendent deity, who yet shows grace and love, and his human Avatar, these have made the Gītā of central importance in the development of Indian theology.

Dasgupta says that 'this doctrine of the incarnation of God, though not dealt with in any of the purely speculative systems, yet forms the corner-stone of most systems of philosophy and religion, and the Gītā is probably the earliest work available to us in which this doctrine is found . . . For the God of the Gītā is not a God of abstract philosophy or theology, but a God who could be a man and be capable of all personal relations.'[2] But it can be questioned how widespread the idea of incarnation is, even in India, and this will be considered. Further, is it really incarnation, does God become 'a man'? The theological implications of this question will be discussed in the final section of this book.

[1] MBH 16, 16–51.   [2] *A History of Indian Philosophy*, ii, p. 525.

4

Philosophical Comments on Avatar Doctrine

AVATAR AND MONISM

The Avatar doctrine, as it appears in the Epic, and even as refined in the Gītā which does not discuss the mythology of other Avatars than Krishna, needs examination in the light of dominant Hindu philosophies. In popular theology the doctrine developed considerably, and attention will be given later to some of its ramifications. But before turning to these theological and mythological developments, it is important to see how some of the greatest Indian thinkers in the Vedāntic tradition considered the religious thought of the Gītā. For the Gītā, though taking some account of popular religion, has the background of the philosophies of the Upanishads and tries to remain true to them, even when a change is being made.

It has seemed to some Indian writers, past and present, that the concept of Avatars is an unnecessary complication, if not a betrayal of the non-dualism of the Upanishads. If the cardinal assertion of monism, 'thou art that', is true then all men are divine. It is hard to see a difference between an Avatar and other people. At most, it appears that the Avatar knows his identity with Brahman, whereas others are yet unaware of it, though potentially they are the same as he is.

The Avatar doctrine, however, as illustrated in the Epic and later works, seems to demand some degree of transcendence. The Avatar is a heavenly being, who comes to earth to manifest grace, to restore right and destroy wrong. Such transcendence, though found in Vedic and popular religion, is not harmonious with Vedāntic monism. Therefore, since thorough-going non-dualists have tried all down Indian history to maintain belief in the

48

undifferentiated unity of divine and human, their comments in the Avatar doctrine of the Gītā, however respectful, have been weak.

The appeal that monism still has comes from its apparent unity, simplicity and refinement. It does away with mythology and crude theological symbols. In place of a transcendent deity, a God 'up there', it teaches a universal Mind, with which the human mind is one. The universe appears to be informed by intelligence, indeed to be all mind, and man *is* that mind. Religion and worship disappear along with superstition. It goes without saying that there is no room for incarnation. Nor indeed is there room for revelation, prayer, or anything that suggests a transcendent Deity.

The difficulties of maintaining such a position consistently are great nevertheless. It denies the important doctrine of evil, if all is divine and the divine is all. The most that can be accepted is 'ignorance' (*ajñāna*). This further implies, at least in the Indian context, a denial of the reality of the material world, which is transient 'illusion' (*māyā*). However attractive this might be to idealists, it would be rejected both by the modern scientific minds and by Jewish-Christian-Muslim thought. Further, belief in the unreality of the world leads to a view of the relativity of good and evil, and this in turn to a complete other-worldliness, wherein the only fully liberated man is the ascetic who is beyond good and evil, and cares for neither foe nor friend.

Some European forms of monism seem to get rid of God altogether. If there is mind, it is 'this-worldly', seen in the universe and man, but there is no need to postulate a divine consciousness, somewhere 'out there' or 'in the depths'. Hindu monism, generally, made the opposite assumption. The divine was the only reality, and the human was but the pale temporary shadow or 'play' (*līlā*) of the divine. There was a difference after all. No one could possess all the divine attributes even now; the mystic could not yet claim to be omniscient and omnipresent – unless he was mad.

The Hindu monists did not deny the existence of the gods, but they also were part of the divine 'play'. In like manner the Jains and Buddhists included the gods in their mythology, but as subservient to the enlightened men, Jinas and Buddhas, and they were finally irrelevant to their scheme of salvation.

ŚANKARA

The struggles of the monists with the Avatar doctrine are well illustrated in the philosopher Śankara, to many Hindus the leader of Vedānta, the Aristotle of Indian thought. Vedānta, the 'end of the Vedas', is a term first of all applied to the Upanishads. The later Vedānta Sūtra (or Brahma Sūtra) which sought to summarize Upanishadic teaching, and the commentators who followed, represent the Vedānta schools of philosophy, though they differ widely among themselves. Modern western Neo-Vedantists tend to follow the non-dualistic teaching of Śankara's school, rather than the modifications on non-dualism, or its outright rejection, taught in other Vedānta schools.

Śankara (788–820 A.D.?) was an outstanding thinker and author of many works. He commented on the short but most fully non-dualistic Upanishad, the Māndūkya, and on the Vedānta Sūtra. It is a tribute to the importance of the Bhagavad-Gītā, that Śankara wrote a notable commentary on this work. This reveals his attitude to the problems of divine-human relationships and the Avatars.

It is significant that in his commentary on the Gītā Śankara wrote only short notes on the critical verses that deal with the coming of the Avatar, though he went to considerable length in exposition of anything that could be turned to the service of non-dualism. In the cardinal passage (Gītā 4, 6–8) Śankara comments, 'Though I am unborn, though by nature my power of vision (*jñāna-sakti*) is undecaying, yet ruling over by nature, the *māyā* of Vishnu . . . by which deluded the whole world knows not Vāsudeva, its own Self–I appear to be born and embodied, through my own *māyā*, and not in reality, unlike others.'[1]

This seems to deny the reality of incarnation. On the next verse Śankara simply says, 'I manifest myself through *māyā*'. He had noted Arjuna's problem, Krishna's birth was later than others. His attitude is summed up in his terse comment on verse 9, 'my birth is an illusion'. In contrast, his successor and critic Rāmānuja wrote pages of comment on these crucial verses.

[1] A. M. Śāstri, *The Bhagavad-Gītā with the commentary of Śrī Śankarachāryā*, 5th edn., 1961, p. 121.

On later passages of the Gītā which teach the same Avatar (7, 24 and 9, 11) Śankara is equally brief. 'The ignorant think that I have just now come into manifestation, having been unmanifested hitherto, though I am the ever luminous Lord. I am not manifest to all people; that is to say, I am manifest only to a few who are my devotees. I am veiled by Yoga-māyā'.[1]

However, in the introduction to his commentary on the Gītā, Śankara explains his views a little more fully. When there was a growth of lust in the votaries of religion, and irreligion was increasing, then the original creator (ādi-kartri) Vishnu, known as Nārāyana, wishing to maintain order in the universe, 'sent part of himself' as Krishna, begotten in Devakī by Vasudeva. 'Sent part of himself' (*aṁśena saṁbabhūva*) seems to reflect the view that Krishna was only a part of Vishnu, who himself was inferior to the un-differentiated Brahman. But followers of Śankara have had diffi-culty with this notion, since it is generally held that Krishna was the full and perfect Avatar of Vishnu. So the annotator Ānandagiri said that 'part' meant in an illusory form created by the Lord's own will.[2]

Śankara continued that the Avatar came 'for the 'preservation of earthly Brahman, of spiritual life on earth'. This is generally taken to mean scriptures and sacrifices. He said that the Lord, who always possesses infinite knowledge and power, controls the *māyā* which belongs to him as Vishnu, and appears to the world 'as though' he were embodied and helping the world at large. But, Śankara explains, 'really he is unborn' and indestructible; he is the Lord of creatures and is by nature eternal, intelligent and free.

This is virtually all that Śankara can find to say on the Avatar theme in the Gītā, in his commentary. It is remarkable that his comments on the transcendental vision of chapter eleven are very brief and formal.

But in his commentary on the Vedānta Sūtra Śankara's views are developed. He quotes the Gītā in this work, but none of the passages directly about the Avatar. At the beginning he recognizes that some men believe that in addition to individual souls there is an almighty omniscient Lord. But he maintains that the Lord is the self of the enjoyer, that is the individual self whose individuality

[1] *ibid.*, p. 218. [2] *ibid.*, p. 3.

is only apparent, the result of ignorance. He says that the Lord needs no body, and there is no soul different from the Lord.[1]

Yet later, as a concession to religious needs, Śankara admits that 'the highest Lord may, when he pleases, assume a bodily shape formed of *māyā*, in order thereby to gratify his worshippers'. This is a new motive for incarnation. He explains various Upanishadic texts which imply a Lord as object of devotion. But the individual gods, such as 'a certain powerful god called Indra', are spoken of as intelligent selves which denote the highest Brahman. And a popular Upanishadic passage about the two birds on a tree does not really show that the Lord is separate from the soul.[2]

Śankara attacked the Buddhists because, he said, they did not admit of any permanent intelligent being or ruling Lord who created all. On the other hand the Bhāgavatas, devout followers of Krishna, were criticized for holding dependent origination, the creation of all things by Vāsudeva. Śankara admitted that the highest Self 'appears in manifold forms', but not that the soul is originated, for that would mean that it was not eternal. So he held that the soul is a part of the highest Self, just as a spark is a part of a fire. And although the Lord may be contemplated in images, yet he must be understood as the self.[3]

Śankara's concession to popular religion may be seen in the hymns that he composed. There must be few philosophers who have been also hymn writers. R. C. Zaehner has translated a typical hymn, from which two verses may be selected to show how far Śankara went in his imagery. It is in praise of Krishna under his popular title of Govinda, cowherd:

> *If a man study the Bhagavad Gītā a little,*
> *or drink only a drop or two of Ganges waters,*
> *or worship Krishna (Murāri) only once,*
> *how should death pay any attention to him?*
> *Worship Govinda, worship Govinda, worship Govinda,*
> *deluded man.*

[1] *The Vedānta-Sūtras with the commentary of Śankarācārya*, translated by G. Thibaut, 'Sacred Books of the East', 1904, I, I, 2; I, I, 5.
[2] Śankara I, I, 20; I, I, 29; I, 3, 7; Śvetāśvatara Upanishad, 4, 6f., etc.
[3] Śankara 2, 2, 42; 2, 3, 43; 4, I, 3.

Chant songs more than a thousand times,
think always of the form of Vishnu (Śrī),
meditate in the company of good men,
give your property to the afflicted.
Worship Govinda, worship Govinda, worship Govinda,
   deluded man.[1]

It might seem that this religious devotion contradicted all the monism that Śankara taught, and many of his followers at least have engaged in fervent worship to a personal God. But for Śankara himself religious worship was simply a means to an end beyond itself. It was a useful technique for concentrating thoughts, like the invocation of the Lord in the Yoga-sūtras of Patañjali. Even the apparently fervent chorus 'worship Govinda', is used, like telling beads, for its mental disciplinary value.

For Śankara, as for many other Hindus, the gods that men worship are useful helps, 'a god of one's choice' (*ishta-devatā*). The notion of choosing one's own god, balancing one against another, is repugnant to those brought up in the Semitic religions, and reflects a view of the divine nature which may be congruous with monism but seems alien to belief in transcendence.

Śankara's meaning comes through in the last verse of this hymn, where he says, 'though you perform pilgrimages, keep vows and give alms, all this without knowledge is worthless'. Worship and good works are for spiritual beginners, and are temporary. The essential is 'knowledge', that key word of the Upanishads, which the Gītā struggled to surpass. The knowledge is of the truth, of the eternal nature of the soul and its identification with the divine, and is worth far more than cultus or morality.

Śankara, for all his attention to the Gītā, does not accept the full implications of either the incarnation or the transcendent deity of grace shown there. He is unhappy in his comments on *bhakti*, recognizing that the way of knowledge is hard, but elevating it above every other way. He uses the Gītā, like other writings and his own hymns, to support a persistent teaching of the non-duality of human and divine.

[1] *Mysticism Sacred and Profane*, 1957, p. 178.

RĀMĀNUJA

Rāmānuja (eleventh century A.D.) was very different and really grappled with the problems of the Avatar belief. It is important to consider his teachings, to show that there are other teachers of Vedānta than Śankara and of as high quality. Dasgupta lists sixty-one objections that Rāmānuja made to the teaching of Śankara. Not only was he a critic of complete monism, but Rāmānuja supplied serious justifications for a theism that was of great value to popular religion.

For Rāmānuja the supreme God is Vishnu, who is identical with the Brahman of the Upanishads. The individual soul is not the same as Brahman, but neither is it entirely different from it. The soul stands in a relationship of 'difference-non-difference' (*bhedābheda*) to Brahman, in so far as it is a 'part' (*aṁśa*) of Brahman. This provides what is called 'qualified non-dualism' (*viśishtādvaita*). God, souls and the world form a unity; souls and the world are the body of God and are real, but they depend on God and are nothing apart from him. 'The Brahman to be reached by the meditating devotee must be something different from him'.[1]

This theism made Rāmānuja much more at home than Śankara with the doctrine of Avatars, and he quotes the Gītā constantly, equally with the oldest scriptures. The Lord takes human form through compassion, so as to make himself understandable to his followers. 'This essential form of his the most compassionate Lord by his mere will individualizes as a shape human or divine or otherwise, so as to render it suitable to the apprehension of the devotee and thus satisfy him.' The *māyā* by which the Lord is manifested means the 'purpose', the knowledge of the Divine Being.[2]

But Rāmānuja does not yet seem to be clear on the reality of the incarnation. It is true that he says that 'in order to fit himself to be a refuge for gods and men, the supreme Person, without however putting aside his true nature, associates himself with the shape, make, qualities and works of the different classes of beings, and thus is born in many ways.' But he also says that 'in the Mahābhā-rata the form assumed by the highest Person in his avatars is

[1] *The Vedānta-sūtras with the Commentary by Rāmānuja*, trs. G. Thibaut, 1904, I, I, I; I, I, 16.
[2] *ibid.*, I, I, 21.

said not to consist of Prakriti (nature), "the body of the highest Self does not consist of a combination of material elements".'[1]

Rāmānuja justified the Bhāgavata devotees of Vishnu in their teaching that the highest Brahman, which they called Vāsudeva, voluntarily abides in various forms. Brahman divides itself into aspects, or hypostases, such as the 'subtle' (*sūkshma*), the 'division' (*vyūha*), and the manifestation (*vibhava*). These terms recall the Buddhist doctrine of the Trikāya, or three forms of Buddha, of which more will be said later. The 'manifestation' form of Brahman is the aggregate of the Avatars, like Rāma or Krishna, in whom the highest Being becomes manifest.[2]

In his commentary on the Bhagavad-Gītā, Rāmānuja gave more attention to the theory and purpose of the Avatars than Śankara ever did. 'The Lord of Śrī . . . willed to assume forms similar to those of his creatures, without abandoning his own essential nature, and repeatedly made descents as Avatars in the several spheres.' The object of the Avatar coming was to relieve the earth of its burden, as the Epic had said, but Rāmānuja added that at the same time it was no less the Lord's intention that he should be within the reach even of people of our description. To fulfil this purpose he manifested himself on earth, so as to be actually the object for all human eyes to see. He performed other wonderful acts, so as to captivate the hearts and eyes of all creatures, high and low. He delighted the worlds by his looks and language, over-flowing with the nectar of friendship and love.[3]

Rāmānuja continued that under the pretext of persuading Arjuna to fight, Krishna had promulgated the doctrine of Bhakti-Yoga, led up to by Jñāna-Yoga and Karma-Yoga. That path of loving devotion was the burden of all Vedānta teaching, he says rather optimistically, by which Krishna is indicated as the only object of love. Then, being loved, Krishna is the means of leading man to the climax of his aims, which is salvation.

On the Avatar teaching of Gītā 4, Rāmānuja says that Arjuna's introductory question, 'How can I understand that it was you who taught this Yoga in the beginning?' was put purposely in

[1] *ibid.*, 1, 3, 2.   [2] *ibid.*, 2, 2, 42.

[3] *Śrī Bhagavad Gītā with Śrī Rāmānujāchārya's Visishtādvaita Commentary*, trs. A. Govindacharya, 1898, introduction.

order to evoke an exposition of the meaning of Avatars. Were the Avatar births determined by Karma, as gods and men are determined? Were the Avatars real, or illusory like magic (*indrajāla*)? Under what circumstances do Avatars take place? What is the nature of the body that is assumed? And at what times do they take place?

That Avatars are real is shown by the statement, 'I have had many births'. And this is supported by adding Arjuna's birth, 'so have you as well', which was both real and historic. The Avatar comes by the Lord's own free choice, for he says, 'by my power I come to being'. A number of verses are quoted from the Upanishads, to show that the Lord takes on forms of gods as if he were of their nature. But whereas all creatures are impelled by *karma* God acts of his free will.[1]

The times of the Avatars are not fixed, but 'whensoever right declines' then the Lord manifests himself in Avatars. However there is not necessarily only one Avatar for each age (*yuga*), as suggested by the Epic and Purānas, but the Avatar comes freely when needed. 'Age by age' (*yuge-yuge*) implies that the Lord becomes incarnate whenever he chooses, not that his Avatars are confined to any particular age, such as the *krita*, or the *tretā*.

The purpose of incarnation is 'for protection of the virtuous', those who seek out the Lord as their shelter, those who feel that without seeking him they cannot live or support their being. Yet the Lord is not confined to manifestation in Avatars, for the Gītā declares:

> *In whatever way men seek me*
> *By that way I grant them favour.*[2]

So 'not only by the method of Avatars, in the forms of gods and men and so on, but by any other method or form, which it may be to their pleasing option to select. Whatever that is, to that I adapt myself. By whatever conception they choose to seek me, I manifest myself to them in that mode . . . I suit myself in such a manner that I am to them not only a visible demonstration, but that they may enjoy me by every one of their sense faculties, and in all diverse ways'.[3]

---

[1] Govindāchārya's translation, pp. 138f.   [2] Gītā 4, 11.
[3] Govindāchārya's translation, p. 143.

Rāmānuja gives full treatment to the Epic teaching on Avatars, and adds ideas from his own theology. The theism which he struggled at length and with great subtlety to maintain, is well illustrated in the beautiful passage which concludes his commentary on the Vedānta Sūtra, and which other theists can appreciate:

'We know from Scripture that there is a Supreme Person whose nature is absolute bliss and goodness; who is fundamentally antagonistic to all evil; who is the cause of the origination, sustenation and dissolution of the world; who differs in nature from all other beings, who is all-knowing, who by his mere thought and will accomplishes all his purposes; who is an ocean of kindness as it were for all who depend on him; who is all-merciful; who is immeasurably raised above all possibility of any one being equal or superior to him; whose name is the Highest Brahman.

'And with equal certainty we know from Scripture that this Supreme Lord, when pleased by the faithful worship of his devotees . . . frees them from the influence of Nescience which consists of *karma* . . . and allows them to attain to that supreme bliss which consists in the direct intuition of his own true nature . . .

'We need not fear that the Supreme Lord, when once having taken to himself the devotee whom he greatly loves, will turn him back to *saṁsāra* (transmigration). For he himself has said, "To the wise man I am very dear, and he is dear to me".'[1]

Madhva

There were other notable critics of Śankara. Probably before Rāmānuja a commentary on the Vedānta Sūtra was written by Bhāskara, in which he accused Śankara of upholding Buddhist views because he thought the world had come from *māyā* and not from some modification of Brahman. And in the thirteenth century Madhva declared even more strongly that Śankara was a crypto-Buddhist, because there was no difference between his qualityless Brahman and the 'void' (*śūnya*) of the Buddhists.[2]

[1] Rāmānuja 4, 4, 22.
[2] Dasgupta, *History of Indian Philosophy*, iii, 1; iv, pp. 69f.

Madhva (1197–1276 A.D.) held that God, souls and the world exist permanently, but the latter are fully dependent on God and ever subordinate to him. He said that Brahman denotes Vishnu, for 'all the Vedas declare him only', and in the Epics and Purānas, 'in the beginning, in the middle and at the end, yea, everywhere, Vishnu is sung'. This supreme Lord pervades and actuates all beings, but is unmixed with matter and untouched by qualities. But it is clear that this Brahman is not the embodied self, for the latter is not omnipresent. Their power differs, and 'there is no equality in experience between the Lord and the self; for the Lord is all-knowing, all-powerful, and absolute; while the self is of little understanding, of little power and absolutely dependent'.[1]

Madhva wrote a commentary on the Bhagavad-Gītā, and on chapter four he asked, 'why should the Lord create such bodies as Vāsudeva, and so on, out of nature under his control and enter into them?' The answer is in the words 'directing my own nature', namely, I follow my own nature without any ulterior purpose, in manifesting myself to the world. Thus the birth of the Lord was of a quite different description from that of the soul (*jīva*). Madhva held that though the souls are parts of God, they are not parts in the same sense as the Avatars are parts of God. The Avatars are parts of the essential nature of God (*svarūpāṁśa*), whereas the souls though parts are different from the essential nature, and are reflections of God.[2]

According to Madhva the purpose of the Avatar is not that the Lord had a motive for himself, but his appearance in the world was full of purpose, in establishing right and eradicating wrong. This was intimated by the Lord in pointing to the times when he appears in the world. In discussing 'age by age I come into being' Madhva said that it is possible for God, without manifesting himself to the world, to accomplish the work of protecting the righteous. But that he does appear in the world is simply his supreme pleasure and mercy to do so. He does this by virtue of his very nature, but not under any necessity. Similarly his divine birth

[1] *Vedanta Sutras with the Commentary of Sri Madhwacharya*, trs. by S. Subbha Rao, 2nd edn., 1936.

[2] *Bhagavad Gītā translated according to Sri Madhwacharya's Bhashyas*, by S. Subbha Rao, 1906, pp. 102f.; Dasgupta, *A History of Indian Philosophy*, iv, p. 147.

is not subject to the karmic laws which give the birth of creatures, but it is the effect of his free will and grace.

Not all the critics of Śankara agreed with Madhva, and his school has also been regarded as too intellectualist by followers of Rāmānuja and other Vaishnavites. But his disciples regarded Madhva himself as an Avatar of the wind, Vāyu, sent with the express purpose of destroying the injurious teachings of Śankara, which were like those of the Jains and Buddhists, but even more obnoxious. Madhva himself wrote that the Buddhist texts had been sent by Vishnu to bring confusion, and those of the Śaivites were sent for the same purpose by Śiva at the command of Vishnu.[1]

Madhva's theism and devotional teaching made some European writers think that he was influenced by Christian teaching, perhaps by the Syrian Christians of South India. But there is no evidence that he knew any Christian teachers or writings, or that Indian Christians were important enough to have influenced him. Madhva claimed that all his teachings were based on the Vedānta and Epics, and his theistic and *bhakti* ideas can be traced back to these sources, which are old and pre-Christian.[2]

OTHER VIEWS

The doctrines of the Pañcarātras were ancient and important in the development of Vaishnava thought. Their theories of incarnation were based on the notion of *āveśas*, 'entrances' or 'possessions' of the god into mundane forms, and this fitted in with the idea of the pervasiveness of Vishnu, which enabled him to be identified with all gods and beings, and helped to assimilate him to the personal aspect of the pervasive Brahman. The 'entrance-Avatar' (*āveśāva-tāra*) was produced by the divine will in human or animal form. It was of two kinds; the 'power-entrance' (*sakty-āveśa*) when Brahmā or Śiva were occasionally endowed with special powers, and the 'own form entrance' (*svarūpāveśa*) in Krishna, Rāma and the like. But superior to these were the 'primary incarnations'

[1] Dasgupta, *A History of Indian Philosophy*, iv, pp. 52, 27.
[2] G. A. Grierson, *Mādhvas*, in *Encyclopaedia of Religion and Ethics*, vol. 8; but see Dasgupta, *op. cit.*, iv, pp. 92f.

(*sākshād-avatāra*) which came directly from the Lord and were non-mundane. However, there were differences of opinions as to which these transcendent forms were. The pure manifestations (*vyūha*) of Vishnu created the world, protected beings, and helped devotees to final liberation.[1]

Quite different views of the function of Avatars are found in the logical Nyāya school. The Nyāyas taught a rational theology in which the existence and unity of God were accepted on a principle of parsimony; but they believed that souls as well as God are uncreated and eternal. Jayanta (A.D. 850–910) admitted that the Vedas are authoritative and conform to experience to some extent. But so do the scriptures of other faiths, and if they seem to contradict one another, so do many Vedic passages. If other scriptures differ from the Vedas they may agree with some parts of the Vedas which are not known at present, and also the texts of Buddhists, Jains, and Sāṁkhyas may have been given by God in previous Avatars. All scriptures are authoritative, said Jayanta, and so they must be the work of omniscient beings, but it is better to say that one God is the author of all scriptures than to posit numbers of beings. All scriptures agree on the need for liberation, and this comes from God who sees the misery of beings, and out of compassion he teaches them the way of salvation. He knows that not all can follow the same path, and so he takes on different bodies, called by such names as Mahāvīra, Buddha, Kapila, and so on. Jayanta quoted Gītā 4, on the purpose of the divine manifestation, and he added that the compassion of God was shown most fully there to the greatest number of people, for it is suitable to the majority.[2]

Reference to popular modern reaction to Avatar doctrine will be made later, but two important philosophical writers may be noted here. K. S. Murty has made a penetrating criticism of Śankara's commentary on the Gītā. He picks up Śankara's statement that the creator Nārāyana was 'partially' (*aṁśena*) born as Krishna. As God could not have any parts, in Śankara's philosophy the use of the word 'partially' can only mean that although God became an Avatar as Krishna, yet he has not ceased to be the

[1] Dasgupta, op. cit., iii, pp. 37ff.
[2] K. S. Murty, *Revelation and Reason in Advaita Vedānta*, 1959, pp. 232ff.

creator and sustainer of the universe, and he is both omnipresent and omniscient. Therefore although he became Krishna, the form of Krishna did not exhaust him.

Śankara accepted the theory of Avatar and believed that Krishna was the Lord (*Īśvara*) himself. Krishna existed prior to his birth on earth, but many did not worship him, not knowing him to be the immutable Lord. So 'it is clear from this that Śankara accepts the theory of Incarnation'. But in his criticism later Murty declares that, to be consistent with his non-dualist theory, 'Śankara cannot accept the theory of *avatāras*'. For since all individuals are Brahman, in what way is an Avatar superior? Śankara's reply would be that the appearance of an Avatar is an illusion in a double sense, while the appearance of a soul (*jīva*) is an illusion in one sense only. An Avatar as a phenomenon of the empirical world is already an illusion, but since God does not really become a man the appearance is a double illusion.

Śankara, following the Gītā, explained that while an Avatar knows his identity with Brahman, others do not. But if this is so, then great sages who knew of this identity would be Avatars, though they are not claimed as such, and they did not appear in special ages to redress the balance of right and wrong. Or, if the Avatar is only a knower of Brahman, who cannot be reborn when he has gained this perfect knowledge, how can he be born in every age?

So it is concluded that Śankara's whole teaching of non-dualism 'breaks on the rocks of the theory of incarnation'. This shows that Śankara's attempts to absorb the conception of the Lord, and give his system an air of theism, is untenable. But Śankara's treatment of Brahman and Īśvara is uneven. His followers, who regarded Brahman as the Absolute, had to speak of it as beyond any relationship with the world, and so Īśvara became the universal cause. But Śankara himself seemed to leave the question open. Brahman was supreme and pure of qualities, which are postulated of Īśvara, but Brahman was somehow the cause and connected with Avatars.[1]

Yet in a logically monistic system there is no room for either Īśvara or Avatar, any more than for worship and prayer. On the other hand the theistic teachers, like Rāmānuja and Madhva,

---

[1] *ibid.*, pp. 7ff., 278f.

regarded the Avatars as real occurrences. Īśvara was Brahman, the world was his body and dependent on him, the Avatars were divine descents to bring souls to salvation.

Surendranath Dasgupta also criticizes Śankara seriously at the conclusion of his study of his philosophy. Dasgupta says that 'there seems to be much truth in the accusations against Śankara . . . that he was a hidden Buddhist himself. I am led to think that Śankara's philosophy is largely a compound of . . . Buddhism with the Upanishad notion of the permanence of self superadded.'[1]

This is a large superaddition, and P. D. Devanandan thinks that Dasgupta is too harsh. He quotes Śankara's severe condemnation of Buddhist theories as having no foundation, and giving way on all sides 'like the walls of a well dug in a sandy soil.' Moreover, although the forms of the external world were illusory to Śankara, yet he believed that they all had a permanent background in the Brahman, which was the only reality.[2]

Yet the Brahman of which Śankara wrote is so characterless as to be not unlike the 'void' of Buddhist philosophers, and Śankara attacked the Nyāya writers who believed in an eternal God as well as eternal souls. For him, as for much of the Vedāntic tradition, the ultimate reality was the self. No doubt this was an advance on Buddhism, which denied or ignored the existence both of God and souls, but it was hardly adequate to allow for a proper interpretation of the Gītā.

Śankara spoke of the Lord (Īśvara) as a useful image, a help for those who need him, as the Yoga writers said, but with no ultimate reality. But in the Bhagavad Gītā the Lord is the ultimate reality, beyond Brahman itself, transcendent and eternal. It is this eternal God who manifests himself personally and visibly, showing grace and compassion to his creatures. The Avatar doctrine, therefore, demands a positive theism and a more thoroughly religious exposition than some of the classical commentators gave to it.[3]

[1] *A History of Indian Philosophy*, i, p. 494.
[2] *The Concept of Māyā*, 1954, pp. 108f.
[3] R. C. Zaehner has shown how the theism of the Gītā has been misinterpreted by monists, from Śankara to modern Neo-Vedāntists, *The Bhagavad-Gītā*, pp. 3ff.

5

Avatar in Rāma

The Rāmāyana of Vālmīki

Belief in Avatars developed in connection with Rāma as well as Krishna. The story of Rāma (Rāma-chandra) is one of the most popular of all Indian historical legends and religious myths; it is a noble tale and relatively straightforward. It occurs in several versions in the Mahābhārata. Rāma first appears there dwelling in the woods with his brother Lakshmana, and ranging the hills with his bow. Then it is said that for the destruction of the demon Rāvana, Vishnu in his own body took birth as Rāma, son of king Daśaratha. He was challenged by Paraśu Rāma (with the axe) to draw a celestial bow. This Rāma did easily and, in anger, to rebuke the vanity of Paraśu Rāma, he was transfigured as Vishnu, with all the gods in his body. Later still Rāma appeared with the monkey god, Hanuman, campaigning in Ceylon (Lankā), the kingdom of the demon Rāvana who had abducted Rāma's wife.[1]

The Rāma narrative may have some historical origins, and he was perhaps a chief of the forest regions to the south-east of the Delhi plains where much of the Great Epic took place. The tale, much overlaid with legendary and mythical detail, is told more fully in the other great epic, the Rāmāyana, the 'story of Rāma'. This is about a quarter of the length of the Mahābhārata, and is much more of a unity. The first and last of its seven books are probably later additions and are chiefly didactic. The Rāmāyana is attributed to the sage Vālmīki, and may have been written a little before the Christian era.

In the first book of the Rāmāyana Rāma is seen most clearly as the Avatar of Vishnu. His wife Sītā is an Avatar of Lakshmī, the

[1] MBH 3, 25; 3, 99; 3, 146f.

consort of Vishnu. It is said that all castes may read this story and he who studies it with devotion will become free from sin. Then Daśaratha is introduced as king of Ayodhyā, performing the great horse-sacrifice for the birth of a son. The gods gather at the sacrifice, including Vishnu with his conch, discus and mace, and dressed in yellow robes. The other gods implore him to destroy Rāvana who is oppressing all beings, and Vishnu decides to become incarnate as the four sons of Daśaratha. A great red being comes out of the sacrificial fire bearing a celestial dish, of which the king's three wives partake. So Vishnu is born as their sons, with limitless splendour as Rāma, and with a portion of his glory in the others. Then follow accounts of Rāma's exploits and marriage. His wife Sītā is daughter of the Earth; her name means 'furrow', and she rose from the earth when her adoptive father was ploughing the land for a sacrifice. Rāma broke the celestial bow, defeated Parasu Rāma, and deprived him of glory so that he retired to the mountains.[1]

In the second book old king Daśaratha is about to name Rāma as regent, when his second wife reminds him of a promise to make her son king. The king objects, but Rāma himself insists on the word being kept, and he retires to the forest with Sītā and his brother Lakshmana. So the little party sets out for an ascetic life. It is particularly interesting to note the occasional comments which the Rāmāyana makes on the hardships suffered by the princely Avatar, which shows his humanity, in some degree. Sri Rāma enters the forest like a common man, dresses as an ascetic with clothes of bark and with matted hair, hunts deer and feeds on roots when hungry, and sleeps on straw or on the ground. He offers a sacrifice of a black deer, adores Rudra and Vishnu, erects altars in eight directions for different gods, offers oblations for expiation of sins, and takes ritual baths. When the news of his father's death reaches him, Rāma faints, then weeps bitterly, and calls himself worthless and wretched that he had not been able to perform the funeral rites.[2]

In the third book Rāma and his brother kill many demons, who afflict villagers and ascetics, and this so annoys their master Rāvana that he plots revenge. Disguised as an ascetic Rāvana comes to the

[1] Rāmāyana 1, 16–18.   [2] *ibid.* 2, 51ff., 102f.

hermitage during Rāma's absence, and carries off Sītā in his aerial car (*vimāna*) to his castle in Ceylon. Rāma weeps in despair, then is angry, and gathers allies for the pursuit. The monkey Hanuman, son of the wind, leaps over the straits between India and Ceylon and wreaks havoc in Rāvana's palace. Rāma's army crosses the sea on a causeway made by the monkeys with rocks; Rāvana is slain and Sītā rescued. But Rāma then repudiated Sītā, since she had lived in another man's house. Sītā chose to undergo an ordeal by fire; she entered the flames but was untouched and the fire-god Agni restored her to Rāma. So the pair returned to Ayodhyā, where Rāma was crowned and ruled ten thousand years.

The last and later book of the Rāmāyana recapitulates the struggles of Rāma and Rāvana. Sītā is again repudiated, and when she pleads her innocence before Rāma a throne appears from the earth and she descends in it to her mother Earth. Then death, disguised as an ascetic, calls on Rāma to say that his task is accomplished, he may stay among mortals or return to the gods. Rāma declares that he has achieved the purpose of his earthly being, he came for the good of the worlds, now he will leave without delay. After issuing his last commands, Rāma goes with his people to a river, where the gods, headed by Brahmā, hail him as Vishnu. Rāma steps into the water, to the sound of music, and enters Vishnu's abode with his younger brothers.[1]

The story of Rāma is largely narrative, interspersed with religious expressions. It has been taken ever since as an example of heroism and noble conduct. The married bliss of the royal couple, and Sītā's chastity, are patterns of true love and wifely devotion. But it is more than an example. Rāma is one of the greatest Avatars, a being of pure character, both human and divine. The name Rāma is a favourite title of the deity, chanted on many occasions, especially at the time of death. For some it is the chief name of the Supreme Being.

Apart from the first and last books there are other passages, whether later additions or not, of religious praise. When Rāma doubts Sītā's purity the gods come to rebuke him for being ignorant, though he is divine. Rāma asks them, 'I think myself a man, Rāma, son of Daśaratha, but who am I really?' He is told

[1] *ibid.*, 7, 104ff.

that he is Vishnu, the boar, the dwarf, Krishna, creator of Indra and the gods, Purusha, OM, the Vedas, the Himalayas, the imperishable Brahman itself.[1]

This assumption is behind all the story, as it is cherished now, whatever basis there may have been of a historical figure called Rāma. Now he is divine, a great Avatar, a supreme object of devotion, whose story is cherished by millions. Every year the Daśarā (ten-day) festival, in September–October, celebrates Rāma's battle against Rāvana, in which the Avatar had the help of the goddess Durgā. Huge cardboard figures of Rāma and Rāvana are paraded in cars and arrows are shot from one to the other, the climax coming when Rāvana's image, filled with crackers, explodes and shows the defeat of evil.

THE RĀMĀYANA OF TULSĪ DĀS

Down the ages the popularity of Rāma has increased and has been the subject of devotional stories and hymns. The great poet Kālidāsa (5th-6th century A.D.) dedicated one of his greatest poems, the Raghuvaṁśa, the 'race of Raghu', to this story. He followed in the main the narrative of Vālmīki, though the birth of Rāma was not placed till the tenth chapter. Then Vishnu says that he himself will become the son of Daśaratha, and the luminous principle (*caru*) of Vishnu comes to the king's wives in the vessel from the fire. The story follows the traditional pattern till the ascension of Rāma to heaven in a celestial chariot.[2]

Many centuries after Vālmīki a great poet, Tulsī Dās, made his own version of the Rāma story in Hindi and ensured it even more popularity. Tulsī Dās lived from 1543 to 1623 A.D., much of it in Benares (Varanāsi, Kāśī). His 'Holy Lake of the Acts of Rāma' (Rāma-charita-mānasa) gives new touches to the story particularly to its theological implications. Though written so much later, than Vālmīki's Rāmāyana, it can usefully be discussed here, while the Avatar of Rāma is being considered.

In the Holy Lake, from the outset, Rāma is called Lord Hari (Vishnu), Hari in human form, the Supreme Spirit who has taken bodily form 'simply to do his faithful servants good, a Lord of

[1] Rāmāyana, 6, 119.   [2] See *Le Raghuvaṃça*, trs. by L. Renou, 1928.

perfect grace who loves his suppliant people'. He took the form of man and 'endured suffering to make the good happy'.[1]

Tulsī stresses the importance of devout repetition of the name of Rāma. There are two forms of the Absolute, the personal and the impersonal, but the Name is greater than both, for it makes them both known. Although the Absolute dwells in all hearts yet men are sad, but by utterance of the Name the Lord becomes manifest. Tulsī feels his own wickedness, and is afraid, but Rāma does not take sin into account; he looks for motive and faith. So his story is a Lake into which a soul should plunge and find refreshment.[2]

The Holy Lake is said to be related by the god Śiva to his wife Pārvatī. Several times the goddess questions how Rāma, the prince, who wept at the loss of his wife Sītā, could really be the Absolute Brahman that knows no origin. How could the impersonal qualityless (*nirguna*) Brahman assume a personal (*saguna*) form? It must be some other Rāma who is the hero. The reply is given by Śiva that there is no difference between personal and impersonal, so all the Vedas and sages say; for the impersonal and invisible becomes personal for love of his devotees. Rāma, 'as all the world knows', is the Absolute, everlasting God.[3]

The cause of the coming of Avatars is the decay of righteousness and the rise of arrogant demons. Then the Lord in grace puts on various bodily forms to relieve the distress of the faithful. He appeared as boar, man-lion, and Rāma. Each Avatar has its story. The tale of the birth of Rāma then begins, though it is not a mere translation of Vālmīki. Tulsī wonders that the infinite Lord, in whose every hair a universe dwells, rested in his mother's womb, and that 'the Lord of lords became a child and began to cry'. Rāma did indeed transfigure himself before his mother, so that she said, 'I held the Father of the world to be my son', but he warned her not to repeat what she had seen.[4]

But Rāma played childish tricks, and he whom the Vedas call 'not this', whom Śiva regards as infinite, would struggle with his mother, or come in from play covered with grime. He went to study under a teacher, but this was a good jest, for his natural breath was the four Vedas. Rāma's body was dark, his eyes like

---

[1] W. D. P. Hill, *The Holy Lake of the Acts of Rāma*, 1952, pp. 10, 16.
[2] *ibid.*, pp. 16ff.   [3] *ibid.*, pp. 57f.   [4] *ibid.*, p. 89.

lotuses, and he carried bow and arrows. He broke the celestial
bow, and Paraśu Rāma recognized his power. At Rāma's wedding
with Sītā the gods came in troops, and Vishnu gazed lovingly on
his Avatar.[1]

Tulsī brings out more human-divine traits when Rāma went
into exile. He who had not hitherto known sorrow now came to
know it at his exclusion from the throne. As a king may dream he
is a beggar, so Rāma really came to sleep on the ground. When he
arrived at the Ganges the ferryman refused to take him across, and
Rāma had to beseech him, whereupon the boatman washed his
feet and the gods rained flowers from heaven. Rāma who had
never known pain now roamed the woods on foot, and fed on
roots and fruit. When Sītā had an ominous dream Rāma's eyes
were filled with tears, and when the news came of his father's
death he was distressed, and was comforted by a sage. When Sītā
was abducted Rāma wept, acted, and spoke 'like an ordinary
man'.[2]

Tulsī comments later that the Lord exhibited 'all sorts of illusory
feats' like a showman. He let himself be bound for a time in battle.
But can he, 'the omnipresent home of the universe, be brought
into bondage?' 'It is idle to argue about the actions of Rāma as
personal, whether by the power of reason or by speech; and that
is why mystics and ascetics worship him without disputation'.[3]

Tulsī's insistence on belief in a personal God comes out clearly
towards the end of his work. 'Now all the sages whom I questioned told me that God is present in all creation; but this doctrine
of the impersonal did not satisfy me; I became ever more attached
to the Absolute made personal'. He argued with a sage who gave
'a matchless account of Hari, but he demolished the doctrine of
the personal and expounded the impersonal. But I would have
nothing of the impersonal and persisted in expounding the personal'. So he revolved all sorts of questions in his own mind: 'Can
there be anger without duality, or duality without ignorance? Can
a soul that is limited and brutish, a prey to illusion, be like God?'[4]

The Vedas, says Tulsī, in the form of bards, drew near to Rāma
and sang his perfections: 'O thou who art personal and imper-

[1] Hill, *Holy Lake*, p. 93.   [2] *ibid.*, pp. 202, 242, 261, 394f.
[3] *ibid.*, p. 400.   [4] *ibid.*, pp. 484f.

sonal . . . descending in the form of man, thou hast rid the earth of its burden. . . . Let those who contemplate the Absolute . . . speak of It and know It; we, O Lord, hymn thy glory unceasingly as personal'.[1]

Tulsī had said that 'there is no religious duty like doing good to others, no vileness like doing them harm'. But at the end the emphasis is upon simple faith and repetition of the divine Name. Sing and meditate only on Rāma. Even the most defiled by sin are purified 'if they repeat but once the name of Rāma whom I adore.' Rāma alone is beautiful, and he looks with love on the destitute.

Tulsī Dās reacted against some of the reformers of his time, Kabīr and Nānak and their followers, who neglected the Vedas and denied the doctrines of Avatars. It is true that he spoke, like them, of the Brahman without qualities, who can only be described as 'not this'. But practically Tulsī stressed the 'with qualities' (*saguna*) form of God, with the attributes of Avatar. He resembles the Smārtas, a syncretistic group who believed especially in the 'remembered' scriptures (*smriti;* law books, Epics and Purānas), and worshipped popular deities. But Tulsī was not devoted as they were to Śiva and his associates, so much as to the Avatar of Vishnu in Rāma. He attacked those who scorned the Epics and Purānas and left the path of devotion.

The descriptions of Rāma, given in the Holy Lake, are continued in a long poem by Tulsī called from its metre the Kavitāvalī. Here he gives a few reasons for the Avatar, which are partly traditional but show some advance.

> As a bridge for religion,
>   for the sake of the earth's well-being,
> And to lighten the load of earth
>   did He take incarnation as a man;
> It is the Master's way to care
>   for order, faith and affection.[2]

The praises of Rāma are sung by Tulsī Dās at length in the Vinaya-patrikā, the Petition to Rām. The fifty-second chapter of this poem lists the ten Avatars of Vishnu, beginning with the Fish. Rāma is the seventh Avatar in this list, and Krishna the eighth.

[1] *ibid.*, pp. 438f.   [2] *Kavitāvalī*, trs. F. R. Allchin, 1964, p. 178.

The ninth Avatar is 'compassionate Buddha' who came to 'set aside the entire complex of sacrifices and karma.'[1]

These poems contain delightful words on the child Rāma, and others on his youth and exploits. Although the other Avatars are mentioned, yet all Tulsī's devotion is to Rāma. He is spoken of as mother, father, sister, brother, teacher, disciple, servant, companion, and God.

> *He is Tulsī's love – dear as life,*
> *what more than this is there for me to say?*[2]

[1] *The Petition to Rām*, trs. F. R. Allchin, 1966, pp. 118f.
[2] *Kavitāvalī*, p. 145.

6

Growth of the Krishna Cult

LIFE STORIES

In the Mahābhārata Krishna appeared in various roles. He was chief of cowherds, a hero, counsellor of Arjuna, a god incarnate. His actions varied from the use of treachery to obtain his ends, to complete detachment from worldly affairs. Clearly numerous strands were woven into the story, and although Krishna appeared again and again in the Epic he was hardly the dominating character. The lofty teaching of the Bhagavad-Gītā was the result of long reflection on the relationships of God and man, but a number of its teachings are not developed in the Epic.

Even after the eighteen long books of the Mahābhārata have closed there are questions about Krishna that have scarcely been considered, particularly his birth and youthful exploits. So a number of later works were composed to deal with these matters.

The Harivaṁśa, 'the family of Hari' (Vishnu), was added as an appendix to the Mahābhārata, perhaps about the sixth century A.D. Like the Epic in some places, the Harivaṁśa speaks of an incarnation as a 'manifestation' (pradūrbhāva) rather than avatāra, which is the popular term. After quoting the Gītā 4, 7, it states that one form of Vishnu, the best one, abides forever in heaven practising austerities. The second form sleeps on his couch, for the creation and destruction of beings, meditating on his mysterious self. After sleeping a thousand eons he becomes manifest for the purpose of action, at the end of a thousand years, as the god of gods, the Lord of the world. Then eight incarnations of Vishnu are related, but the last, Kalkin, is called the tenth and this shows that ten Avatars were accepted.

71

The Harivaṁśa is in three sections, the first of which gives the history of Krishna's ancestors, the second relates Krishna's exploits and the third tells of the corruptions of the future Kali age, the fourth age of the world. It also enunciates the doctrine of the Tri-mūrti, the three forms in one, of Brahmā, Vishnu and Śiva. This teaching, aimed at reconciling different schools, is not prominent in the literature, but it is found also in some of the Purānas, notably the Padma and the Mārkandeya Purānas.

The Purānas, 'ancient tales', are epic works serving particular didactic purposes. At the end of the Mahābhārata, and in the Harivaṁśa, it is said that there were eighteen Purānas. These have not survived in their original form, for the ones that exist are mostly later than the Mahābhārata, though no doubt containing legends from it and other sources. There are Purānas of the Fish, Tortoise, Dwarf and Boar Avatars of Vishnu. The Mārkandeya Purāna, related by a sage of that name, discusses the Avatar of Krishna, chiefly in narrative. The Vishnu Purāna treats of this among cosmological and mythical stories. The Padma ('lotus') Purāna is also strongly of the Vishnu school. The most popular of all is the Bhāgavata Purāna, which goes into the fullest detail about Krishna.[1]

The Vishnu Purāna was perhaps compiled about the sixth century A.D. It praises Vishnu as the Supreme Being, the creator, preserver and destroyer of all. Other gods, Brahmā, Śiva and the rest, are the energies of Vishnu. Vishnu's Avatars in fish, tortoise, boar and man-lion are mentioned. Vishnu resides in these Avatars in different lands, though he pervades all places. Further, when Vishnu descends among men in various shapes his consort Śrī Lakshmī does this too; so she was Sītā for Rāma and Rukminī for Krishna.[2]

The Krishna story begins in the fifth book of the Vishnu Purāna, and it is called 'the Avatar of a part of a part' of Vishnu (aṁśāṁ-śāvatāra). This might seem to diminish his dignity, but commen-

---

[1] The Matsya (fish) Purāna gives ten Avatars of Vishnu, including the Buddha (47, 46). The Varāha (boar) Purāna also gives ten Avatars, the Bhāgavata Purāna gives twenty-two, and the Ahirbudhnya Saṁhitā gives thirty-nine. Vaishnavites generally consider that only Krishna is a full incarnation (*pūrnā-vatāra*).

[2] Vishnu Purāna 2, 2.

72

tators explain that the term applies only to Krishna's human condition, and not to his power, though it is a mystery how the Supreme Being should assume the form of a man. The meaning seems to be that Krishna comes from the personal Vishnu, who is a part of the impersonal and unmanifested. As the Gītā had said, 'I transcend the perishable and the imperishable, and am called the Highest Person'.[1]

The reason for the Avatar is the complaint of Earth that she was suffering demonic oppression. Brahmā led the gods to report this to Vishnu who plucked two hairs from his body, one white and the other black, and said that his hairs would descend to earth. The white one was Krishna's elder brother, Bala-rāma (Rāma the Strong) sometimes listed as an Avatar of Vishnu or of the divine serpent Ananta on which he sleeps. The black hair of Vishnu became Krishna.

Kaṁsa, a demon incarnate, was cousin of Krishna's mother, Devakī. A celestial voice told him that Devakī's eighth child would kill him, and so Kaṁsa tried to destroy all Devakī's children. When Bala-rāma was born he was smuggled away. Krishna was the eighth child and his parents fled with him, whereupon Kaṁsa ordered all male babies to be massacred.

The Vishnu Purāna goes into raptures over the child Krishna and his mother. When Devakī was pregnant nobody could bear to look at her, for the light that filled her. The gods praised her continually, as infinite Nature (Prakriti), parent of the gods, and mother of the universe. 'Have compassion on us, O goddess, and do good to the world. Be proud to bear that deity by whom the universe is upheld.[2] When Krishna was born, at midnight, there was moonlight over the whole earth, the winds were hushed, celestial nymphs sang, and the gods dropped flowers on the earth. The child was as black as the dark leaves of a lotus, but had four arms and the 'favourite of Śrī' mark on his breast. Having hailed him as God of gods, his parents besought him to forgo his four-armed shape. Then they changed him for a baby girl born to a cowherd's wife, Yaśodā. When Kaṁsa dashed this child against a stone, it rose up as a huge goddess with eight arms and told the tyrant that his destroyer had been born.[3]

---

[1] *ibid.*, 5, 1; Gītā 15, 18.   [2] Vishnu Purāna, 5, 2.   [3] *ibid.*, 5, 3.

So Krishna grew up among the cowherds, and his mischievous childhood is recounted. As a baby he sucked the life from a female fiend. He overturned a waggon, and broke all its pots and pans. He stole butter, pulled the cows' tails, and dragged trees from their places, laughingly showing his little white teeth. With Balarāma he indulged in many games, playing the pipes of the cowherds, driving out the calves, and dancing with the milkmaids. Krishna fought snakes and demons. He defied the god Indra, telling the cowherds not to worship Indra but rather revere the mountain where they grazed their herds. Indra in anger sent a storm, but Krishna lifted up the mountain and sheltered his friends beneath it. Indra then came and paid homage to Krishna.[1]

Every so often there is a reminder that though Krishna is human, and plays childish tricks, yet he is eternal and the centre of creation. His pranks are but part of his eternal play (*līlā*). The cowherds exclaim in astonishment, 'we cannot believe you to be a man; your boyhood and humiliating birth among us are contradictions that fill us with doubt, for the gods would have attempted in vain the deeds which you have wrought'. Krishna declares that he is neither god nor demon (he is of course the Supreme Being) and they must be satisfied with him as their kinsman. Then he went out to dance with the cowgirls (*gopīs*) and each one thought him to be dancing with her alone. Each *gopī* meditated on Krishna, with closed eyes and entire devotion, so that all sin was expiated and 'all acts of merit were effaced by rapture'. This became a favourite scene for later devotion.[2]

After a victorious reign Krishna is wounded in the foot by the hunter Jaras (old age), and unites himself with his own unborn and imperishable spirit. He abandons his mortal body and re-enters his own sphere of Vishnu. After his cremation by Arjuna, the dark Kali age descends on the earth.[3]

THE BHĀGAVATA PURĀNA, WITH TWENTY-TWO AVATARS

The most popular Purāna is the Bhāgavata, compiled perhaps somewhere about the ninth or tenth centuries. It says more of other Avatars, and of the youthful adventures of Krishna, than

[1] *ibid.*, 5, 5; 5, 10.   [2] *ibid.*, 5, 7; 5, 13.   [3] *ibid.*, 5, 37.

other Purānas, and its tenth and eleventh books which give details of Krishna have been translated into many Indian languages. The tenth book of the Bhāgavata Purāna is the most popular and is called in Hindi 'the ocean of love' (Premsāgar).

Bhāgavata means relating to or coming from Bhagavat, blessed Lord, Vishnu or Krishna. It begins with a request to recite the stories of the Avatars of Hari, 'whose descent is for the welfare and prosperity of beings'. This indeed is 'the greatest Dharma, by which there will be devotion to Hari'. It then proceeds to list, not merely the traditional ten Avatars of Vishnu, but twenty-two. And it adds that the Avatars of Vishnu are innumerable, like rivulets flowing from an inexhaustible lake. This seems a great extension of the Avatar idea, though in fact it does not detract from the primacy of Krishna.[1]

The twenty-two Avatars are: (1) Purusha, primeval man; (2) the Boar, Varāha; (3) Nārada, a great sage; (4) Nara and Nārāyana two saints, names sometimes applied to Arjuna and Krishna; (5) Kapila, founder of Sāmkhya philosophy; (6) Dattātreya, a saint; (7) Yajña, the sacrifice; (8) Rishabha, a righteous king; (9) Prithu, a king; (10) the Fish, Matsya; (11) the Tortoise, Kūrma; (12) Dhanvan-tari, a divine physician; (13) Mohinī, an enchantress; (14) the Man-lion, Nara-simha; (15) the Dwarf, Vāmana; (16) Parasu-Rāma, with the axe; (17) Veda-Vyāsa, compiler of the Vedas; (18) Rāma, the king; (19) Bala-rāma, elder brother of Krishna; (20) Krishna; (21) Buddha; (22) Kalkin, yet to come.

This list adds to the Avatars of the Mahābhārata respectful references to teachers, doctors and rulers. The Harivamśa had included Dattātreya, and the Matsya (fish) Purāna included him and a king Māndhātri, and also Veda-Vyāsa and the Buddha.

The inclusion of the Buddha seems to have been intended to attract Hindus away from Buddhism. Some writers have denied that Gautama Buddha is meant, and the title Buddha is not uncommon. But it is said that the Buddha Avatar came as the embodiment of illusion to mislead men of low birth, and so hasten the end of the present world cycle and prepare for Kalkin

[1] There are few translations or abbreviations of the Bhāgavata Purāna; see M. N. Dutt, *Bhāgavata Purāna*, 1896; E. Burnouf, *Bhāgavata Purāna*, 1840–1898; V. Raghavan, *Srimad Bhagavata*, n.d.

who would restore all things. This is the most popular Hindu reference to the Buddha, though it has been seen that some of the philosophers criticized Buddhist doctrines, and the Vishnu Purāna speaks of their delusions.[1] But the Buddha is an undoubted historical figure and his presence among the Avatars, alongside the historical kings and sages, strengthens the belief in the historicity of Avatars.

The Bhāgavata Purāna gives details of the other Avatars which it has listed, calling them 'sportful Avatars' (*līlāvatāra*). Hari was partially manifested as Rāma and his three brothers. But Krishna is the Lord himself (*bhagavān svayam*), the Supreme Spirit; later he is called a 'dwelling place' (*dhāma*) of Vishnu. The Lord enters the mind of Vasudeva, Krishna's father, by his yogic power, and appears with four arms in all the glory of Vishnu. But, afraid of the tyrant Kaṁsa, his parents implored him to become an ordinary child. Marvellous legends are told of his childhood. His mother tried to tie him to a mortar, as if he were an ordinary person, but out of pity Krishna let himself be bound, though in his mouth she saw all the universe.

So the story continues, with childish pranks, youthful adventures with cowherds, killing demons, including Kaṁsa, reigning as prince, marrying, and finally returning to Vishnu by simply sitting in silence and entering his own abode. The story veers between human actions and an ever-present divine power. This affects the most human traits, as when the imperishable Lord washes the feet of a friend who visits him.

Most significant for the whole development of the Krishna cult are his relationships with the cowgirls. This is the Brindāban *līlā*, the divine sport taking place for the time among the *gopīs* of Brindāban. The Bhāgavata Purāna says that they implored the goddess Pārvatī to make Krishna their Lord, and they took ritual baths in winter for that purpose. Krishna saw them bathing in a river, stole their clothes, and climbed a tree. He made the girls join their hands in salutation over their heads, before returning

---

[1] Wilson, *Vishnu Purāna*, p. 271. The Matsya Purāna 47, 247 and the Agni Purāna 16 refer to the Buddha Avatar. A common belief of Hindus was that Buddha appeared to mislead men, but sometimes he is spoken of as compassionate.

their clothes to them. Then the dances of Krishna with the *gopīs* followed their love for him which captivated their hearts. Krishna played on his flute and so possessed their minds that the *gopīs* left their homes to seek him.

Krishna appears in crown of peacock feathers, yellow robe, and shining blue-black skin. He reproaches the *gopīs* for leaving their husbands, saying that love for him comes more through singing and contemplating than through physical proximity. They reply that they come full of devotion to the Primal Spirit (*ādi-purusha*). Krishna laughs, and in compassion dances with them. Then the cowgirls become proud, so that Krishna disappears taking one girl with him, and when she takes liberties he vanishes. Then the *gopīs* all pray, 'you are not the son of the cowherd, you are the inner soul of all beings'. Finally Krishna returns, as their most 'beloved Lord', and they rise up with their eyes glowing in love.

Krishna danced the circular (*rāsa*) dance, and multiplied himself so that each woman thought she danced with him alone. They all bathed in the river Jumna and returned home secretly. This erotic dance was repeated a number of times; and even when Krishna was ruling, and had many wives, his brother Balarāma returned to the cowgirls of Brindāban. He found some of them reproaching Krishna for absence and others still passionate for him, and he danced with them the circular dance.

Similar passion is shown in the relationships of Krishna with his first wife, Rukminī, and other wives, in the Bhāgavata Purāna. Their palace, clothing, and bed are described in lavish terms. Krishna teases Rukminī, saying that he is poor and has only been loved by the poor, and she should seek a rich king. Rukminī collapses at the suggestion, and Krishna embraces and consoles her, and vows never to leave her. Rukminī adores him as the Lord of boundless greatness. But Krishna uses his delusive powers with his other wives, to make each think he is with her alone. They are filled with frenzied love for him, and all sixteen thousand bear him ten sons and a daughter each.

In these popular stories new and powerful themes have been introduced into the Avatar doctrine, moulded by the stories of Krishna. The Avatar no longer occurs simply to restore righteousness and destroy demons. Passionate love (*prema*) is here the chief relationship of God and man. As the union of love is the highest point of human life, so it is of human-divine relationships. Krishna shows that romantic love is the highest symbol, and that impassioned adoration of God is the best road to salvation.

GROWTH OF LOVE SYMBOLISM

In the centuries following the Bhāgavata Purāna the Krishna story developed further on this new path. The Purāna had said that during the dance Krishna disappeared with a single cowgirl. She is not named, but soon she is called Rādhā, most beautiful of the *gopis*, and occasionally regarded as an Avatar of Lakshmī, Vishnu's consort. Rādhā leaves her husband for Krishna, though she was Krishna's first love. This romantic but adulterous love was spontaneous, more exciting than the formality of battles and righteous reigns. In it the emotions of passion, jealousy, reconciliation and consummation are all illustrated.

But however frankly erotic the literature may appear, it was composed to demonstrate religious purposes. Krishna is God and Rādhā is the soul. Sexual passion is a symbol of the intensity of desire for God. Rādhā leaving her husband for Krishna illustrates the priority of love for God over human ties. Taking away the clothes of the cowgirls showed that the soul must appear naked and pure before God. Krishna multiplying himself for each paramour, proves that God loves every soul individually. Even the harsher parts of the tale, Krishna's desertion of his loves, indicate the disciplines of the spiritual life, the 'dark night of the soul', and the necessity of fidelity even when the presence of God is not visible or felt.

These remarkable developments, which swept India and remain powerful today, appear first clearly in the Gīta-Govinda, 'the Song of the Cowherd', written in Sanskrit by a Bengali poet, Jayadeva, in the twelfth century. This is a series of lyrical monologues, of Krishna, Rādhā, and her confidante, describing love, jealousy, estrangement, and final reconciliation of the lovers. It is full of sensual description of Krishna embracing beautiful women, and Rādhā longing for him, the master of her heart, in a fever of love, till Krishna is smitten with 'the arrows of love', and returns to her embraces and full union. Yet this poem of exuberant love is given an allegorical explanation, and those who listen to it are exhorted to place 'for ever in their hearts, Krishna the source of all merit', and many verses express the longings of the soul for God under the imagery of separated lovers.

Jayadeva listed the appearances of Vishnu in a Hymn to the Ten Avatars (*Daśāvatāra-stotra*), and here the tender-hearted one in the body of the Buddha defied the Vedic sacrificial rites where slaughter of cattle is taught. But it is Krishna who is supreme and all nature witnesses to the rapture of his love-making with Rādhā.[1]

Other poets took up this theme, in different languages. In Bengal in the fifteenth century Vidyāpati described the youth of Rādhā, her awakening to love, doubts and fears and union. Rādhā is shown in her maiden beauty and Krishna is implored to cast aside his moods, and cease turning his face away. Chandi Dās, also in Bengal, wrote of Krishna's ruses to show himself to Rādhā. Disguised as a flower seller he bargained with the girl, threw a garland over her head and kissed her. When Rādhā was sick with love Krishna went as a doctor, said that the water of love was rotting her heart, and showed himself as the cure.

In western India Princess Mīra Bāi, in the sixteenth century, began a popular movement of bhaktas of Krishna, though it led to her own persecution and leaving home. She sang the praise of the Lord as Hari, Rāma, the Name, and the cowherd playing his flute in Brindāban.

Sur Dās employed the thirty-six traditional modes of Indian music to make from each a love poem about Krishna. Different schools of painting delighted in depicting the loves of Krishna and Rādhā, all of it symbolical of the love of man for God and God for man. The erotic language and painting may appear surprising, but there are some parallels in the Song of Songs, and its use by the Church, and elsewhere. The relationships of man with God were thus spoken of in the most personal and human terms. For his devotees Krishna was the supreme Avatar, the only one in which God was fully revealed, and his story was told endlessly at all levels

[1] *Gīta Govinda*, trs. G. Keyt, 1947, pp. 14f.

of society. It gave new conceptions of the nature and personality of God, and of his love for mankind.[1]

ĀLVĀRS AND OTHERS

The Bhāgavata Purāna speaks of great devotees of Vishnu in south India. These had flourished at least after the Bhagavad Gītā and before the philosopher Rāmānuja. From that day to this Śrī-Vaishnavism has been strong in Tamil country, as well as elsewhere. Many Śrī-Vaishnavas memorize long devotional hymns to Vishnu, and these are also used in temple worship.

The oldest Vaishnava saints of the south are probably the Ālvārs, a name that means those who have deep knowledge of God or are immersed in contemplation of him. They claim to go back thousands of years and regard their early saints as Avatars of Vishnu or his companions. Their Tamil hymns are chanted in the temples along with the Sanskrit Vedas. The Prabandham, a devotional classic, is called the Tamil Veda, and verses from it are recited in processions, and on special occasions such as marriages and funerals.

In the Ālvār hymns Rāma and Krishna are the two chief Avatars, though others such as the Boar are mentioned. Krishna fighting Kaṁsa's demons and Rāma conquering Rāvana's hosts are often praised. Krishna's birth is contrasted with his divine majesty:

> He is adored by all the lords of heaven,
> He measured the globe in two strides,
> Yet it was he who came to birth among the cowherds.

And again,

> He wields the discus and the conch-shell,
> Yet it was he who wept when his nurse beat
> him and called him a butter-thief.[2]

[1] D. Bhattacharya, *Love Songs of Vidyāpati*, 1963; D. Bhattacharya, *Love Songs of Chandi Dās*, 1967; B. Behari, *Bhakta Mira*, 1961; W. G. Archer, *The Loves of Krishna in Indian Painting and Poetry*, 1957. The *Jnāneshvari*, the most notable work of Marathi literature, reproduces the Gītā, but significantly on the Avatar verses comments that it is 'as though I were incarnate'. See the translation by V. G. Pradhān (1967), pp. 105, 226: 'they erroneously identify me with this body'.

[2] J. S. M. Hooper, *Hymns of the Ālvārs*, 1929, pp. 78, 85; and see Dasgupta, *History of Indian Philosophy*, iii, ch. xvii.

The baby Krishna's mother describes the child rolling in the dust and calling for the moon, yawning for drowsiness; yet he must not be despised because he is a child, for in his great hands he wields discus, club and bow.[1]

Therefore the grace of the Lord is stressed. He pities one who is dull or of lowly caste, and calls him friend. Krishna is said to have created all the world for the joy of delivering them. The incarnation of Krishna as a mischievous child, 'a butter-thief', is hard even for the gods to understand, but it shows his condescension to human weakness. He hides himself at times in order to intensify devotion. The devotee also pleads that Rāma, who did so much to deliver Sītā, should have pity on those who are in deep grief.[2]

The Ālvār poets referred to Krishna's life at Brindāban, and came to make emotional identifications of the devotees with Krishna's foster-mother Yaśodā, his companions, or the Gopīs. This identification with characters in the Krishna story is a new phenomenon, which is not found in the Harivaṁśa, the Vishnu Purāna or even the later Bhāgavata Purāna. Dasgupta says that 'the idea that the legend of Krishna should have so much influence on the devotees as to infuse them with the characteristic spirits of the legendary personages in such a manner as to transform their lives after their pattern is probably a new thing in the history of devotional development in any religion. It is also probably absent in the cults of other devotional faiths in India.' It is important for its prominence later in the life of Chaitanya in Bengal.[3]

The Ālvār hymns, however, do not mention Rādhā, Krishna's paramour, and so they avoid the eroticism of later times. Other Śrī-Vaishnavas also recognize all the Avatars of Vishnu, but do not concentrate on the Rādhā-Krishna cult.

In like manner the Mādhvas, followers of the dualistic philosopher, accept the Bhāgavata Purāna and teach *bhakti*, but give no place to Rādhā since she does not come in the Purāna.

Nimbārka, a Telugu philosopher of about the twelfth century, exalted Rādhā from being a chief cowgirl to the rank of eternal consort of Krishna, becoming an Avatar with him at Brindāban.

[1] Hooper, *op. cit.*, p. 38.
[2] Hooper, *op. cit.*, pp. 41, 58, 71, 87.
[3] Dasgupta, *History of Indian Philosophy*, iii, p. 81.

This was a dignified conception, and less erotic than some. Nimbārka himself was regarded by his followers as an Avatar of Nārāyana. He taught a kind of dualistic monism, 'difference-non-difference' (*bhedā-bheda*, or *dvaitā-dvaita*). Souls can never be different from God, though they may forget their unity with God and feel themselves independent. Yet even when emancipated there is the difference, of parts from the whole, between the blissful souls and God for they spend eternity in contemplation of him.[1]

Another important philosopher was Vallabha, of Telugu family, born in Benares in 1481. He appears to follow Nimbārka in his view of the roles of Avatar played by Krishna and Rādhā. The Vishnu-swāmīs also worshipped Rādhā along with Krishna. Vallabha's views seem at times to be monistic, but like Rāmānuja he held that the existence of God cannot be inferred by reason, but only from the texts of the Upanishads. And the Gītā is the greatest text, since Krishna son of Devakī is the only God; any doubts in the Vedas are solved by the words of Krishna in the Gītā. The best way for the wise man is *bhakti* devotion, which is overwhelming affection for God, and can alone lead to salvation. Bhakti comes from 'affection' or 'love' (*prema*) which is due to the divine grace. This leads up to a 'passion' (*vyasana*) which is the inability to remain without God, and finally demands the renunciation of worldly attachments, though not in the direction of asceticism.[2]

CHAITANYA AND AVATAR THEORY

Against this kind of background arose the powerful Chaitanya movement in Bengal. Chaitanya was a Vaishnava reformer succeeding Nimbārka, and a junior contemporary of Vallabha. Not only these philosophers, but the poets Jayadeva, Vidyāpati and Chandī Dās had long been popular in Bengal for their praise of the loves of Krishna and Rādhā.

---

[1] *ibid.*, pp. 399f., 413ff.; and see M. T. Kennedy, *The Chaitanya Movement*, 1925, p. 7.
[2] Dasgupta, *History of Indian Philosophy*, iv, pp. 320ff., 382ff.; and see Kennedy, *The Chaitanya Movement*, pp. 7f.

Chaitanya was born Viśvambhar in 1486, of devout Vaishnava Brahmin parents, at Navadvīpa in Bengal. He studied Sanskrit and some poetry, but chiefly the Bhāgavata Purāna. At the age of twenty-two Chaitanya visited a Vishnu *tīrtha*, a holy place, of the Visnhupad, Vishnu's foot at Gayā. Here, under the influence of a Mādhva *sannyāsi*, Chaitanya turned from study to a life of religious devotion. He fell into trances, which were first regarded as insanity, but became characteristic of his whole life of absorption in Krishna. In the musical worship of *kīrtans*, Chaitanya sang and danced of the love of Krishna and Rādhā, entering into an ecstasy of communion with the beloved or breaking off from the circle and calling out the name Hari.

There was a wave of *bhakti* devotion, which developed from small groups into public processions, not only engaged in the intoxicating *kīrtan* song-dance, but also singing from door to door, telling men to call on Hari and lead holy lives. It became a popular movement, despite the opposition of scholars. Chaitanya went into ecstasies, imitating episodes from Krishna's life as told in the Purānas, and sometimes acting the part of Rādhā, dressed as a woman. He came to be regarded himself as an Avatar of Krishna and received secret adoration.[1]

Dasgupta says that 'the religious life of Chaitanya unfolds unique pathological symptoms of devotion which are perhaps unparalleled in the history of any other saints that we know of. . . . His love for Krishna gradually so increased that he developed symptoms almost of madness and epilepsy.'[2]

However, there was some check to the early fervour when Chaitanya became a *sannyāsi*, took the name Krishna Chaitanya, and left his home on a pilgrimage to the ruined Krishna centre of Brindāban in north India. At his mother's request, nevertheless, Chaitanya made his chief centre in the south, at Purī, and the reclamation of the sacred sites at Brindāban, the building of a great Vaishnava temple city there, was left to his successors.

At the famous Jagannāth temple at Purī Chaitanya danced and then swooned before the crude images, and his fervour led to the revival of *bhakti* movements. Then he went on a tour of sacred

---

[1] Kennedy, *The Chaitanya Movement*, pp. 17ff.
[2] Dasgupta, *History of Indian Philosophy*, iv, pp. 389f.

sites to the extreme south, at Rāmesvaram, back to Purī, and then to Brindāban. He visited Śaivite shrines as well as Vaishnavite, but he disputed with monists and Buddhists. He recognized the Mād-hvas, but said they had no devotion. His visits were a stimulus to the southern Vaishnavites, but the chief centres of his work were in Orissa and Bengal. Chaitanya lived his last years in Purī, and may have died by drowning in a fit of ecstasy, about 1534.[1]

It seems that Chaitanya wrote nothing and gave few instructions. Yet this influence on literature and life was enormous. The most authoritative exposition of his life and doctrine was written in Bengali verse by an elderly Brahmin, Krishna Dās Kavirāja (or Kavirāja Goswāmī). He was not a contemporary of Chaitanya, but knew many of his followers and wrote the 'immortal or nectarous deeds', the Chaitanya Charitāmrita. The development of the Avatar doctrine, and its application to Chaitanya, appears clearly in these verses.

The teachings of the Vedānta are recognized but given new applications. What the Upanishads call one Brahman without a second 'is the halo of the body of Lord Chaitanya'. The Paramāt-man, supreme soul, is but a 'partial manifestation' of him. He is himself the Lord, Bhagavat, and there is 'no higher principle of truth than Chaitanya-Krishna'. Chaitanya is held to be the primordial cause of all creations, one without difference from Hari, the Avatar of great Vishnu.[2]

Kavirāja is particularly interesting in his discussion of the nature of Avatars. Krishna is the primary principle of all Avatars. He manifests himself in the partial Avatars of the Fish, Tortoise, Man-lion and Dwarf. But Krishna is the Supreme God (Parameś-vara), who has incarnated himself as the Lord Chaitanya, and the latter is therefore 'the supreme ultimate principle'. Krishna (Govinda) and Rādhā are then praised, seated on a throne in a jewel-decked mansion in Brindāban, and his grace is invoked, he who called the cowgirls to the *rāsa* dance at the sound of his flute.[3]

Krishna has love (*prema*) for his servants and companions, and plays with them, enraptured with love. Though men may wor-

---

[1] Kennedy, *op. cit.*, p. 51.
[2] *Sri Sri Chaitanya Charitamrita*, trs. by N. K. Ray, 2nd. edn., 1959, i, p. 1.
[3] *ibid.*, pp. 3, 25.

ship him with knowledge, or fear his power, yet without love there is no salvation. Krishna thought within himself; 'I have not conferred *prema-bhakti* for a long time. Unless one practises *bhakti* himself others cannot find it, as the Gītā teaches. So I shall teach *bhakti* by practising it myself.' Hence in his last 'play' his name was Chaitanya, who made all men blessed by giving the knowledge of Krishna.[1]

It is true that one purpose of the Avatars was to kill all demons, and this Krishna did. But that was only 'an incidental action'. The two chief grounds of the Avatar were, firstly to taste the essence of love (*prema*), and secondly to teach devotion to the 'path of spontaneous love' (*rāga-mārga*). Therefore Krishna came to propagate the way of devotion. He appeared as Lord Chaitanya with his devotees, and tasted the sweetness of love in the *kīrtan* devotions, assuming the feelings of the devotees, and preaching *bhakti* by practising it.

It is further said that the Avatar appeared for three reasons: to taste the glory of the love of Rādhā, to know the sweetness in himself which Rādhā enjoys through that love, and to know the bliss which she experiences. These three feelings the Lord 'could not taste in his former incarnation as Krishna', though 'he attempted to do so'. But he tasted them when he 'took the feeling of Rādhā into himself in this Avatar (as Chaitanya)'.[2]

Rādhā and Krishna are said to be one and the same, assuming two bodies and sporting eternally to taste their mutual sweetness, and appearing in one body as Chaitanya. His heart was a picture of the feelings of Rādhā, her sentiments of pleasure and pain at union and separation arose therein.[3]

The width of the appeal of the Avatar is shown plainly. 'Here on earth he came to grant, without any distinction of caste or creed, without any distinction as to who is virtuous or who is a sinner, that sweet name and that sweet love which were not given to mankind for thousands of years.'[4]

It followed naturally that if Chaitanya was a full Avatar of Krishna, there should be devotion to him. This happened already during his life. Images were made of him, probably after his

[1] *ibid.*, pp. 28ff. [2] *ibid.*, i, p. 2; ii, pp. 37f.
[3] *ibid.*, i, p. 47. [4] *ibid.*, ii, p. 566.

death; but they were not black like Krishna, since Chaitanya was held to incarnate both the dark Krishna and the light-skinned Rādhā. In Chaitanya works of ritual, directed to Krishna, there are invocations of Chaitanya at the beginning of every chapter. The many temples that have been built, particularly at Brindāban, contain images of Chaitanya among others.[1]

Other followers of Chaitanya examined the problems of Avatars in different ways. Jīva Goswāmī wrote a commentary on the Bhāgavata Purāna, in a larger work giving most of his ideas, and providing theological explanations of episodes in the Purāna. Krishna's human body, his dress and ornaments, the milkmaids with whom he dallied, even the cows and trees of Brindāban, were physically existent in limited forms and also unlimited in the essential nature of God.

The Avatars are said not to be necessary for God to maintain the world, but they come in order to satisfy the devotees. God knows the sufferings of men but he does not share them, for he is omnipotent, and so he cannot be called cruel in not releasing all men from suffering. When the texts suggest that God is dependent on the devotee, what is meant is that *bhakti* is the essence of God's power and that the devotee through *bhakti* holds the essence of God within him.

So the Avatars come in response to human prayers, to fulfil the desires of devotees. The works of God are independent and self-determined, but they also reward or punish the works of man. God is beyond *māyā*, but in showing mercy he expresses himself apparently in terms of *māyā*. There are various 'manifestations' (*vyūhas*) of God, but the Lord of the Purāna is the principal manifestation.[2]

---

[1] *The Chaitanya Movement*, pp. 64ff., 176, 181ff.
[2] Dasgupta, *A History of Indian Philosophy*, iv, pp. 410, 410ff.

7

Similarity and Opposition

ŚIVA AND ŚAKTI

Although the belief in Avatars is confined chiefly to the followers of Vishnu, who is the pervasive and incarnating god, yet there are some similarities in cults of other Indian gods. Apart from Avatar belief, there are personal manifestations of the gods and responses of faith and devotion.

In the Mahābhārata many gods had their 'manifestations' (*prādurbhāva*). In course of time some of these divinities declined in favour, but some increased. Śiva, and his consort Śakti-Durgā-Kālī, gained millions of followers (perhaps they were originally Indus Valley or forest fertility gods), and today they form with Vishnu the three most powerful deities of India.

There are few real Avatars and little Avatar doctrine in Śaivism, but Śiva is a complex character, and he makes visible appearances as a personal god, as Guru or in another character. He is time and death (Mahākāla), haunting cemeteries. Śiva is also Lord of the Dance (Naṭarāja), one of his most popular appearances in art where he dances surrounded by a ring of flames. He is Lord of Beasts (Paśupati), like his prototype who appears on some Indus Valley seals. The regular representation of Śiva to this day is the *linga*, a phallic symbol, a short stone pillar with rounded top on which offerings are made. Yet along with these symbols of energy Śiva also appears as the great ascetic (Mahāyogī), sitting on Himalayan slopes in meditation, with matted hair from which flows the river Ganges, and with a third eye in his forehead. His body is smeared with ashes and a trident is by his side. The bull Nandi is his devoted attendant and his son is the elephant-headed Ganeśa.

87

Although there were clashes of Vishnu and Śiva in mythology, and fierce sectarian differences, yet there were also attempts at reconciliation and identification of these great deities. In imagery Hari-Hara statues show Vishnu and Śiva as two halves of one figure. There are also androgynous statues of Śiva and his wife Pārvatī, at Elephanta, Ellora and elsewhere.

In the Kūrma Purāna, devoted in the main to the Avatar of Vishnu as Tortoise (*kūrma*), the first eleven chapters of the second part are devoted to Śiva, and are called the Īśvara-Gītā, the Song of the Lord. This is directly inspired by the Bhagavad-Gītā, but though it praises Vishnu it recognizes Śiva as supreme God. Its date is perhaps somewhere between the seventh to eleventh centuries A.D.

The author of the Īśvara-Gītā calls Vishnu (Nārāyana) the soul of the universe, the eternal supreme Spirit, who revealed himself formerly under the form of the Tortoise (*kūrmarūpina*). Śiva also is the great God (Mahādeva), the supreme Lord. Those who consider that Vishnu and Śiva are different do not obtain deliverance from rebirth. Then, in response to questions, a throne descends from heaven, and Śiva sits there with Vishnu.[1]

Śiva has a thousand forms, taking the bodies of Brahmā, Vishnu and Rudra, creating, sustaining and destroying the universe. The assembled sages see him dancing, with their own eyes, to show his divine aspects. To others full of devotion he appears as the Yogi, a being full of light. Then in a fearful vision Śiva is manifested in many forms, and when they see him the sages bow with joined hands and chant his praise; he who is in all gods and sung by all the Vedas. This follows closely on the vision in the Bhagavad-Gītā, and there are parallels of words and ideas. Śiva proceeds to explain how he is everything in everything.[2]

The proper attitude to this god, manifested in all being, is devotion. Those who see him as the Supreme Being, one or many, are identical with him. The *linga* should be adored as symbol of

[1] Īśvaragītā, 1, 46; see also Dasgupta, *A History of Indian Philosophy*, iii, pp. 482ff.
[2] Īśvaragītā, 4, 20; 5, 1ff., 5, 21ff.

the Lord, for all the universe is established in it. People of lower castes who have this *bhakti* are saved also.[1]

But there is no Avatar, properly speaking, in the Iśvara-Gītā, and although much of it follows the Bhagavad Gītā, especially in the transfiguration scenes, yet there is no verse comparable to the Avatar texts of Bhagavad-Gītā 4, 6–8. But the deity is manifested in visible forms to his devotees and he has material symbols which evoke their fervour.

Followers of Śiva have occasionally spoken of him as appearing in Avatars. The Linga Purāna speaks of a number of these, but they are pale copies of those of Vishnu. Some of the sects of south Indian Śaivism claim an Avatar of Śiva for their founders. Laku-līsa, who originated a Śaivite philosophy, is said to have been an Avatar of Śiva with a staff in his left hand and a citron in his right. His work begins with a dialogue of Śiva and Pārvatī, in which Śiva relates his Avatar. Other myths tell of his wondrous child-hood. Some of the Śaivite works say that their doctrines were given by Śiva in successive incarnations. But in the main the Avatar doctrine is reserved for followers of Vishnu.[2]

Among the many Śaivite works an important manual of reli-gious doctrine in Tamil is the Śiva-jñāna-bodha, by Meykanda Deva in the thirteenth century. This begins by denying the com-plete identity of God and souls. The word *advaita* means 'not two', but it does not mean that there is one, but that which thinks it is one. It denies, not that two exist, but that they are distinct. So God is soul and not soul. God is not a One, a That, an object to be known. He is one with the soul's knowledge.[3]

God teaches souls as a Guru. To some he appears as true know-ledge, to others standing before them, to others concealing him-self. But who could know him 'if he did not reveal himself, taking visible form?' Devotion to the feet of the Lord brings union with him. 'Those who say not "I" but "He", the Lord brings to his feet, and he appears himself to them'. So God reveals himself,

---

[1] Iśvaragitā, 10, 8; 4, 10; 11, 96; Śiva also loves men: 'I love (*bhajāmy*) those who call upon me' 11, 72; to those who are full of *bhakti* the Yogī appears in sleep, 5, 6; and 'the devotees that I love most' (*ishta*) are those who seek me by knowledge, 4, 24.

[2] Dasgupta, *History of Indian Philosophy*, v, pp. 7, 155.

[3] *ibid.*, v, 24f.; Śiva-Ñāna-Bōdham, 2, 1; 6, 2.

'as a Guru in his own form as Śiva, four-armed, three-eyed, black-throated, and performing his three functions'. The Lord is seen in his shrines and is one with the visible form of the *linga*.[1]

Such revelations were expressed more passionately in many Tamil poems, and those of Māṇikka Vāchakar, in his Tiru-vāchaka of the ninth or tenth centuries are particularly noteworthy. In the opening stanzas of praise Śiva draws near in grace and comes down to his worshipper.

> *Thou didst seek me in grace,*
> *didst come to earth,*
> *didst show thy glorious feet . . .*
> *Thou art the essence of tender love,*
> *more beloved than a mother.*[2]

Śiva is seen dancing the dance of life in his sacred city, revealing his myriad qualities, abiding in countless souls, unfolding knowledge, so that intense love may flow from their hearts. He gives vision (*darśana*) in many forms, taking unto his own the nature of every one. He appeared to Māṇikka as king of kings, riding a horse, sounding a drum, and then performing his mystic dance with an elusive smile on his face.[3]

The appearances of the Lord are spoken of at the same time as his infinity: 'he came as a Brahmin sage, yet he is without name and form'. The divine condescension is emphasized. Śiva came down to earth as a sage and called me, freed me from misery, filled my heart with love and taught me the truth. 'He mingled in my mind and will, and in gracious love changed my way of life to his'. Such a revelation of divine love brings a realization of human unworthiness.

> *False is the play of my heart and mind . . .*
> *Dear Lord, perfect my love*
> *and draw me in grace to thee.*[4]

[1] Śiva-Ñāna-Bōdham, pp. 21, 25, 28, 59, 77.
[2] Dasgupta, *History of Indian Philosophy*, iii, p. 84; v, pp. 149ff.; and R. Navaratnam, *Tiruvachakam*, 1963, p. 54.
[3] *Tiruvachakam*, pp. 68f., 70ff.
[4] *ibid.*, pp. 149, 144, 194, 114.

The Śaiva singers of south India flourished about the time that the Ālvārs and their followers were singing of the Avatars, and the tender love of the deity. The Śaivites tended to stress the falsehood of man and the need of his submission to God, rather than the rapturous passion of the Vaisnavites. The Śaiva hymns 'are full of deep and noble sentiments of devotion which can hardly be excelled in any literature; but their main emphasis is on the majesty and the greatness of God and the feeling of submission, self-abnegation and self-surrender to God'.[1]

It is not surprising that similarly fervent devotions have also been addressed to the Great Mother Goddess, for she is the wife of Śiva, under many names. She is his Śakti, potency or strength, and the female *yoni* accompanies the male *linga*. As Umā or Pārvatī she is the gracious daughter of the Himalayas. As Durgā and Kālī she is terrible and 'black', with lolling red tongue, armed with many weapons, decked with skulls, and standing on the body of her husband Śiva.

The Tantra scriptures of the Śāktas, worshippers of Śakti, are akin to the Purānas, and the goddess in addition to her other activities is identified with the Absolute. Tantric worship is referred to in the Bhāgavata Purāna, and involves complex ritual and the use of sacred texts. The left-handed Tantra sought release through indulgence in forbidden things.

Besides the worship with formal texts and rites, and the representation in horrific symbolism, there is passionate devotion to the goddess under more gracious forms. Bengali poets in particular celebrated both her fear and her love. Rāmprasād Sen in the eighteenth century prayed to the goddess to show a mother's love, though recognizing that she may send evil and often does not seem to hear a call.

> Mother, I cry, and yet again, Mother,
> but you are deaf and blind.[2]

The Dark Goddess is reproached for being stony-hearted to prayer, even a delusion, yet she is called the supreme Deity, for

---

[1] Dasgupta, *A History of Indian Philosophy*, iii, 84.
[2] E. J. Thompson and A. M. Spencer, *Bengali Religious Lyrics*, Śākta, 1923, p. 35.

whose sake faith and works alike are abandoned. The manifestation of the Goddess is implored, even though she is of many and
unimaginable forms.

> *Mother of the universe, art thou male or female?*
> *Who can say? Who knows thy form?*
> *In whatever form men think of thee,*
> *in that form do thou, universal One,*
> *appear to them.*[1]

Both the grace and the presence of the Goddess are known.

> *I know you are present,Mother,*
> *Have you not cared for me, and clothed me?*[2]

There is revelation and compassion here, even if there is no true
Avatar, though the devotee may call himself Rāma. But the
goddess is personalized, and references to the mythology show her
activity in the world on behalf of her followers. This is something
of the background to modern Bengali saints, such as Ramakrishna
and Rabindranath Tagore, who both revered the Mother, and
also used the Avatar idea.

KABĪR AND THE SIKHS

Early and medieval Indian movements of devotion and love to
God arose naturally from the Epics, the Gītā, and the Purānas.
There is no need to suppose foreign influence. But Islam entered
India long before some of the later movements that have been
mentioned, and its extent and influence gradually grew. The stern
monotheism of Islam, its categorical denial that God has any
associates, or can be represented by any images, came as a shock
to Indian religion and temple-building. When Mughal rule was
established there were periods of fierce persecution of Hindus,
Buddhists and Jains. The final suppression of Buddhism in India
can be assumed from this time.

Despite the antagonism, there was considerable interaction of
Hindu and Islamic religious life and thought, borrowing from as
well as criticizing one another. Marginal groups sought some kind

[1] *ibid.*, p. 78. [2] *ibid.*, p. 81.

of religious synthesis, in traditional Indian fashion. It is these, the movements of Kabīr and Nānak, that are particularly significant for the ideas of Avatars.

According to tradition Kabīr was brought up a Muslim weaver in Benares (1440?–1518). He became a disciple of the Hindu teacher Rāmānanda, who taught that God should be worshipped under the name of Rāma with fervent devotion. Kabir refused Muslim circumcision, put on the dress of a Vaishnava ascetic, and adopted the title of Rāma for God.

Kabīr held to the unity of God, which he learnt from Islam, but he used any name to show the oneness behind apparent diversity. In addition to Rāma, he used the names of Hari, Govinda, Nārāyana, Brahmā and Allāh.

> *Whether Allāh or Rāma, I live by thy Name . . .*
> *Hari dwells in the south, Allāh has his place in the west . . .*
> *Kabīr is a child of Rāma and Allāh*
> *and accepts all gurus and pīrs.*[1]

Though Kabīr used myths of the gods this never implied for him recognition of their separate existence. He taught a firm monotheism: God is one, there is no second. In a remarkable verse he said that other gods died like men, and only God is immortal.

> *Dead is Brahmā, Vishnu, Maheśa;*
> *dead is Ganeśa, the son of Pārvatī . . .*
> *Hanumān is dead who built the bridge.*
> *Dead is Krishna . . .*
> *Only one did not die – the Creator.*[2]

Kabīr went on to deny explicitly the Avatars and personal representations of divinity.

> *In Mathura died Krishna, the cowherd:*
> *One by one died the ten Avatars.*
> *One by one died the founders of devotions:*
> *Those who know Him in qualities and without qualities.*[3]

[1] F. E. Keay, *Kabīr and his Followers*, 1931, p. 69.
[2] ibid, p. 70.　　　　　　　　[3] ibid., p. 82.

This is an attack on the widespread movements of devotion to Avatars and personal deities. To Kabīr God was 'without qualities' (*nirguṇa*). He is so mighty that he cannot be described, his form and outline cannot be explained for there is no second who has seen him.

Kabīr has been called a monist whose teaching confirms that of Śankara's Vedānta. But while there are passages in his poems that suggest this, there are many others which indicate rather a 'modified non-dualism', similar to that of Rāmānuja. Although the Rāma worshipped by Kabīr was not the Avatar of Vishnu, but the Supreme Being 'without qualities', yet qualities do appear in the relationships of God with creation and his devotees.

For Kabīr taught a devotion which implies some degree of subject-object relationship. He spoke of God as his Beloved, using the refined language of affection.

> *By devotion I have obtained the Lord . . .*
> *I cast down my eyes and take the Friend into my heart,*
> *I enjoy every pleasure with my Beloved.*[1]

Further, Kabīr insisted on the need for a spiritual teacher, a *guru*, an idea that also came from the *bhakti* movements. The True Guru (*Sat Guru*) is God himself, but earthly teachers are also needed. His followers gave almost divine honours to Kabīr and his Gurus, in a manner reminiscent of the Avatars themselves.

Similar ideas appear with Nānak and the Sikhs. Guru Nānak was a younger contemporary of Kabīr (1469–1539), and exercised his influence chiefly in the Punjab, where the Sikhs are strongest still. For Nānak it was the True Name (Sat Nam) that was the designation of God, and pious repetition of the Name was the true religion. At the creation, he said,

> *There were no gods to inhabit the highest heavens,*
> *No Brahmā, no Vishnu, no Śiva . . .*
> *Krishna was not, nor were his milkmaids,*
> *Neither were tantras and mantra Śaktis . . .*
> *There was no one to think of any one,*
> *Except God to think of himself.*
> *God was his own emanation.*[2]

---

[1] *ibid.*, p. 85.
[2] *Selections from the Sacred Writings of the Sikhs*, trs. by Trilochan Singh and others, 1960, p. 104.

God is the formless One, dwelling in the realm of truth. Yet he is also and often, by Nānak and his successors, called the Beloved, the Friend, and the Bridegroom of the soul. There is both personal devotion to God, and exaltation of the Guru to the highest place.

> *The Guru is Śiva, Vishnu, Brahmā,*
> *The Guru is theMother Goddess . . .*
> *The Word of the Guru is the highest scripture.*[1]

Nānak held that God is unborn, non-incarnated (*ajūnī*), because to be incarnate would involve death which is characteristic of this world but the very antithesis of the eternal being of God. For Nānak God was the Formless One, and he rejected not only Avatars and images, but any anthropomorphic ways of describing God. But although God could not be revealed by an Avatar he was omnipresent and dwelt in the human heart.[2]

Guru Nānak is said to have declared that only the Gurus and God are without error. Later the ten Gurus of the Sikh succession were taken as models of devotion. Each Guru was identical with his predecessors, and always signed himself Nānak. The Sikh assembly came to be regarded as the embodiment of the Guru. The believer was said to live in the embrace of the Guru, who lived within him. 'The Guru lives within his Sikhs'.[3]

The tenth Guru, Govind Singh, founder of the Khālsa community, was just as determined as Nānak to turn men's thoughts away from the Avatars to the one God. 'Some say that Ram is God some say Krishna, some in their hearts accept the Avatars as God. But I have forgotten all vain religion and know in my heart that the Creator is the only God.' And again, 'God . . . unlike Ram or Krishan, hath no male or female nurse. . . . What book wilt thou read? Will it be the Bhāgavat Purāna or the Gītā? Wilt thou hold on to Ram or clutch at Krishna for protection? The gods whom thou deemest supreme have all been destroyed by death'.[4]

These are taken from teachings written by or sanctioned by Guru Govind, and from a similar source came translations and

[1] *ibid.*, p. 31.
[2] W. H. McLeod, *Gurū Nānak and the Sikh Religion*, 1968, pp. 172ff.
[3] For references see my *Worship in the World's Religions*, 1961, pp. 75f.
[4] M. A. Macauliffe, *The Sikh Religion*, 1909, v, 68, 76f., 318.

abridgements of tales from the Purānas on the twenty-four Hindu
Avatars:

> *They who are called the twenty-four Avatars*
> *Have not found a trace of thee O God . . .*
> *Thou wert never born in the world . . .*
> *Vishnu and Shiv—what are the wretched beings? . . .*
> *I never meditate on Krishna or Vishnu . . .*
> *Ram, Krishna, and the Prophet—. . .*
> *Where live they now in the world? . . .*
> *If he whom we call Krishna were God, why was he subject to*
>   *death . . .*
> *Why did he who called himself the eternal and the unconceived,*
>   *enter into the womb of Devaki?*[1]

Why indeed? The Gītā and the Purānas give plenty of reasons, and
the question is important for theology in general. That it was
contradicted so fiercely shows the strength of the Avatar doctrine.
And while the Sikh Gurus in general, like Kabīr, opposed the
Avatars yet statements came to be made about the Gurus themselves which show the persistence of Avatar beliefs. Guru Govind
is said to have declared, 'At the command of God I received
mortal birth, and came into the world . . . In the town of Patna
I received a body.' A later Sikh historian said of the birth of Guru
Govind, 'It has been usual that, when God sees his people suffering,
he sends a saviour into the world.' And Bhai Guru Das even
declared that 'Guru Govind appeared as the tenth Avatar . . . he
established the Khālsa as his own sect.'[2] At the popular Goindwa
Sikh shrine wall paintings still depict the Fish and Boar Avatars of
Vishnu.

It was about this time that Tulsī Dās promulgated his great
devotion to the Avatar in Rāma, to which reference was made
earlier. Contemporary with Tulsī Dās, though less known, was
Dādū (1544–1603). He was a Hindi *bhakti* writer, approaching to
ethical monotheism, who gave interesting teachings on the Avatars.
He used both Hindu and Muslim names for God; Parameśvara,
Rāma, Govinda, Hari, Allāh, Rahīm. Yet Dādū never used the

[1] *ibid.*, v, 306ff.
[2] M. A. Macauliffe, *The Sikh Religion; a Symposium*, 1958 edn., pp. 139, 143;
and *The Sikh Religion*, 1909, iv, 357.

names of the gods Vishnu, Siva, and Rudra for the Supreme Being, and his words seem to suggest a monism becoming monotheism.

> *Brahmā and Śankara didst thou form,*
> *and made Vishnu incarnate* (avatāra) . . .
> *Thou thyself remainest aloof* (nirañjana)
> *the changeless Beholder.*[1]

There is a great deal of personal religion in the poems of Dādū, thirsting for love, and holding to God as the hope of the fatherless and stay of the destitute. God reveals himself truly, being moved with compassion at human needs, and suffering with men.

> *In a moment he in truth reveals himself, if his worshipper cries to*
>   *him;*
> *When he beholds the humble in affliction, then is he greatly*
>   *moved.*
> *He accompanies him behind and before, taking his burden upon*
>   *himself.*
> *When the saint suffers, then does Hari suffer: such is the*
>   *Creator.*[2]

With such new apprehensions of the divine nature, born both of mingling religious traditions and of further intuition, preparation was made for the modern period.

[1] W. G. Orr, *A Sixteenth-century Indian Mystic*, 1947, p. 135.
[2] *ibid.*, p. 90.

8

Modern Indian Thought and Christianity

REFORM MOVEMENTS

In the development of Hindu beliefs there may occasionally be discerned resemblances to Christian belief in Incarnation. But any Christian influence before the nineteenth century seems unlikely, or vague at best. From the beginning of the last century, however, Christian influence on Indian thought became significant.

Christian missions had followed European trade from the sixteenth century. Success was very small and there were only a few missionaries who began to understand Indian life and thought. Roberto de Nobili (1577-1656), a Jesuit, was perhaps the first European to learn Sanskrit and study the Vedas, but he had few followers. Not till 1785 did Charles Wilkins publish an English translation of the Bhagavad-Gītā, and in 1806 the Baptist missionary William Carey translated the Rāmāyana.[1] The number of Christian converts remained tiny, but the indirect effect of Christian thought and education on Hindus increased.

The reform movements in Indian religion in the nineteenth century owed their inspiration to several teachings. Ram Mohun Roy (1772-1833), the founder of the Brāhmo Samāj, came from a Bengali Brahmin family which followed Chaitanya. He studied both the Vedas and the Bible, wrote a book entitled, *The Principles of Jesus*, and maintained that the Upanishads taught pure theism, untainted by the later Hindu idolatry. The worship of the Samāj, from 1828, was theistic, almost deistic, in which much of popular Hinduism was banned.

[1] William Blake made a drawing of 'Mr. Wilkin translating the Geeta . . . part of the Hindoo Scriptures'.

98

Keshab Chandra Sen (1838–1884) who followed Roy, also came from a Bengali Vaishnavite family. He entered even more profoundly under Christian influence, so that some claimed him as a Christian. But there were other forces at work on him. Keshab broke with the original Brāhmo Samāj, and introduced forms of *bhakti* devotion that were popular in Bengal. *Sankīrtana* chorus singing, and public town processions (*nagarkīrtana*), used by followers of Chaitanya, were adopted with great success. Then Keshab came under the sway of the holy man of modern, though traditional, Hinduism, Rāmakrishna, of whom more will be said later. Keshab called God Mother, and recognized a form of the Durgā Pūjā in her honour. He compiled a hymn of praise of 108 names of God, in imitation of Vaishnavite hymns with 108 names of Vishnu. At the same time forms of baptism and the Lord's Supper were introduced into the ritual of his New Dispensation.

Keshab's attitude to Avatars was complex. In a lecture, *Jesus Christ: Europe and Asia*, he spoke of Christ as 'the Son', 'an emanation from Divinity'. At the apex of faith, he said, is 'the very God Jehovah, the Supreme Brahma of the Vedas'. Yet as there had been a Jewish Dispensation, a Christian Dispensation, and a Vaishnava Dispensation through Chaitanya, so there had now come the New Dispensation through Keshab Chandra Sen. It is not surprising that some followers of Keshab came to pay him divine honours, as the latest Avatar. For inherent in the Avatar doctrine is its repetition in every age.[1]

The Ādi Brāhmo Samāj continued under the leadership of Devendranath Tagore (1817–1905). His *Autobiography* is a moving story of spiritual search. He declares his conviction of the oneness of God behind different names, but insists that 'our relation to God is that of worshipper and worshipped'. He rejected not only the contradictions of the Vedāntic texts, but also the monism of the Upanishads and Śankara. 'When in the Upanishads I came across "I am He" and "Thou art That", then I became disappointed in them also. These Upanishads could not meet all our needs; could not fill our hearts.' So he sought a religion based on the intuition of God dwelling in the heart, and more practically

[1] J. N. Farquhar, *Modern Religious Movements in India*, 1915, pp. 63ff.

compiled a collection of Brāhma Dharma, made up of scriptural texts supporting this view.[1]

Devendranath affirmed 'the relation of friendship subsisting between God and the soul, and that they were constantly together: hence the doctrine of Monism was denied'. But he had noted the rivalry of the Vaishnava and Śaiva sects, and the Brāhma Dharma said, 'He did not become anything'. (Kaṭha Upanishad 2[18] 'This one has not come from anywhere, has not become anyone'. This is altered in the Gītā, see p. 46.) This was taken to mean that God did not become the material universe, not trees, birds, beasts or man. 'Hence the doctrine of Incarnation was denied.' Devendranath was grieved one day to find one of his teachers trying to prove from the Brāhmo Samāj scriptures 'the fact of the incarnation of Ramchandra, King of Ayodhya. This struck me as being opposed to the spirit of Brāhma Dharma. In order to counteract this, I arranged that the Vedas should be read out in public, and forbade the exposition of the doctrine of incarnation.'[2]

Forthright denial of the Avatar doctrines is found in a number of the modern movements, no doubt partly in a reaction against excessive emotionalism and idolatry: in the Ādi Samāj teaching, 'God has never become incarnate'; in the official statement of the Prarthana Samāj of western India, 'God does not incarnate himself'; and in the Ārya Samāj, 'the doctrine of *avatāras*, or divine incarnations, is denied'. The Ārya Samāj, founded by Swāmī Dayānanda in 1875, stands in contrast to the Brāhmo Samāj. Rather than being eclectic, it is conservative Hinduism and is opposed to both Islam and Christianity. It teaches that 'the Vedas are the books of true knowledge, and it is the paramount duty of every Ārya to read or hear them read, to teach and preach them to others'. It insists on belief in Karma and rebirth, but condemns as later and popular corruptions idolatry, animal sacrifices, pilgrimages, temple-offerings, and Avatars. Today the Samāj aims at being the church militant of Hinduism, a church founded on the authority of the Vedas.[3]

[1] *The Autobiography of Maharshi Devendranath Tagore*, trs. by S. Tagore and I. Devi, 1916, pp. 160f., 175.
[2] *ibid.*, p. 76.
[3] Farquhar, *Modern Religious Movements in India*, pp. 71, 80, 120f. and see D. S. Sarma, *Hinduism through the Ages*, 1956.

Rabindranath Tagore (1861–1941), son of Devendranath, was a great poet and a Nobel prize-winner. His Gitanjali, 'Song Offerings', translated by himself into English from Bengali, remains his best known writing and one of his finest. Though he followed his father, Rabindranath was more broad-minded and less iconoclastic than some members of the Ādi Brāhmo Samāj. In his writings he quotes from Upanishads and Bhagavad-Gītā, but also from Christian and Buddhist works, and his *Religion of Man* is strongly theistic. He was influenced as a poet by the songs of the *bhakti* poets Vidyāpati and Chandi Dās, and other Vaishnavites, as well as by the Baul sect which dispenses with temples and rituals and simply sings of God as a lover.

Tagore's religious poems avoid sectarian names and mythology, and speak of God as bridegroom and lover, but not clearly as Avatar. Yet the Avatar symbolism permeates Bengali religious poetry so deeply that it comes out in his verse.

Gitanjali opens with the divine Lord playing his flute, the stream of his music running from sky to sky, and commanding his follower to sing, until

> *Drunk with the joy of singing I forget myself*
> *and call thee friend who art my lord.*[1]

God is 'the innermost one', who 'weaves the web of this *maya*', and lets his feet peep out 'at whose touch I forget myself'. He is the king of kings who appears like Śiva in a golden chariot, but stoops to ask a beggar for a grain of corn from his bag. He comes down to stop at a cottage door, with a flower for a prize to a poor singer. He wanders abroad on a stormy night on a journey of love to his friend. Then most strikingly comes this thought,

> *Here is thy footstool and there rest thy feet*
> *where live the poorest, and lowliest, and lost.*[2]

So the worshipper must leave his chanting and singing and telling of beads in the dark corners of temples, and see where God is at work outside with the stone-breakers 'covered with dust'.

[1] R. Tagore, *Gitanjali*, 1928, edn., p. 2.
[2] *ibid.*, pp. 67, 43, 42, 18, 8.

Our master himself has taken joyfully upon him
the bonds of creation;
he is bound with us all for ever . . .
Meet him and stand by him
in toil and in sweat of thy brow.[1]

These are powerful new notes, freed from sectarian religiosity, but using the best of the old religious language with a free adaptation from other sources.

MAHĀTMA GĀNDHI

M. K. Gāndhi (1869–1948) was contemporary with Rabindranath Tagore, but although Tagore supported the struggle for Indian independence, and wrote an important book on *Nationalism* he was primarily a poet and mystic. Gāndhi was the great political leader, though the deep religious forces that played upon him are well known. His family were worshippers of Vishnu, and there was also strong Jain influence in Gujerat. He learnt to recite hymns invoking the protection of Rāma, and was so impressed by hearing the reading of the Holy Lake of the Acts of Rāma, by Tulsī Dās, that Gāndhi said later, 'that laid the foundation of my deep devotion to the Ramayana. Today I regard the Ramayana of Tulasidas as the greatest book in all devotional literature.' He also heard recitations of the Bhāgavata Purāna, but spoke of it more coldly; 'today I see that the Bhagavat is a book which can evoke religious fervour'. During one of his periods in prison Gāndhi published a collection of translations from *bhakti* poets.[2]

Gāndhi had a great love for the Bhagavad-Gītā, but he did not read it till he came to England and then studied it first in Sir Edwin Arnold's English translation as *The Song Celestial*. During his second year of law studies in London, Gāndhi was invited by two Theosophists to read the Gītā with them. He said later that

[1] *ibid.*, p. 9.
[2] *Mahatma Gandhi: His Own Story*, ed. C. F. Andrews, 1930, pp. 37, 51f.; *Songs from Prison*, 1934. Gāndhi practised the repetition of the Rāmanāma as a mantra, and told his readers, 'I myself have been a devotee of Tulsīdās from my childhood and have, therefore, always worshipped God as Rāma' (*Harijan*, 24.3.1946).

'the book struck me as one of priceless worth. This opinion of the Gītā has ever since been growing on me, with the result that I regard it today as the supreme book for the knowledge of Truth. It has afforded me invaluable help in my moments of gloom'.[1]

Gāndhi also studied the Bible, and was particularly impressed by the Sermon on the Mount, though he later declared that he found greater help in the Gītā than in the Bible. He could not accept the Christian doctrine of one Incarnation. 'It was more than I could believe that Jesus was the only incarnate Son of God, and that only he who believed in Him would have everlasting life. If Jesus was like God, or God Himself, then all men were like God and could be God himself . . . I could accept Jesus as a martyr, an embodiment of sacrifice and a divine teacher, but not as the most perfect man ever born.'[2]

Gāndhi did not seem to set much store by the Avatar doctrine. He admired the Rāmāyana and the Gītā, but their teachings of divine grace apparently did not impress him so much as the doctrines of non-violence and action without attachment. The coming of the divine Avatar age by age is not singled out as significantly different from the divine presence in the world all the time. Gāndhi dedicated himself to 'the God of Truth', praying that he would grant the boon of non-violence 'in thought, word and deed'. But his followers have commonly regarded Gāndhi himself as an Avatar; his bust stands in many Indian towns decorated with marigold flowers, and his grave is a place of pilgrimage.[3]

It has become common in modern times to call any great person an Avatar, no doubt weakening the original idea that the Avatar came once or only a few times in each age. Already in 1920 S. C. Bose said that in some parts of the country the Mahātma 'began to be worshipped as an Avatar'. And in 1930 the captain of the Bombay Youth League said, 'Gandhi is now marching as Buddha marched through India. . . . When you walk with him a light seems to emanate from him and fills you with its deep radiance. It is a new phenomenon, the present incarnation of Gandhi. . . . It was not the politician but the saint Gandhi, a new incarnation of Buddha.'

[1] *ibid.*, p. 71. [2] *ibid.*, p. 121. [3] *ibid.*, p. 335.

The comparison with Buddha is significant, as expressing the compassionate side of a historical man who is increasingly honoured today in India, but assimilated to the Avatar theory But it is difficult to discover what Gandhi himself thought about his identification with the Avatars, and his views on one Incarnation and the historicity of such an event, are made difficult of interpretation because of his occasional use of the Avatar idea. The complexity of Gāndhi's religious thought may be illustrated from his writings. In *Young India* in 1921 he wrote, 'I call myself a *Sanatani* Hindu because I believe in the Vedas, the Upanishads, the Puranas, and all that goes by the name of Hindu scriptures, and therefore in avatars and rebirth'. In the same place in 1925 he said 'I worship Rama, the perfect being of my conception, not a historical person, facts about whose life may vary with the progress of new historical discoveries and researches. Tulsidas had nothing to do with the Rama of history'. And again in 1925, 'My Krishna has nothing to do with any historical person . . . I believe in Krishna of my imagination as a perfect incarnation, spotless in every sense of the word, the inspirer of the Gītā and the inspirer of the lives of millions of human beings'.

In the *Gita according to Gandhi*, on Gītā 4, 6 he notes that 'God by his mysterious power–maya–assumes the garb of prakriti and looks as though he was born'. There is no commentary on verse 7. But on verse 8 he translates, 'I am born from age to age'. He comments then, 'Here is comfort for the faithful and affirmation of the truth that Right ever prevails . . . Inscrutable Providence–the unique power of the Lord–is ever at work. This in fact is *avatara*, incarnation. Strictly speaking there can be no birth for God'.

Every so often Gāndhi asserts his belief in Avatars, but then calls them unhistorical, the perfect beings of his own thought. God appears, yet is not born, he is manifested in many forms, which are not unique. This appears in R. M. Datta's summary of Gāndhi's philosophy. He quotes Gāndhi as saying that 'God manifests himself in innumerable forms in this universe and every such manifestation commands my spontaneous reverence.' And again, 'God is not a person. To affirm that he descends to earth now and again in the form of a human being is a partial truth which merely signifies that such a person lives near to God.'[1]

Gāndhi's closest living disciple, Vinoba Bhave, has published *Talks on the Gita*, in which the eighteen chapters are given expository comment. Vinoba is a Bombay Brahmin and a Sanskrit scholar. The Avatar theory is not discussed in chapter four of his book and the Krishna that is spoken of later is the one seen in the Purānas. It is said that 'the most charming part of Krishna's life is his childhood', and his life as a cowherd. Vinoba is also fond of the Holy Lake, of Tulsī Dās, and he recommends the constant repetition of the name of Rāma. He discusses both Brahman without qualities and with qualities, but declares that 'Hari-bhakti, devotion to the Lord, is essential'.[2]

Vinoba counters criticism of Avatar devotion. 'The young people of today say, "We don't understand all this about Rama-*nama*, Rama-*bhakti*, and Rama-worship. But we shall do God's work".' He answers that the way to do the work of God is shown in the examples of the Rāma stories. If one has no dealings with God it is hard to live the life of self-control. But when one is devoted to God, even when separated from him this separation is assimilated and transformed by doing God's work. Devotion to God consists in doing duty, but we need 'the living warmth of the symbol'.[3]

The motive of religious service had appeared in some circles before the nineteenth century. Some of the followers of Vallabha had taught 'service' (*sevā*), bodily action inspired by love. But this was chiefly service to God, and service to other people was alien to much of the world-denying quest of salvation or the emotionalism

[1] I am indebted for references in these paragraphs to the thesis of C. P. Mc-Kinnon on *The Religious Ideas of M. K. Gāndhi*. He refers to *Young India* 6/10/21; 27/8/25; 1/10/25; *Gītā according to Gandhi*, on 4, 6–8; and R. M. Datta, *The Philosophy of Mahatma Gandhi*, pp. 27, 79. Gandhi also said that 'in as much as God is omnipresent he dwells within every human being, and all may therefore be said to be incarnations of him. But this leads us nowhere. Rama, Krishna, etc., are called incarnations of God because we attribute divine qualities to them. In truth they are creations of man's imagination. Whether they actually lived on earth does not affect the picture of them in men's minds.' (*Harijan* 22/6/1947.)
[2] V. Bhave, *Talks on the Gita*, 1960, pp. 117, 169.
[3] *ibid.*, pp. 168f.

which sought to be rapt away in the beloved. Service for others received its greatest impetus from Gāndhi and his associates. But they discovered sources of inspiration for their action in the Gītā and the Rāmāyana. To act, in the name of God, for the sake of others rather than personal gain, became the highest form of *bhakti*. So Vinoba stresses knowledge and devotion, non-violence and service. The Lord feels pity for Arjuna, inviting him to come for refuge. He gives him rest with the thought, 'Not my will, but his, be done'.[1]

RĀMAKRISHNA

The most outstanding priest to be looked upon as an Avatar in modern times is undoubtedly Rāmakrishna (1834–1886). He was born Gadādhar Chatterji, of a poor Brahmin family in Bengal, and received no formal education. It is remarkable that in view of his wide interests later, he knew virtually no Sanskrit and only a little English.

Gadādhar's elder brother was appointed chief priest of a new group of temples at Dakshineśvara in north Calcutta. Most of the shrines there are dedicated to Śiva, but there are shrines of Kālī, and of Krishna with Rādhā. Young Gadādhar became assistant priest and fervent worshipper of Kālī, often passing into ecstatic trances (*samādhi*). His devotions and visions of the Mother became central to his life. He was greatly encouraged by a nun (*sannyāsinī*), versed in Tantric lore, who seems to have been the first to regard Gadādhar as an Avatar. His latest biographer says that, 'she came to the staggering conclusion that Rāmakrishna was other than mortal; that he was actually an incarnation of God upon earth'. This conclusion was based upon two special powers of an Avatar which Rāmakrishna demonstrated: the ability to remain for long periods in a state of *samādhi*, and the power of transmitting spiritual virtue to another person simply by touching him.[2]

Bhairavī, the ascetic, disappeared and Gadādhar's family took him home and had him married. He was twenty-five and his bride

[1] *ibid.*, p. 268; and see Dasgupta, *A History of Indian Philosophy*, iv, p. 351.
[2] C. Isherwood, *Ramakrishna and his Disciples*, 1965, p. 94; and Farquhar, *Modern Religious Movements in India*, pp. 188ff.

six years old, but the marriage was never consummated. Back in the temple the young priest went into trance again. He also sought Vaishnava ways of love to God, and at one period thought of himself as Rādhā, dressed as a woman like Chaitanya, and lived among the women. Yet he was helped by another *sannyāsi*, Totā-puri, who taught the monism of Śankara. Strangely enough the priest accepted this monism and himself became an ascetic. Yet he took a new name from the two greatest Avatars, Rāma-Krishna, and his disciples later added the title Paramahaṁsa, 'highest ascetic' (literally, 'greatest swan').

The story of Rāmakrishna and his followers cannot be followed here in detail. A movement gathered strength round him, and grew after his death, chiefly due to two of his most educated followers: Keshab Chandra Sen and Vivekānanda. The latter gave it world fame by his lectures at the Parliament of Religions in Chicago in 1893. The movement, significantly named Mission, was founded in 1909.

The teaching of Rāmakrishna and his disciples is remarkable in that while it accepts Śankara's monism, it also teaches the manifestation of the impersonal Brahman in the world in all the Avatars. These Avatars are not confined to Hinduism. Despite Rāmakrishna's limited education and travel, he was sensitive to the presence of Islam, Buddhism and Christianity in India, and he tried earnestly to learn about other religions. At one time he went to live with a Muslim holy man, dressed like him, observed Muslim practices, and had a vision of Muhammad. Later he listened to readings from the Bible and learnt of Jesus (Śri Īśa). He saw rays of light coming from a picture of Mary and Jesus, had a vision of a tall fair-faced foreigner, and heard a voice saying, 'This is Jesus Christ, the great yogī, the loving Son of God and one with his Father, who shed his heart's blood and suffered tortures for the salvation of mankind'.[1]

Swāmī Vivekānanda said that Rāmakrishna 'would speak of himself as the same soul that had been born before as Rāma, as Krishna, as Jesus, or as Buddha, born again as Rāmakrishna'. He said that he was free from all eternity, and that the ascetic practices in which he engaged, and the struggles after religion which he endured, were only meant to show people the way to salvation.

[1] Isherwood, *Ramakrishna and his Disciples*, p. 148.

107

'He had done all for them alone. He would say that he was a Nitya-mukta, or eternally free, and an incarnation of God himself.'[1]

In a collection of sayings called *The Gospel of Śrī Rāmakrishna*, which gives many of his conversations, in language often modelled on the Gospels, there are only occasional references to his thought about Avatars. On one occasion he said that 'an avatar is one who grants salvation. And there are ten, or twenty-four, or an infinite number of avatars. . . . Wherever there is a special manifestation of God's power, there is an avatar.' He declared that it is 'extremely difficult to recognize the divine incarnation', unless all desire has vanished from the mind. And to an inquirer who found it difficult to believe in Avatars he said, 'it does not matter. . . . It is enough if he believes that God exists and that all beings and the universe are his manifestations.'[2]

Not only Rāmakrishna himself, but his closest disciples are also regarded as Avatars. His wife, Sarada Devī, followed him to Calcutta when she was eighteen, became his devout pupil, and revered him as the Avatar for the present age. In return Rāmakrishna referred to his wife as the goddess Sarasvatī, and worshipped her formally as the Divine Mother. In recorded conversations, 'the Mother said: "People say I am Klāī"'. To a disciple who asked if the Master was Lord, Bhagavat, who appears regularly, she replied without hesitation: 'I am Bhagavatī, the Divine Mother of the universe.' On another occasion she referred to the cyclic appearances of Avatars. 'The Holy Mother said: "This repeated journey to the earth! Is there no escape from it? Wherever is Śiva there is Śakti. They are always together. It is the same Śiva again and again, and the same Śakti too'.'[3]

The headquarters of the Rāmakrishna Mission, at Belur Math north of Calcutta, is an interesting mixture of old and new. It has motifs in architecture from different religions, though the central

[1] M. Müller, *Rāmakrishna, his Life and Sayings*, 1951 edn., p. 58.
[2] M. N. Gupta, *The Gospel of Śrī Rāmakrishna*, 2, pp. 317f. Elsewhere he said that God sends his Avatar wherever religion declines, and 'it is one and the same Avatāra that, having plunged into the ocean of life, rises up in one place and is known as Krishna, and diving again rises in another place and is known as Christ.' See M. Müller, *op. cit.*, p. 109.
[3] S. Nikhilananda, *Holy Mother*, 1963, pp. 186ff.

force is that of modern Hinduism. Relics of the founders of the mission are preserved, and show its historical roots. But in the main sanctuary (*garbha-mandir*) the central figure, where divine images would be in other Hindu temples, is a marble image of Śrī Rāmakrishna in meditation on a stone lotus pedestal. The official guide book calls this 'the presiding Deity'. There are also temples, with images, of Swāmī Vivekānanda, the Divine Mother Sarada Devī, and Swāmī Brahmānanda the first president of the mission.[1]

MODERN PHILOSOPHERS

Developments of Avatar doctrines, under the influence of Christian thought, can be seen not only in popular religious movements but also in the writings of philosophical theologians. This may be illustrated from two outstanding thinkers. Dr. Sarvepalli Radhakrishnan and Śrī Aurobindo Ghose.

Dr. Radhakrishnan (born 1888), late President of the Indian Republic, and first Spalding Professor of Eastern Religions and Ethics in the University of Oxford, is one of the most persuasive exponents of Indian philosophy. He is almost unequalled among Indians in his knowledge of Christian thought. His writings on Indian philosophy, and translations and commentaries on the Upanishads, Brahma Sūtra and Bhagavad-Gītā, are full of references to the widest range of parallels: from Plotinus to Wordsworth from St. Teresa to Jean-Paul Sartre.

Radhakrishnan has aimed at a deliberate synthesis of the best in all religious thought and in this is typical of many modern Indian writers. His work begins at home, in trying to reconcile the different Hindu teachings. He accepts the non-dualism of Śankara, and this is really his fundamental position. But by re-interpreting the doctrine of *māyā*, Radhakrishnan has tried to show that the world is not 'illusion'. This is not what Śankara meant by *māyā*, he claims. The empirical world is real. It is not ultimate reality, of course, but neither is it unreality. Its basis is in the Absolute Brahman, which is the source of its many transformations, but these do not affect the integrity or the absoluteness of Brahman. He comments on the Upanishadic text, 'Thou art That', by saying

[1] S. Tejasananda, *The Ramakrishna Movement*, 1956, p. 19.

that it is 'a simple statement of experienced fact', and then trying
to support it by verses from the Bible and European philosophers,
which suggest union with God. He admits that there are those
who emphasize the transcendence of the Supreme, with whom the
individual cannot be assimilated, and who are haunted by a sense of
otherness and divine grace. Christian mystics and the author of the
Gītā belong to this type. But having noted the contrast Radhakrishnan is content to assert that 'there cannot be a fundamental
contradiction' between the philosophical idea of an all-embracing
God and the devotional idea of a personal God.[1]

Despite his name, Rādhā-Krishna, one has to search out his
exposition of Avatar doctrines. They are certainly not prominent
in his thought, and do not figure in a number of his most popular
expositions of the fundamentals of Indian religion. Yet there are
Avatar theories, and these are presented in interesting ways.
Radhakrishnan writes critically of the Mahābhārata. 'Vyāsa made
the best of a bad bargain and wove into a colossal poem the
floating mass of epic tradition, hero worship, stirring scenes of
strife and warfare, dressing up the new gods of uncertain origin
and doubtful morality in the "cast off clothes" of the Vedic
deities'.[2] He then discusses the question whether Krishna was the
only full manifestation of the Supreme, as the Bhāgavata Purāna
maintained, or a partial manifestation, as Śaṅkara held. No decision
is taken, but the theory of Avatars follows.

The Avatars are 'the militant gods struggling against sin and
evil, death and destruction'. The words of the Gītā which teach
the constant manifestation of the Avatar are an eloquent expression of the laws of the spiritual world. 'If God is looked upon as
the saviour of man, he must manifest himself whenever the forces
of evil threaten to destroy human values.' Hindu mythology
shows this in the stories of the demonic Rāvana and Kaṁsa being
overthrown by the Avatars Rāma and Krishna. However, the
work of divine redemption is a constant activity, though on
occasions the normal self-manifestation of God 'becomes emphatic'
when the order of the world grows disproportionately evil.[3]

[1] *An Idealist view of Life*, 1929, pp. 16, 107.
[2] *Indian Philosophy*, 2nd edn., 1929, i, pp. 480, 544f.
[3] S. Radhakrishnan, *Indian Philosophy*, i, p. 545.

An Avatar is a descent of God into man, says Radhakrishnan, differently from Aldous Huxley, not an ascent of man into God. Every conscious being is a descent of the divine, but this is veiled in most creatures who are shrouded in ignorance, while the Avatar is a fully self-conscious divine being. Yet a human being is 'as good as an avatar', provided he crosses the *māyā* of this world and transcends his imperfection. So it is really 'indifferent' whether we say that God limits himself to take the form of a man, or man rises to God through the knowledge of his own true nature. However, an Avatar 'generally' means a limitation of God for some purpose on earth.

A further strand is added, though it seems with weakening effect, in pointing out the example of the Avatars, as men. They are like moulds into which the seeking soul tries to fit itself, to help its progress towards God. So, 'what has been achieved by one man, a Christ or a Buddha, may be repeated in the lives of other men'. The Avatars mark crises in earthly progress; the animal Avatars of Vishnu showing growth from the sub-human level, then the brutish Paraśu Rāma was followed by the spiritual Rāma. Krishna exhorted us to the warfare of the world, and the Buddha worked compassionately for the redemption of mankind. The Avatar to come, Kalkī, is the militant God fighting injustice with the sword.[1]

After its early promise this is rather disappointing. More would be expected from Radhakrishnan's commentary on the Bhagavad-Gītā. But even here the Avatar theme is not expounded in the long introduction, scarcely mentioned on the Avatar verse 9, 11, and not at all on 15, 8. However the commentary on the crucial verses, Gītā 4, 7–9, contains important and partly new ideas. First the Avatar is called a descent so that man may ascend. The divine comes down to the earthly plane in order to raise it up to a higher level. 'God descends when man rises.' This is almost an eschatalogical aim. The purpose of the Avatar is to bring in a new world, a new *dharma*. But it is also personal, for by his teaching and example, the Avatar shows how a human being 'can raise himself to a higher grade of life'. So when Krishna came as a descent of the divine into the world, he revealed the condition of being to

[1] *ibid.*, p. 546.

which human souls should rise, showing their essential divinity. 'The avatāra helps us to become what we potentially are.'[1]

This is illustrated from Hindu and Buddhist teachings of regular Avatars and Buddhas. It is said that 'these have no servitude to historic fact', and 'do not believe in any exclusive revelation at one unique instant of time'. This is an indirect criticism of Christian doctrine, but it may be partly compensated by a short but clear emphasis on the reality of incarnation, which owes something to Christianity.

For the Avatar reveals several beliefs. It shows that there is no opposition of world and spirit, but it is man's duty to redeem the world. The Avatar also shows the way in which men can rise, from the animal to the spiritual mode of existence. But, most important, the divine nature is not revealed in its absoluteness, but it is mediated through manhood. The omnipresent Lord appears in order to teach mortals through his own experiences. 'He knows hunger and thirst, sorrow and suffering, solitude and forsakenness.' He overcomes them all and asks us to take courage from his example.[2]

Such human suffering of the Avatar does not appear in the Gītā and only slightly in the Purānas. It is clearer in the story of Rāma, though almost always qualified by an immediate reassurance that the Avatar is divine after all. A much plainer reference would be to the Gospel, with which Dr. Radhakrishnan is well acquainted. But this theme is more explicit in a few words of the writings of Aurobindo.

Śrī Aurobindo Ghose (1872–1950) was a philosopher-saint who combined, like Radhakrishnan but in different ways, both ancient and modern, east and west. Aurobindo was brought up in England and like European scholars he learnt Latin and Greek before going on to Sanskrit. He underwent Christian influences in a Roman Catholic school in Darjeeling, then with a Congregational minister in Manchester, and later at the Anglican St. Paul's school in London. He went to Cambridge on a classical scholarship, but got caught up in politics and did not take a degree.

Yet despite this strongly English and Christian environment, the writings of Aurobindo appear to show much less of this influence than do those of most Indian philosophers of his time.

[1] S. Radhakrishnan, *The Bhagavadgītā*, 1948, p. 157.   [2] *ibid.*, p. 156.

Whereas Radhakrishnan ranges easily from Plato to Teresa, and
Exodus to Eckhart, Aurobindo rarely mentions European philosophers or the Bible. In his masterpiece, *The Life Divine*, every one
of the fifty-six chapters is headed with quotations from the Hindu
scriptures, and Christianity is mentioned only a few times.
Rather than importing the West into India, Aurobindo seems to
be interpreting India to itself. But this first impression is misleading.
For Aurobindo not only tries to draw out the best in India, and
modernize it, he also has so deeply absorbed Christian thought that
it conditions much of his life and teaching.

Aurobindo taught a synthesis, in which the Absolute is said to
develop through grades of reality, from matter up to the supreme
spirit. The *māyā*, 'illusion', of Śankara was rejected as both foreign
to the Vedānta and to Aurobindo's own view of reality. The descent
of the power of Brahman into the finite is fundamental, and this
seemed to be virtually denied by Śankara's negative interpretations.
All reality is infused by the divine, and this is shown by the
power of evolution through which lower forms grow into
higher. Man is to progress from mind to super-mind, to achieve
what Aurobindo called Gnostic Being or Life Divine. The goal is
a super-race, on earth, a new order of beings and a new earth-life.[1]

To achieve identity with the divine Aurobindo taught a discipline of Integral Yoga, which was meant to be inclusive of the
various states of the individual and society. This is given practical
expression in the Aurobindo Ashram at Pondicherry, where
education, physical and mental, libraries, agriculture, building,
crafts, printing, and publishing, are developed alongside meditation
and spiritual exercises. Here the body of the saint lies in *samādhi*,
incense, flowers and devotions are offered daily, and the Mother of
the movement gives occasional audience (*darśana*).

In *The Life Divine* there is passing reference to 'the Son of Man
who is supremely capable of incarnating God'. But this Son of
Man turns out to be the ancient Manu, the Purusha, 'the soul in
mind of the ancient sages'. There is little here, or in most of his
other extensive writings, about Avatars.[2]

[1] Śrī Aurobindo, *The Life Divine*, 1955 edn., pp. 189ff., 324ff., etc.
[2] *The Life Divine*, p. 56; see E. G. Parrinder, 'Śrī Aurobindo on Incarnation
and the Love of God', in *Numen*, June 1964.

Avatar doctrine does occur, as would be expected, in the two volumes of *Essays on the Gita*. Here also references to Christ are most frequent. The idea of Avatar is claimed as the special property of India, which has held to it strongly from ancient times. Whereas Europe has never taken to belief in incarnation properly, 'because it has been presented through exoteric Christianity as a theological dogma, without any roots in the reason and general consciousness and attitude towards life'. If there had been more teaching on the immanence of God, belief in incarnation would have taken deeper root in Europe.[1]

Aurobindo, like Gandhi, seems to think it is a mistake to insist on the historical character of the Avatar. This is a help with the stories of Krishna. No doubt there was a historical Krishna, perhaps the founder, restorer, or at least an early teacher of the devotional school. But though this may be of historical importance, it has no theological value, for 'it is the eternal avatar, this God in man, the divine Consciousness always present in the human being, who manifested in a visible form speaks to the human soul in the Gītā'. And the same consideration applies, roughly, to Christian belief. The external aspect is merely of secondary importance. 'Such controversies as the one that has raged in Europe over the historicity of Christ, would seem to a spiritually-minded Indian largely a waste of time.' It might have some historical importance, but no religious value. 'If the Christ, God made man, lives within our spiritual being, it would seem to matter little whether or not a Son of Mary physically lived and suffered and died in Judea.'[2]

This seems categorical enough, yet it is more complicated than that. Aurobindo used Christian technical language at times, and was aware of its implications. He speaks of the Avatar as a descent, 'a birth of God in humanity, the Godhead manifesting itself in the human form and nature'. The Avatar stands as a gate, making through himself the way men must follow. So each incarnation holds before men his example, declaring of himself that 'he is the way and the gate', for 'the Son of Man and the Father above from whom he has descended are one'.[3]

[1] Śrī Aurobindo, *Essays on the Gita*, 1959 edn., p. 15.
[2] *ibid.*, pp. 17f.   [3] *ibid.*, p. 200.

Moreover, the Avatar is a true incarnation, not a mere appearance or supernatural wonder-worker. The object of the coming of the Avatar is 'precisely to show that human birth, with all its limitations, can be made such a means and instrument of the divine birth and divine works'. But this would not be accomplished unless the Avatar were real. 'A merely supernormal or miraculous avatar would be a meaningless absurdity.' This does not exclude the manifestation of supernormal powers, or miracles of healing, for these are within the scope of human nature. 'The Avatar does not come as a thaumaturgic magician, but as the divine leader of humanity and the exemplar of a divine humanity. Even human sorrow and physical suffering he must assume and use, so as to show, first, how that suffering may be a means of redemption – as did Christ – secondly, to show how, having been assumed by the divine soul in the human nature, it can also be overcome in the same nature.'[1]

Aurobindo says that a rationalist might find the whole notion of Avatar or incarnation absurd, and its height to be in the suggestion of divine suffering. But this is where he is most foolish. 'The rationalist who would have cried to Christ, "If thou art the Son of God come down from the cross", or point out sagely that the avatar was not divine because he died and died too by disease, – as a dog dieth, – knows not what he is saying: for he has missed the root of the whole matter. Even, the avatar of sorrow and suffering must come before there can be the avatar of divine joy; the human limitation must be assumed in order to show how it can be overcome.'[2]

Despite these strong words Aurobindo remains within the Indian tradition in speaking of many Avatars. He often writes of 'the avatar, the divinely-born Man', the 'secret Godhead', the 'divine manifestation of a Christ, Krishna, Buddha,' Yet he indicates some differences between Avatars. The early Avatars of Vishnu were manifested to destroy some evil. But, 'if this outward utility were all, we should have to exclude Buddha and Christ whose mission was not at all to destroy evil-doers and deliver the good, but to bring to all men a new spiritual message and a new law of divine growth and spiritual realization'.[3]

[1] *ibid.*, pp. 221f.   [2] *ibid.*, p. 222.   [3] *ibid.*, p. 229.

Further, Aurobindo justifies belief in Avatars along traditional lines. To many people in India and the West, the concept may appear a degeneration from the purest ideas of the impersonal God. 'To the modern mind Avatar-hood is one of the most difficult to accept or understand'; it is 'to the heathen a foolishness and to the Greeks a stumbling-block'. The materialist dismisses the idea of incarnation because he does not believe in any God. The rationalist or Deist does not allow God to intervene in the affairs of the world. The dualist sees God as wholly other, with a nature utterly different from that of man. The monist regards him as pure spirit which cannot be a creature born into the world. The writer of the Gītā knew of these objections. He knew the divine to be unborn, yet assuming birth. 'The Gītā is able to meet all these oppositions and to reconcile these contraries because it starts from the Vedantic view of existence, of God and of the universe'.[1]

[1] *ibid.*, pp. 202f.

9

Analysis of Avatar Doctrines

HINDU AND CHRISTIAN BELIEF

Hindu beliefs in Avatars are more than two thousand years old and appear in diverse forms in succeeding ages. For the greater part of their history they ran parallel to Christian beliefs in Incarnation. They showed some, even if few, similarities. The fact does not of itself prove any communication or borrowing until modern times. It used to be suggested that the entire Indian sect organization, in so far as it is founded on the exclusive worship of a single personal God, owes its origin to Christian influences. And it was therefore assumed that 'the whole avatar system originated in an imitation of the Christian dogma of the descent of God'.[1]

The evidence is all in the other direction. The oldest traces of the Avatar doctrine are fully Indian. It appears in the Mahābhārata, and not only or chiefly in the Bhagavad-Gītā section of it. The development of the Avatar belief through the Purānas into Vaishnavism, greatly helped by the philosophical justification given by Rāmānuja, followed naturally from the Epics, and the developments were characteristically Indian. It has been seen above that Grierson's theory of Indian Christian influence on Madhva is unlikely. It is not impossible that there was some Christian influence before the nineteenth century, but it is not proved.

Whether the Avatar doctrine was only Hindu and not Buddhist, assuming that they can be differentiated in the early centuries, is also problematical. The story of the Fish is one of the oldest in the cycle of myths, and is pre-Buddhist, but while it occurs in the

---

[1] Albrecht Weber said this as long ago as 1868 and it was often repeated, see *Über die Krishnajanmashtami*, quoted by R. Garbe, *India and Christendom*, trs. L. G. Robinson, 1959, p. 255.

Brāhmana it is identified with Prajāpati first in the Epic and only later with Vishnu. Vishnu is a dwarf in the Śatapatha Brāhmana, but hardly yet an Avatar. Both the Tortoise and the Boar are forms of Prajāpati in the Brāhmana. The identification of these as Avatars of Vishnu is again the work of the Epic.[1] This question of Hindu or Buddhist priority will have to be considered again when discussing Buddhism.

Modern assessments of the Avatar doctrine do not usually claim a Christian origin for it, but often try to differentiate it as much as possible from Christian belief. Rudolf Otto considered at length possible comparisons of Christian and Hindu doctrines in several books. Curiously enough he brushed aside the characteristic differences of Avatar and Incarnation, although he was anxious to stress other dissimilarities. He said, 'it is not the essential difference between Christ and Krishna and Rāma that he is a "mediator" only, for they were mediators too. Neither is the doctrine of the "incarnation" the special doctrine of Christianity. India possessed doctrines of incarnation long before Christianity. But that Christ was a "propitiator" is the profoundest meaning of his coming, and all speculative doctrines about his person derive their special meaning and the theological criterion of their validity from this fact.'[2] (see p. 238 below).

It is strange that in his book specifically written on the Bhagavad-Gītā, Otto says little about the Avatar doctrine. It is not listed in the index and is mentioned only two or three times. It is however shown to be particularly appropriate to Vishnu, whose name is interpreted as the great 'Pervader'. Because Vishnu has this capacity of pervasion he is especially the god of *avatāras* and *āveśas*, 'enterings'. He is the god present in artificial images (*arcās*), natural objects like the sacred black stone (*śālagrāma*), *tulasi* plants, and 'other fetishes'.[3]

Perhaps Otto did not regard the Avatar doctrine as particularly important in the Gītā, since it did not occur in what he called 'the Original Gītā'. It only comes in the seventh of the eight treatises

---

[1] See Chapter 2 above.
[2] R. Otto, *India's Religion of Grace and Christianity compared and contrasted*, 1930, p. 105.
[3] *The Original Gītā*, pp. 249, etc.

which he supposed to be traceable in the Gītā. The Gītā, he thought, was primarily revelation, in which chapters ten and eleven are central, and so the Ur-Gītā was like many other divine manifestations in the Epic. But such a radical curtailment relies chiefly on theological presuppositions and the Gītā is far richer than this. In it the teaching of the descent of the Lord follows naturally upon Arjuna's problems of action.

Otto does have an important note on the Avatar verses in chapter four of the Gītā. The verses have 'an intentionally paradoxical character'. That the Lord is 'unborn and unchanging' is contrasted with 'I come to being'. It is apparently impossible that God who exists beyond all change and becoming, and is the Lord of those who have come into existence, should himself enter into becoming. This seems to contradict his nature as one who has not become. But God is superior to his own nature, in that by resorting to it his *māyā* is the 'capacity to render the impossible actual'.

Otto insists, importantly, that Gītā 4, 6 is not 'docetic', an illusory or unreal incarnation, as some have suggested. The coming into being of 'one who has not become' is not a 'mere appearance'. *Māyā* has not that sense of 'illusion' here. It is deliberately intended to be shown as an 'actual miracle', really occurring by *Yoga-māyā*. This is virtually the 'free will of God', who is not even bound by the absoluteness of his own nature. So even monistic commentators have called this action 'the supernatural and wholly incomprehensible *śakti* of the Supreme Lord'.[1]

Few other Christian theologians have discussed the Avatars in comparison with the Incarnation of Christ. H. H. Farmer seems to agree that an Avatar may be a real incarnation, but that makes him dissatisfied with the word 'incarnation'. For this word is too apt to denote merely 'taking a bodily form', and this suggests 'a divine being who merely drops into the human scene in an embodied form from the realm of eternity, unheralded, unprepared for, without roots in anything that has gone before in history, and without any creative relationship to the unfolding of events in what comes after'.

Farmer prefers to speak of the 'inhistorization' of God. The Christian faith is in an incarnation of a fully historic individual

[1] *The Original Gītā*, pp. 287f.

human person, a Jew of the first century. He attacks Aldous Huxley's identification of Avatars with incarnation. Huxley, indeed, had not been content to say that all Avatar beliefs were alike, he criticized the 'error of Christianity' in believing in only one Avatar. It is too pre-occupied with history and it believes its Avatar to be unique.[1] Farmer retorts that these, if they are errors, are one and the same. For 'history is essentially the sphere of the singular, the unique'. History does not repeat itself, and the uniqueness of the Incarnation comes from its being fully historical. So he says that it is dangerously misleading to assert that an Avatar is the same as Incarnation, for the latter is the 'inhistorization' of God, which the former is not. This argument must be examined more at length at a later stage, but some of the strands of Avatar belief can now be disentangled.[2]

Twelve Characteristics of Avatar Doctrines

It is time to summarize the various beliefs which appear to be necessitated by the Avatar doctrine in the Hindu traditions. Otto's treatment is far too scanty, though some of his words on the related problems of 'India's religion of grace' are important. But his denial of the 'docetic' character of the Avatar is a good starting place for a study of the principal implications of Avatar teaching.

1. *In Hindu belief the Avatar is real.*
That is, it is a visible and fleshly descent of the divine to the animal or human plane. It is an incarnation or at least a theophany. In the Gītā Krishna is the charioteer of Arjuna, speaking to him as Blessed Lord, with a superior voice, but in the battle scene at Kurukshetra. His supernatural form is hidden, except in the transfiguration in chapter eleven. And though one verse speaks of Krishna's natural shape as four-armed, yet Krishna has truly been Arjuna's comrade: eating, sitting, playing and sleeping. So it is in the rest of the Epic. Krishna plays various roles, but they are bodily and visible. In the later Purānas, although there is an increase of the miraculous, yet the bodily nature of the Avatar is

---

[1] A. Huxley, *The Perennial Philosophy*, pp. 60ff.
[2] H. H. Farmer, *Revelation and Religion*, 1954, pp. 195f.

not in doubt. This is just as clear in the story of Rāma. These are the two great Avatars, and central to devotion down to this day.

2. *The human Avatars take worldly birth.*

This happens in various ways, but through human parents. In the Mahābhārata Vishnu simply decides to be born of Vasudeva and Devakī, the latter being the name of a woman given in the Chāndogya Upanishad as mother of a student Krishna. In the Vishnu Purāna the two Avatars, of Krishna and his brother, are said to come from a black and a white hair from Vishnu's body, but they have human parents. In the Bhāgavata Purāna it is said that Vishnu entered the mind of Krishna's father. In the Rāmāyana the king's wives ate of a divine dish before conceiving. Even so, it is not suggested that these divinely sent children had no human fathers; it may be said that the power of the god rested on their parents. These are few, if any, real parallels to the infancy stories of the canonical Gospels, or even of the apocryphal Gospels.

3. *The lives of Avatars mingle devine and human.*

In the Purānas the pranks of the child Krishna, his youthful loves, manly exploits, marriage and reign, all show humanity even when demonstrating some power of divinity. Similarly in the story of Rāma; the youth, marriage, renunciation, sufferings and triumph all make up a human picture, the details of which are cherished by millions. The Avatars are divinity incarnate, and miracles occur during their lives on earth. But it would be strange if there were no miracles, and the abundance of marvellous story surrounding Krishna is closely comparable to that told of the childhood and manhood of the Buddha, who was almost certainly a historical personage.

4. *The Avatars finally die.*

Krishna was fatally wounded in the foot by an arrow from the hunter Jaras ('old age'), before ascending to heaven. Rāma walked into a river, a symbol of death. His wife Sītā descended into her mother Earth, or in another version she entered the cremation fire lit for Rāma's obsequies. Death came when the purpose of the Avatar's coming was accomplished; evil is overthrown and righteousness strengthened. The end of the mortal episode must be completed, for it if is real it is only occasional. God is not always visible, though he constantly maintains the world by his power. But his appearances are exceptional, and limited in time as in bodily form.

5. *There may be historicity in some Avatars.*

The animal Avatars are mythical, though visible and bodily. They are important for cosmology. The Tortoise supported the earth, the Boar delivered it from floods, and the Fish saved mankind. The Man-lion, the Dwarf, and Rāma with the axe, fight demons. So do Krishna and Rāma-chandra, but they alone can be claimed as historical. Indian thought generally has not given the same prominence to history as did the Jews and Greeks to the west, or the Chinese to the east. Krishna is a complex figure, and few western historians would venture to fix a date for his career, or careers. Yet his family and clan are named, and the sacred sites at Mathurā and Brindāban are cherished for their many historical associations. Rāma seems more clearly historical, though he also could hardly be dated within hundreds of years. But Rāma's genealogy, from his father Daśaratha back to the primordial Manu, and his city of Ayodhyā, are remembered and held as real.

The inclusion of the Buddha among the Avatars, in the later Purānas, help to strengthen belief in the historical character of some Avatars. Few people doubt that Gautama Buddha, son of a ruler in the foothills of Nepal, really lived on earth. The same applies even more forcibly to other saints now commonly regarded as Avatars, from Chaitanya in the sixteenth century, down to well documented saints of modern times, like Śrī Rāmakrishna and Mahātma Gāndhi.

6. *Avatars are repeated.*

It is both a strength and a weakness of the Avatar doctrine that the divine descent to earth is constantly repeated. This has been taught from the Gītā onwards: 'from age to age I come into being'. The strength of this belief was that it made possible the inclusion of mythical beings of the past, and heroes of the present, within the same system. Perhaps the success of the doctrine of the Krishna

Avatar, in the Gītā and later, led to Vālmīki equating Rāma with Vishnu in his Rāmāyana. Later the Buddha was added, but with the sectarian purpose of disparaging his cult or absorbing it into Vaishnavism.

The weakness of this constant repetition of Avatars is that it tends to give the whole theory a mythical air. The all-embracing catholicity brings in some strange bedfellows. Que font-ils dans cette galère? Terms such as 'incarnation', and 'in the flesh', can at most only be applied to the human Avatars; Krishna, Rāma, and later figures.

Yet the repetition does give some continuity. The Avatars do not just 'drop into the human scene', as Farmer maintained, without roots in anything that came before or relationship to what comes after. Each Avatar, in theory, appears 'whenever there is a decline of righteousness'. He maintains harmony. He is in a succession, of those who have gone before. He is in turn succeeded, and since early days there has been a looking forward to the Avatar to come. Kalkin is an eschatological figure who will destroy the old and inaugurate the new order. But the repetition fits the idea of reincarnation, and this has a great effect which will be considered later.

7. *The example and character of the Avatars is important.*
'Christ is not, at bottom, the same as Krishna', says Otto, in another place.[1] This is a truism, but it needs to be said. The character of Krishna is many-sided, and both character and history are very different from those of Christ. It is easy to smile at the infant prodigies of the child Krishna in the Purānas, or perhaps lament enviously his adventures with the milkmaids, and frown at the ecstasies of the Rādhā-Krishna cult. Yet in considering the character of Krishna the dominance of the Bhagavad-Gītā must be remembered, and here Krishna is noble, moral, active and compassionate.

Rāma affords even more patterns of conduct in nobility, affection and long-suffering. Both he and Krishna are examples of virtuous life and teachers of righteousness, because they are thought really to have lived on earth. So the Avatar doctrine is both religious and moral.

[1] *Mysticism East and West*, trs. B. L. Bracey and R. C. Payne, 1957 edn., p. 165.

123

8. *The Avatar comes with work to do.*
The divine descent has a purpose, it is not mere 'play'. These purposes range from slaying demons and delivering earth, men and gods, to showing the divine nature and love. The great purpose is to establish *dharma*, to restore right and put down wrong. *Dharma* is a great central concept of Hindu thought, and its importance in the Avatar doctrine shows that this is thoroughly native to India. It is the harmony of human society and the universe, and Arjuna's dejection at the beginning of the Gītā was precisely because he saw that useless slaughter would destroy society and its harmony. Krishna's answers were intended to show that Arjuna was taking a short-sighted view. Perhaps this was not proved, and later in the Epic king Yudhishthira himself, Arjuna's elder brother, son of *Dharma*, and King of Righteousness (*dharma-rāja*), takes up the problem again. He denounces the *dharma* of the warriors, in favour of the *dharma* of his own conscience and the claims of compassion. There are great moral problems, which the Avatar doctrines try to solve.

9. *The Avatars show some reality in the world.*
It is often said that Indian thought teaches the unreality of the world; history is unimportant, there is no progress, and both religion and morality are world-renouncing. There is some truth in all these assertions. Certainly to the monist if the world is not complete 'illusion', it is unreal or lacking objectivity. But in the Gītā *māyā* is not 'illusion'; it is a divine power, by which the Avatar becomes a human person in the material world. The Avatars come into the world, live and suffer in it. They teach *dharma* for this life. The Gītā constantly insists on the importance of action, which is better than inaction, and disciplined activity which is superior to asceticism. The examples of the Avatars are encouragement to noble life on earth. The harmony of society is the object of the actions of all classes of people.

10. *The Avatar is a guarantee of divine revelation.*
It is sometimes thought that only the Semitic religions believe that they have revelations, which tend towards exclusiveness, and that Hindus accept anything and believe that anybody can be saved by

doing, or not doing, what any religion teaches. But Hindus have been as insistent as Christians and Muslims that they have a divine relationship which is the only way to salvation. It has been noted above that Śankara believed that only the Vedas could give knowledge of Brahman. They are 'heard' (*śruti*) by the ancient sages from God himself. Buddhists and Jains also claimed to have the final truth; the Jains holding that he alone is righteous who believes the true teaching, and Buddhists that anything which contradicted the Buddha's teaching could not be true. 'So modern exponents of Hinduism should make it explicit that such statements as "All religions are true" are made only on their own authority, and do not represent the orthodox Hindu tradition.'[1]

The Avatars give revelations of God. They are 'special revelations', which are both divine teaching and the self-manifestation of the divine to human persons. Yet they do not deny that there is some knowledge of God already, an awareness of God in the mind. So in the Gītā Arjuna tells Krishna that he believes him to be true, first because Krishna has revealed the truth, then because all the sages have testified to him, and finally because he himself perceives that it is true.[2] Therefore Arjuna accepted Krishna as divine because this fitted in with, or at least did not contradict, his previous ideas about the nature of God and his revelation to man.

It is clear that in the many kinds of Hindu scriptures man can have some knowledge of God apart from the Avatars. This might be called 'general revelation', though in scripture, and not only in nature and conscience. Because there was this 'general revelation', the 'special revelation' of the Avatars became possible.

11. *Avatars reveal a personal God.*

It has been seen how uneasy the monists are with the Avatar doctrine. Monism no doubt is a reaction against the crude polytheism of some of the earlier texts. But the Gītā insists both on the real manifestation of Krishna, and that he is the Highest Person, beyond manifestation. Yet if there is that in God which responds to human persons, this aspect of the divine is best revealed to men through a personality. The Avatar reveals God in the life and work

[1] K. S. Murty, *Revelation and Reason in Advaita Vedānta*, p. 219.
[2] Gītā 10, 13–14.

of a human being. It shows that God is concerned with all men, as well as his devotees.

The personal revelation of God brings divine speech to men, in commands and promises. Men spoke to the gods but not the gods to men in the Vedas. The monism of the Upanishads precludes conversation. But in the Gītā God teaches man, directly by audible speech, in a language that he can understand. However, this divine self-disclosure is not automatic. It can be misunderstood, or rejected. The Gītā condemns those who despise the Lord, or blindly rely on ritual, or other gods. The revelation is only fully understood by the devotee, who has faith.

12. *Avatars reveal a God of grace.*

The direct personal encounter is more than a teaching session, or an argument on morality. God is implored to show mercy and grace, to enter into loving communion:

> As father to his son, as friend to friend,
> As lover to beloved.[1]

Rāmānuja went even further, in his commentary on the Gītā. God is 'an ocean of boundless compassion, moral excellence, tenderness, generosity, and sovereignty, the refuge of the whole world without distinction of persons'. By his Avatar God 'can be seen by the eyes of all men', for he 'came down to dwell in the house of Vasudeva, to give light to the whole world'.[2]

The Gītā exhorted the devotee to show love to God, and said that such a one is 'dear' to God, 'very dear', and 'exceedingly beloved'. Rāmānuja added that God needs his worshipper. As the devotee 'who approaches me as his ultimate goal cannot maintain himself in existence without me, so I too cannot maintain myself without him. Thus he is my very soul. . . . Whoever loves me beyond measure, him will I love beyond measure. Unable to endure separation from him, I cause him to possess me.'[3]

THE AVATAR FAITH

Argument alone cannot prove that Avatars are either possible or true. Is there any necessity for an incarnation of God? Not all

---

[1] Gītā 11, 44.   [2] R. C. Zaehner, *Hindu and Muslim Mysticism*, pp. 195f.
[3] *ibid.*, p. 197.

religions have had such ideas, though similarities are more common than is often thought. In India the worshippers of Śiva have sometimes spoken of his Avatars, but only in imitation of Vaishnavite belief. However, they have spoken much more often and spontaneously of the divine manifestation in visible form to men.

From time to time there have been attacks on Avatar belief. Nineteenth-century reform movements in India often threw out the belief as superstition, along with polytheism and idolatry. Some modern Hindus would say that in order to convey authentic revelation of God Krishna did not need actually to be God. In reply the believer can adduce the importance of the life, example and teaching of the Avatar, and the need for personal manifestation of God. But ultimately it is a question of faith. Historians may, or may not, be able to judge of the occurrence of particular events, but only faith can declare whether these events are disclosures of God, in a different way from other earthly happenings.

That reason cannot prove incarnation to have occurred does not mean that it is contradicted by reason, or that it can be fully understood, for the scriptures say that the wisdom of God is unsearchable and past finding out. When Arjuna, with the help of supernatural vision, marvelled that he saw God everywhere, 'infinite of form on all sides', he also admitted that he could not find 'the beginning, middle, or end' of God. And Krishna declared that those who despise his Avatar do so because they are ignorant of his infinite being as the eternal God.

> *Foolish people have despised me*
> *having taken a human body;*
> *they ignore my higher being*
> *as the greatest lord of beings.*[1]

[1] Gītā 9, 11; and see 11, 16.

PART II

BUDDHAS, JINAS, AND SŪFĪS

10

Incarnation of the Buddha

GOD AND GODS

In studying the idea of Incarnation it seems that there must be a Supreme Being to send his Avatars, but where does Buddhism stand in this context?[1] It used to be maintained that early Buddhism was atheistic, but it is now realized that there was no generally accepted belief in a supreme God for the Buddha to deny. It is astonishing that the neuter divine Brahman of the Upanishads is never discussed in the extensive Buddhist scriptures. But numerous other Hindu gods are mentioned favourably, Brahmā, Indra and the like. Because of this Buddhism has been called not atheistic but 'transpolytheistic'. There are gods in plenty, but they are transcended by the Buddha who is often called 'teacher of gods and men'.

Whether 'gods' is the proper translation for *deva* and *devatā* has been debated, and English translators have called them variously 'angels', 'friendly mortals', or even 'brave and pious gentlemen'. But it seems from the Book of Discipline that the *devas* come from a non-human world to take parts in mortal affairs, as such beings are still supposed to do in Ceylon, Burma and the rest. In the Kindred Sayings the first ninety pages are devoted to the gods and their sons, and a further thirty pages each to Brahmā and Indra, not to mention lesser beings, Yakkhas and Māra. But it becomes clear in all the texts that this pantheon provides a background for the acts of the Buddha. The triple world, as in the

[1] According to E. J. Thomas, when B. H. Hodgson was resident in Nepal in 1840 he set a questionnaire with leading questions, such as 'how many avatārs of Buddha have there been?' and so 'it was thus that he got the answer that the last seven Buddhas were avatārs.' *The History of Buddhist Thought*, 1933, pp. 247f.

Hindu scriptures, is peopled with divinities; but in Buddhism the gods are spectators rather than actors, and they surround the Buddha rather than act independently of him.

The Buddha spent his last existence but one in the Tushita heaven, the fourth class of the world of gods, and there the future Buddha Maitreya lives at present. Sometimes the Buddha and his disciples visit the world of Brahmā, and in return the gods descend to question the Buddha, or implore him to preach as Brahmā did at his enlightenment, but the Buddha is always superior to the gods. The pattern of incarnation, therefore, in so far as it exists in Buddhism, is centred on the Buddha, or Buddhas, and not on the gods. In this, as in some other ways, the Buddha has similarities to Vishnu in Hinduism.

Some of the important later Hindu gods, notably the Avatars, are not mentioned in the Pāli canon. Krishna is not in the texts, though in one of the latest books there are two references to Vāsudeva, but it is not clear whether he was identified with Krishna at that time. There would be no reason to suppress any mention of Krishna, for the Buddhists liked enlisting Hindu gods as supporters of the Buddha, and in some later works both Krishna and Śiva appear.[1]

In the Jātakas, the birth stories of the Buddha, which despite their many legends belong to the later part of the Pāli canon, there is a story of the birth of Krishna, under the name of Vāsudeva, which has resemblances to narratives of the Great Epic. The prince Kaṁsa appears, whose sister is Devagabbhā (divine-womb) to whom Brahmin soothsayers declare that a son born of her will destroy the lineage of Kaṁsa. The prince therefore imprisons his sister in a tower, with a servant called Nandagopā. The two women deliver on the same day, the princess a son and her servant a daughter, but they exchange children. In this way ten sons are born and ten daughters, but since all were exchanged in secret Kaṁsa thinks that his sister has only borne daughters. The eldest son was Vāsu-deva, the second Bala-deva, and the ninth Ghata-pandita. The young men set out to fight their enemies, capture the city of Ayodhyā, and finally conquer all India. But then they begin to destroy one another, and in the end only four people

[1] E. J. Thomas, *The History of Buddhist Thought*, p. 199n.

manage to escape: Vāsudeva lies in the shelter of a bush and is hit in the foot by a spear from a hunter called Jarā or Old Age, as in the Krishna story. The king calls him and demands his name, and on hearing it declares that he who is wounded by Old Age will die. So he teaches knowledge and dies that day, and all his remaining friends perish except his sister. Rather strangely the leading figure in the story is not, as usually in the Jātakas, identified with the Buddha, but Vāsudeva is his disciple Sāriputta. The Buddha himself is another brother, Ghata-pandita, who died before the end of the story. The narrative seems confused and a garbled version of the Epic legends, perhaps from earlier accounts and with bits of the Rāma story. But in any case the Buddha is not here an Avatar of Vāsudeva-Krishna.[1]

In later periods Buddhist commentators took account of Hindu cults, and from Nāgārjuna in the second century A.D. onwards they added to older lists of heretics the sectarian followers of Vāsudeva. They described Vishnu as Universal Hearing, with four arms, holding conch and discus and riding a bird with golden wings. It was said that Vishnu claimed to have created the universe, but in speaking thus such gods denied the law of the production in dependence of all phenomena. Vasubandhu in the fifth century said that to affirm the creative activity of a god is to postulate gratuitously an invisible and uncontrollable cause, and to neglect the visible causes whose efficacity can always be seen.[2]

The Buddhist texts are not unlike the Bhagavad-Gītā in accepting the gods but looking far beyond them. The Jains also accepted the popular deities, but taught that their 'conquerors', the Jinas, were far above them. The Gītā, however, is truly theistic in that it teaches a transcendent Brahman which is being, non-being, and yet more. Beyond the personal manifestations, the Avatars, there is the higher state of God, the greatest Lord of beings. It is this transcendence that seems to be lacking in early Buddhism, at least as far as the gods are concerned.

DESCENT OF THE BUDDHA

A study of the life of the Buddha is important for comparison with the Hindu Avatars, and as a pattern for successive Avatar-like

[1] Jātaka 454.   [2] E. Lamotte, *Histoire du Bouddhisme indien*, 1958, pp. 434ff.

Buddhas. That he was a historical figure may be assumed, and this is important for Avatar doctrine. Yet there is a great deal of myth and legend, and it is difficult to establish historical elements. It is not possible to isolate the 'original' doctrines of Gotama Buddha and describe them as 'archaic Buddhism'. Critical estimates of the date of his death range from about 480 B.C. to 370 B.C. All that can be attempted is to discover elements of the common teachings of Buddhist monks as they may have existed in the third century B.C., before the 'scholastic' period of the Abhidhamma texts.

In the Vinaya and Sutta portions of the Pāli canon there are masses of episodes referring to the public ministry of Gotama, but the anecdotes are not in any continuous narrative. They are occasional stories introduced to form a framework of the circumstances in which it was supposed that the Buddha gave a command or imposed a prohibition. Legends expanded in course of time, in order to justify details of tradition. Then the growing reverence for holy places provided the need for developing stories about them and their connection with the Buddha. Later the cult of relics and the growth of religious imagery affected the written tradition. Also great families which had been converted to Buddhism wanted to be attached to the lineage of his Śākya family, and new regions conquered by Buddhism claimed to have been visited by the founder, and so masses of details were added.

Not till the second century of the Christian era are there complete biographies which take Śākyamuni from his descent from the Tushita heaven, through his life, and down to his Nirvāna and funeral. The monks of India and Ceylon were not uninterested in the personal history of their Master. They transmitted the Pāli teachings and narratives without changing them too much, and while they gave a fairly large place to the miraculous, they kept it within reasonable limits, and it is possible to see many human traits peeping through the wondrous story. The Lives borrowed their basic details from the canonical sources: miracles of the conception and birth of Gotama come from the Mahāpadāna Sutta, episodes of the enlightenment are from the biographical sections of the Majjhima Nikāya, and the beginnings of the public ministry are taken from the Vinaya Pitaka.

The Mahāpadāna Sutta says simply that the Exalted One was

born in the world as an Arahant, Buddha Supreme. His father was the rāja Suddhodana, his mother was the rāja's wife Māyā, and they lived in the town of Kapilavatthu. The Exalted One became a recluse, became a Buddha under a fig tree, and set the Wheel of Dhamma rolling. He had 1,250 disciples, of whom the chief were Sāriputta and Moggallāna, and his friend and chief attendant was Ānanda. The span of life of the Exalted One was brief and soon past.[1]

The basic stories are later magnified and in the Ceylon compilers' introduction to the Jātaka birth tales, the Nidāna-kathā or Three Epochs, there are three stages in life of the Buddha. First of all, ages ago, he took a vow under a previous Buddha, Dīpankara, to become a Buddha himself. Then he came down from the Tushita heaven and attained omniscience. Finally there are the various places at which he stayed on earth.[2]

Of his birth, the Jātaka introduction says that the lady Mahā Māyā had taken part in the midsummer festival in the city of Kapilavatthu. Then the gods who were guardians of the world carried her off to the Himalaya mountains. There the future Buddha had become a superb white elephant, and doing obeisance three times to his mother's couch, he gently struck her right side and seemed to enter her womb. However, this was a dream, for next day when she awoke the queen related the dream to her husband. It was not a virgin birth, since she was married, and in this story at least it is a celestial influence rather than a divine seed that enters her. However, there are already signs of that Docetism which affected Buddhism so much. When the child was born he had none of the offensive matter that smears other children. His mother cherished him in her womb for exactly ten months, and then gave birth to him standing. And the future Buddha left his mother's womb erect, 'like a preacher descending from a pulpit'.

The infant stretched out his hands and feet unsoiled. Four great gods (Mahābrahmās) received him in a golden net, and four kings placed him on an antelope skin. He looked round in ten directions and then took seven strides, and in a lion's roar he said, 'I am the chief in the world'. Mahābrahmā held a white umbrella over the

[1] Dīgha Nikāya, ii, 51–2.
[2] *Buddhist Birth Stories*, trs. T. W. Rhys Davids, 1880.

babe, who emerged from the womb holding medicine in his fist
and asking his mother for a gift.

There appears to have been some effort by the old Abhidhamma school to show that there was no essential difference between
the birth of the Buddha and that of other men. Why did he at his
last birth choose to be born in a human womb? It was because he
saw a great advantages therein. This would inspire respect in
people, who would say of him, 'He is a man and so even men can
attain perfection'. If the Buddha had had neither race nor family
people would have asked, 'Who is he? Is he a magical man or a
demoniacal being?' Further, the Buddha wanted to leave behind
him physical relics, through the worship of which thousands of
people could gain heaven and deliverance. However, the Buddha
was not incarnated in exactly the same way as other celestial
beings. These enter a womb under the impression that it is a hut
to protect them from the cold. But the Buddhas enter the womb,
remain there, and leave it, in full consciousness of what they are
doing (the Jains say much the same). Yet the Buddha did not assume
the form of a white elephant to enter his mother's womb, that was
simply a portent of his future greatness.[1]

It is not necessary here to repeat the traditional stories of the
youth of the Buddha, his marriage, the Four Signs, renunciation,
wandering, enlightenment, and teaching for forty years. For our
purpose it is useful to look more closely at those elements in the
story which throw light on belief in the nature of the Buddha, and
which can be compared with beliefs in Avatars and Incarnations.

HUMANITY OF THE BUDDHA

The texts reveal a number of human traits in the Buddha, even
after his Enlightenment, which are important for an understanding of his person. It was suggested that since Gotama even later
stayed in lodgings in the forest therefore he was not devoid of
attachment, aversion or confusion. But this is denied, and explained
for two reasons: one was to provide ease for the individuality that
still remained to him, and the other was in compassion for people
who came after him.[2]

[1] Abhidharma-kośabhashya, Fr. trs., 1914, p. 14.   [2] Majjhima Nikāya i, 23.

To the implied criticism that the ascetic Gotama did not greet Brahmins, neither standing up to them or asking them to sit down, the Vinaya says that in the world of the gods, including the Brahmās and the Māras, recluses and Brahmins, there is no one whom he should greet or rise up for or offer a seat. For if the Tathāgata should greet or rise up or offer a seat to anybody, his head would split asunder![1]

As he himself had preached out of compassion for mankind, he sent his monks to wander for the gain of many, for the welfare of the world of gods and men. He told them to preach the Dhamma, which is glorious in the beginning, middle and end. But the success of the mission among the Kshatriyas of Magadha caused the people to object that the ascetic Gotama made the fathers beget no sons, wives became widows, and families became extinct. The Buddha's reply was that this noise would only last seven days, and if the monks were reviled they should lead men by the power of truth. Then at the request of his patron, King Bimbisāra, he forbade the ordination of men who were in the army or royal service, and also forbade it to slaves and robbers. When he returned home to Kapilavatthu, begging with his alms bowl at his father's house, Gotama's wife asked their son Rāhula to demand his inheritance. In response the Buddha ordained him into the Order. But then at his father's prayer he forbade the future ordaining of a son without the permission of his father and mother.[2]

Possible faults in the conduct of the Buddha are discussed in Milinda's Questions, though the faults are only in his previous lives. The Jātaka tales indicate that there had been earlier lapses which bore fruit in his last life on earth, and these help to explain some of the trials he suffered from Devadatta (god-given), the Buddha's cousin and Judas of the movement. Devadatta threw a stone at him which grazed Gotama's foot, but this was because in a previous life Gotama himself had thrown a rock at two brothers. Devadatta loosed a killer-elephant against him, because Gotama had driven his own chariot against a former Buddha. He once had to eat dried barley, because he had formerly reviled some monks.

[1] Vinaya Piṭaka, Suttavibhanga, 1f.
[2] *ibid.*, 124f.

And Gotama is said to be the only Buddha to practise austerities, because in a previous life he had reviled another Buddha.[1]

The punishment which was decreed for Devadatta raised serious moral and theological problems. Did the Buddha know that Devadatta would split the Order? Did he know that in punishment for this deed Devadatta would boil in hell for an eon? If he did know, then it is false to say that the Buddha is compassionate, and seeks the welfare of all creatures, removing all woe from them. If the Buddha let Devadatta go to hell without knowing it, then he was not omniscient. This is just the dilemma that is brought against the idea of a loving and omniscient God, by the problem of evil.

The Buddhist answer to the difficulty is to reaffirm that the Buddha is both omniscient and compassionate. But suffering will have a useful purpose, for Devadatta will not suffer forever; like strong medicine the punishment will do him good, and in the end he will become a Buddha. In fact, although Devadatta was going downstream to the whirlpools of death, the Buddha made him go upstream to Nirvāna, out of compassion, and to save him from being boiled in hell for hundreds of thousands of becomings. Here are the roots of a universalism which seems to be demanded by the combination of omniscience and compassion, by a sort of divine determinism.[2]

Less speculative and more human traits in the story appear in the Buddha's bodily ailments, which are mentioned a number of times. The Vinaya says that sometimes he was troubled by wind in the stomach. Once a disturbance fell on the humours of his body and he took a purgative. Ānanda rubbed the Master's body with fat for a few days, and he was purged thirty times. These are complaints that are common in hot countries, and both Gotama and Muhammad died of dysentery, at a reasonably old age.

Nāgasena admitted to Milinda that painful feelings arose in the Tathāgata's body, even when all unskill had been burnt up; his foot was grazed by a splinter, he was purged with hot water, and so on. But these sufferings did not affect his perfection, 'for not all that is experienced is rooted in karma', but it may be 'merely

[1] *Milinda's Questions*, trs. I. B. Horner, i, p. xxxiv.
[2] *ibid.*, 108f.

138

sudden' and produces no result. In fact, the Buddha suffered because he remained in the body.[1]

The Buddha met many people of different classes. He talked with gods and Brahmins, with rulers and Jains. He often declared that the only true Brahmin was a man of good life, and not just of superior birth. The courtesan Ambapālī took him into her house, sat down at his side, fed him, was taught by him, and presented her mansion to the Order. It was at the hands of the blacksmith Chunda that the Buddha received his last meal, which poisoned him.

The Buddha really died. Māra (death), the wicked one, had long dogged his footsteps, tempting him at his enlightenment, and saying that he would not escape him. But the Buddha had replied that he was delivered from all fetters and Death was struck down and vanished. At the end Māra came again and said, 'Pass away now, Lord, from existence', and so the Blessed One consciously rejected the rest of his allotted sum of life. But he also told Ānanda that he was old and full of years, he had reached his sum of days, turning eighty years of age. Like a worn-out cart that can only be kept going with the help of thongs, so the body of the Tathāgata could only be kept going by bandaging it up.

Much play is made on Ānanda's failure to plead with the Buddha to stay longer. Even when clear hints were given that the Tathāgata could live for an eon, the venerable Ānanda was incapable of comprehending them, 'so far was his heart possessed by the Evil One'. This is rather hard on Ānanda, and reflects the problem as to why the Buddha died at all. But perhaps, as with the followers of Muhammad, the final onset of the sickness was unexpected and felt to be disastrous.[2]

The Mahā Parinibbāna Sutta gives many details of these last days. When the rainy season came dire sickness and sharp pains, even unto death, afflicted the Blessed One, but he bore them without complaint, and by a strong effort of will he bent the sickness down and kept his hold on life until the time he fixed upon should come. He came eventually to Kusinārā, a 'wattle-and-daub' branch township in the jungle, whose insignificance was a problem to the writers, who would have preferred the Buddha to

---

[1] *ibid.*, 134, 174.   [2] Dīgha Nikāya ii, 100, 102.

die in a more exalted place like Benares. But the inferior name is a
better guarantee of authenticity. He stayed with the blacksmith
Chunda, who prepared for him rice and cakes and a quantity of
boar's flesh. After the Buddha's dysentery this was fatal, and he
told the blacksmith to serve only the rice and cakes to his followers
and bury the rest of the pork, for nobody on earth or heaven
could digest it. This eating of pork is testified in verse from the
oldest tradition, and later times took care to remove the blame
from Chunda because his intentions were pure. There was no
reason, then or now, to forbid eating flesh if it was given to the
monk. But in modern times philologists have sought some other
translation for pork and Rhys Davids rendered it 'a quantity of
truffles'. Foucher remarks that this was 'not more easily digested
but far more distinguished'.[1]

The Buddha then told Ānanda that he was weary and would
rest in a Sāla Grove; he was thirsty and would drink, he was tired
and would lie down. He lay under the trees on his right side, with
one leg resting on the other; as depicted in countless images. He
gave Ānanda some last instructions; not to look at women or
speak to them, and if they addressed him then 'keep wide awake'.
Ānanda stood weeping at the thought of the death of his Master,
but the Buddha consoled him by saying that some may think that
'the word of the Master is ended, we have no Teacher more'. But
they must not look at it in that way. After he was gone the truths
and rules of the Order must be their teacher. Ānanda said that
none of the brethren had any doubt of the Buddha, the Dhamma
or the Sangha. The Buddha replied that he had spoken 'out of the
fullness of faith', and that all the brethren would eventually attain
enlightenment. His last words were a reminder of the decay
inherent in all compounded things and, according to the Pāli
tradition, an exhortation to work out their salvation with dili-
gence. The Buddha then went into four stages of rapture, and
when he passed out of the last stage he expired immediately.[2]

Of course there are plenty of miracles, even in the Pāli texts.
To compensate for the poor locality, the trees under which the
Exalted One lay were covered with flowers out of season, which

[1] Dīgha Nikāya ii, 126f.; *Life of the Buddha*, p. 232.
[2] *ibid*. ii, 154f.

sprinkled themselves all over his body. Heavenly flowers fell from the sky as well, with celestial sandal-wood powder, and music and songs came from the sky out of reverence for the successor of the Buddhas of old. The colour of the skin of the Tathāgata became very bright and clear, like all his predecessors at their deaths. There was a great earthquake when he died, thunders burst forth, and both the gods Brahmā and Sakka uttered verses of praise. Eight chiefs, bathed and in new robes, tried to lift up the body of the Buddha but could not do so until the spirits directed them to the north and east, whereupon the whole town was strewn kneedeep in celestial flowers. The body of the Buddha, it is said, was treated like that of a king of kings, wrapped in five hundred layers of wool, put in oil, in an iron vessel, and cremated on a funeral pyre with all kinds of perfumes.[1]

The interests of the sacred places asserted themselves in the composition of the narrative. There were eight claimants for his relics, and the inhabitants of Kusinārā said that none of his remains should be given away. But a solution was found by a Brahmin who said that since the Buddha taught forbearance, it was unseemly to quarrel over his remains. They should be divided into eight parts and cairns set up in those places, so that 'mankind might trust in the Light of the World'. But it was earlier said that there are four places which believers should visit with special reverence: the place where the Tathāgata was born, where he attained perfect Enlightenment, where he set on foot the kingdom of Dhamma, and where he finally passed away.

GLORIFICATION

The human traits of the Buddha are important, where they can be distinguished, because they show that he was believed to have been a real man, and this is significant for incarnational theories of Buddhism. From the early texts it can be seen that Gotama did not give himself out as a god, but as a seer. In fact he sought to destroy in himself all the impurities which, if they had not been eliminated, could have made him a god in some other birth, or a man or a demon. He effaced himself before the Dhamma which he preached

[1] *ibid.* ii, 138, 166.

and at death he could do no more for his disciples than recommend them to his Dhamma; this would be their island and resort.[1]

Serious attempts were made by the Abhidhamma teachers to hold to the worldly appearances of the Buddha, against the Docetics who held that he only visited this world in a spiritual form. To this it was replied that there are towns and shrines mentioned by the Buddha; he was born at Lumbinī, enlightened under the Bodhitree, preached at Benares, and completed existence at Kusinārā. The Lokottaravādas held that the Buddha's speech was supramundane (*lok-uttara*, beyond the world), but that would imply that his speech was only heard by the spiritual ear and by his disciples alone. Yet it was known that ordinary people were aware of his speech, some were baffled and others offended by it, so that it must have been mundane as well as supramundane. The Docetics held that even the excreta of the Buddha excelled all other fine perfumes. But that would imply that he fed on perfumes, whereas it was known that he ate rice.[2]

Yet despite these strong human assertions, the Abhidhamma asserts that the powers of the Buddha were unique and were not shared by his disciples. He alone was Conqueror, Buddha, Supreme, All-knowing, All-seeing, Lord of Dhamma, Fountainhead of Dhamma, and no disciples had such titles.[3]

The same dual attitude is found from the oldest Pāli texts. He is called the ascetic Gotama, of the Śākya clan, who went out from that family to adopt the religious life. But after his enlightenment the name Gotama is little used and he is called an Arahat, a fully awakened one, abounding in goodness and wisdom, unsurpassed as a guide to mortals willing to be led, a teacher of gods and men, a Blessed One, a Buddha.

Teacher of gods and men. That gives him a more than divine status, and the description continues: He, by himself, thoroughly knows and sees face to face this universe–including the worlds above of the gods, the Brahmās and the Māras, and the world below with its recluses and Brahmins, its princes and peoples; and having known it he makes his knowledge known to others. The Buddha is omniscient, superior to the gods, the only one who can

---

[1] *Histoire du Bouddhisme indien*, pp. 26ff.
[2] Kathā-Vatthu 2, 10; 18, 1; 18, 4.   [3] *ibid.*

bestow knowledge of the saving truth. He is closely similar to the Krishna of the Bhagavad Gītā, and has many of the attributes of the God of the monotheistic religions. In the constantly used Refuge Formula the disciple confesses: 'And now I betake myself to the Blessed One as my refuge, to the Dhamma and to the Sangha. May the Blessed One accept me as a disciple, as one who, from this day forth, as long as life endures, has taken refuge in them.' This faith in Buddha is better than all sacrifices. 'He who with a trusting heart takes Buddha as his guide, and the Dhamma and the Sangha, that is a sacrifice better than gifts and alms and dowries.' It is not surprising that another text remarks that 'a man should worship him from whom he learns the Dhamma, as the gods worship Indra'.[1]

The Pāli texts do not hesitate to attribute divine qualities to the Buddha. The Niddesa gives three classes of god (*deva*). The first are kings and queens who receive honorific titles of gods; the second are all the ordinary gods who are born to this state up to the Brahmā-gods and beyond; the third are the Buddhist Arahats and Pacceka-Buddhas (lonely Buddhas). But the Lord Buddha himself is the super-god (*atideva*), and the god beyond the gods (*devātideva*). He is a god, but only as defined in the Buddhist sense, and he is far above all other divinities, transcendent and supreme.[2]

Further evidences of the transcendence of the Buddhas are the Thirty Two Marks of a Superman (Mahā-Purusha), which are often listed. If a child bears these signs he will become one of two things, and no other. If he stays at home he will become a sovereign of the world, a Lord of the Wheel, reigning over the earth from sea to sea, ruling in righteousness without the use of spear or sword, having a thousand sons and seven royal treasures. But if he goes out to the homeless state he will become a Buddha who removes the veil from the eyes of the world.

Buddhists claimed that Gotama was both a Buddha and a king, a religious king, since he set in motion the irresistible wheel of Dharma. He possessed all the marks of a Great Man, and though in theory universal kings had these too, yet they can be taken as attributes that were attached to the person of the Buddha. The dialogues tell how he convinced Brahmins who were looking for

[1] Dīgha Nikāya i, 87; Sutta Nipāta, 315.   [2] Niddesa 1, 355ff.

the marks, and eventually they were impressed by all his perfections of which even the most secret were revealed by 'psychic power'. These marks were probably not the invention of the Buddhists. But there is no comparable list in pre-Buddhistic priestly literature, and the monks have made the Marks known by applying them point by point to the body of the Buddha at birth and during his life.[1]

In the early centuries Buddhist artists were reluctant to portray the body of the Buddha in sculpture, and the fact that Milinda's Questions have no discussion on imagery suggests that there was none when they were written. At first artists depicted the sandals, throne or umbrella of the Buddha instead of his body. But when, after some five centuries and under Persian and Greek influence, they did begin to portray him then the Marks of the Buddha's beauty and grandeur were shown in plastic form and enabled the devout to concentrate their devotions on him. Today, as for many centuries past, there are millions of images of the Superman, and the one who perhaps would have disliked any representation of his body for worship, probably now has more images than any other figure in human or divine story.

The Questions of Milinda take up a number of problems about the transcendent Buddha that troubled men in the development of religion. He was said to have possessed not only the Thirty Two Signs but also a halo that spread round him for a fathom's length. But surely a son inherits his qualities from his father or mother, and they did not have such marks? The answer is that there is a lotus of a hundred leaves, yet it rises from the mud and thrives in water. Even so the Lord had marks which his parents did not possess. Later it is said that the parents of the Buddha had been determined beforehand, the tree of enlightenment was determined, his son was determined, his attendant determined, his chief disciples determined. The whole life became a fixed pattern, a type, which could be applied to any Buddha.[2]

The Tathāgata is said to have had four additional special qualities which nobody could obstruct. Nobody could break up the halo round his body, break his life-principle, hinder his omniscience, or stop the offering of a gift to him. Even if he suffered

[1] Sutta Nipāta, 548ff.   [2] Milinda's Questions, 75, 193, 225f.

from disease, or undertook ascetic practices, there is no being like the Lord, who is the foremost, eldest and best of beings. Gotama, we know, was a Kshatriya of the ruler caste, but to conciliate Brahmins he was said to belong to them as well. The Tathāgata was a Brahmin in that he put away all unskilled states and passed beyond perplexity. And he was a king, who reigned through Dhamma over men and gods. So the Buddha was incomparable in moral habits, in contemplation, in wisdom and freedom. He had the ten powers, the four confidences, the eighteen special qualities, and the six knowledges, which are peculiar to a Buddha.

'Was the Buddha omniscient?' it is asked. And at first the cautious answer is given that knowledge and vision were not constantly present to his mind, but when he turned his mind to a thing he was omniscient, and that is practically the same. He knew whatever he wanted to know, not through searching it out but as by a latent power. Just as a tree laden with fruit, yet whose fruit had not fallen, would not be called a tree without fruit, so the Buddha would not be called without omniscience when he had not turned his mind towards it. More practically, it was argued that when there was a division in the Order the disciples pacified the Lord by means of a simile of a young calf. But did the Buddha not know of this? Yes, he did know, indeed he knew already and had taught that very simile beforehand to his disciples.[1]

WORSHIP

All of these and many other statements show the development of reverence and worship to the Buddha, as to a god. Yet did the Buddha still exist? This problem was discussed in a number of ways. When the Buddha was staying with the Archers he was asked, 'Does a Tathāgata exist after death?' And the answer given is that, 'this has not been revealed by the Exalted One'. And if men persisted in saying that a Tathāgata did not exist after death, or neither existed nor not existed, or both existed and not existed, they should be answered in the same way,–it had not been revealed. This was typical of the refusal to speculate because it does not lead to good, or true religion, or peace, or Nirvāna.[2]

[1] Milinda's Questions, 102, 209.   [2] Dīgha Nikāya iii, 135

Milinda pressed the matter further when he asked, 'Have you seen the Buddha?' And when Nāgasena admitted that neither he nor his teachers had seen the Buddha, the king retorted that there was no Buddha. This was the kind of elementary argument used earlier to refute those who had not seen Brahmā, and Nāgasena showed the absurdity of replying that since the king had not seen a famous river in the Himalayas there was no such river. But is the Buddha pre-eminent, since you have never seen him? Yes, just as a river plunges into the sea, so from those who have attained final Nirvāna we know that the Lord is pre-eminent. The Lord is known by his Dhamma, as past teachers are known from the writing they left.[1]

Elsewhere when a seeker said he was going to a disciple for refuge, he was told only to go to the Lord. And when he asked where the Lord was now, was told that he was in Nirvāna, so he said he would go to him for refuge. The same theme is repeated and shows that refuge was taken in the Buddha not only in his life on earth but also after his death, and of course this has been continued ever since.[2]

Critics from other sects had objected that if the Buddha accepted homage then he had not attained final Nirvāna; he was still within the world, fettered to the world, and service given to him would be fruitless. On the other hand, if he had attained final Nirvāna and was released from the world, there was no point in giving homage to him, for anyone in final Nirvāna did not accept gifts. The answer was that although the Lord does not need gifts, yet the sects are wrong to say that service rendered to him is barren. As winds die down and fires go out, yet fans can restore the flame, so the relics of the Tathāgata and the jewel of his knowledge are conditions for achieving attainment. Therefore service rendered to the Tathāgata who has attained complete Nirvāna becomes fruitful.[3]

The veneration of relics became very important, and began as soon as the Buddha died, according to the Mahāparinibbāna Sutta. The chiefs who had carried the body were unable to set it alight, until a visiting brother had circumambulated and bowed to the

[1] Milinda's Questions, 70.   [2] Majjhima Nikāya 2, 90; 2, 163.
[3] Milinda's Questions, 95.

body, followed by fire hundred monks who walked round it three times and bowed, whereupon the corpse caught fire of itself. Then the remaining bones were divided among eight stūpas, as already mentioned. But it seems that although the Buddha had given instructions about his cremation and the erection of stūpas, yet he recommended Ānanda and his fellow monks not to hinder themselves by honouring his remains, but to devote themselves to their own good, leaving relic worship to nobles and Brahmins.[1]

Milinda asked how this discouragement of relic-worship could be reconciled with another traditional verse that said if you venerate the relic of him who is to be venerated you will go to heaven. Nāgasena's answer was that this was not said for everybody. Buddha-pūjā, worship of the Buddha himself or of his image, is for others, whether gods or men. But for the monks, the Conqueror's sons, attention must be given to comprehension of the impermanent qualities, warfare against defilement, and intentness on Nirvāna. It is assumed that although people who worship relics will go to heaven, that is not the goal for the monk, whose sole aim should be Nirvāna.[2]

Nevertheless, there grew up *pūjā*, reverence or ritual worship, not only of the Buddha but of disciples who were *nibbuta*, having cooled attachment and attained Nirvāna. Another Milinda discussion says that there are wonders displayed at the relic shrines of some who have attained Nirvāna, and not of others. For the gods (*devatās*) 'out of compassion for mankind', show wonders at some shrines, thinking that 'the true Dhamma will be perpetually supported by this wonder'. And others bring wonders about by their devotion. But even if there are no wonders one should have faith that the saint, this son of the Buddha, has well attained final Nirvāna. At a later date the Mahāvastu says that one may worship the Tathāgata while he is still living, with flowers and incense and so on, or after he has passed away. In either case one will reap an infinite store of merit, which is the purpose of such worship.[3]

The Questions of Milinda are fairly reserved, seeking to reconcile different practices. Nevertheless, the great interest in Buddhology, shown in the problems it discusses, is evidence of the growth

---

[1] Dīgha Nikāya, ii, 141, 163f.   [2] Milinda's Questions, 177.
[3] Milinda's Questions, 309; Mahāvastu, 362.

of the cult of the Buddha. Moreover, although we have been speaking all this time of *the* Buddha, as though he were the only one, it will have been noted that we could not exclude references to other Buddhas and Bodhisattvas. The theme of successive Buddhas, like Avatars, must be considered next.

11

Buddhas and Avatars

BUDDHA SUCCESSION

We commonly speak of Gotama as *the* Buddha, but every Buddhist, Theravāda as well as Mahāyāna, believes that there are numerous Buddhas, past and to come. This would be quite understandable if a Buddha were simply as, the name means, an 'enlightened' man, a wise teacher. Perhaps the notion of a succession arose because teachers were anxious to show that their doctrines had the support of sages of past times, as Krishna said in the Gītā that 'so had all the sages taught', listing a number of them. Gotama himself did not pretend to be an innovator, or a founder of a religion; there were other teachers, though he claimed, or his followers claimed for him, that he was supreme. He realized the Truth, by his own efforts, at his enlightenment. Nevertheless, the assertion of supremacy is found many times in words attributed to him by his disciples.

The idea of a succession of Buddhas is found in the Sutta Pitaka of the Pāli canon. T. W. Rhys-Davids, in the introduction to the translation of the Mahāpadāna Sutta, said that we find here the root of that spreading weed which grew up along with the rest of Buddhism but flourished so luxuriantly that it gradually covered up much of the valuable ancient doctrine and 'finally led to the downfall' of the ancient faith in its home in India. 'The doctrine of the Bodhisatta, of the Wisdom-Being, drove out the doctrine of the Aryan Path. A gorgeous hierarchy of mythological wonder-workers filled men's minds, and the older system of self-training and self-control became forgotten.'[1]

This statement is highly debatable. Not only is the system of

[1] *Dialogues of the Buddha*, ii, p. 1.

self-training still practised among the monks and many of the laity of Theravāda countries, and Mahāyāna as well, but it may be questioned how far Buddhism ever was free from a hierarchy of supernatural beings and wonder-workers. As for the decline of Buddhism in India, there were many causes. In India Buddhism always had to face a highly literate religion, whereas it had virtually a free hand in its more successful campaigns among the illiterates of ancient south-east Asia. Then Hinduism revived and led counter-attacks, with the Vaishnavite and Śaivite devotional movements. Finally it was Islam which ravaged the remaining 'idol temples' of Indian Buddhism and destroyed its monasteries.

Yet the idea of successive Buddhas seems to be specifically Indian, and parallel to that of Avatars. Though religious teachers in many countries have appealed to the examples and doctrines of wise men of antiquity, it is a particularly Indian conception of a Wisdom-Being that appears from age to age 'under similar circumstances to propound a similar faith'. In Indian literature the idea is strongly propounded by the Buddhists, and in Buddhist literature 'its first appearance is in documents of the date of our Suttanta'.[1] But the date of the Sutta cannot be fixed; it may be about the third century B.C., but it could be earlier or later. Krishna is a similar recurring being in the Bhagavad-Gītā, and while most writers consider the Gītā to have been written after the beginnings of Buddhism there are some, including the authoritative Dasgupta, who think that it is pre-Buddhist.

Whether Gotama Buddha himself knew anything of the doctrine of a succession of identical Buddhas is debatable. 'Possibly not', says Rhys-Davids, though the Sutta he translates puts the theory into the mouth of Gotama. But it is true that the notion of a number of Buddhas gives the idea of a Buddha in a different and more exalted light than that of an Arahant (Arahat or Arhat), a perfected or worthy one.

BODHISATTA

The title Bodhisatta (or Bodhisat; Bodhisattva in Sanskrit), the Wisdom-Being or Being of Enlightenment, is used of Gotama in

[1] *Dialogues of the Buddha*, ii, p. 2.

the Pāli canon. Here it means the one who was determined to win enlightenment after his renunciation. It occurs frequently in the Middle Length Sayings, where Gotama remarks: 'before my Awakening, and while I was yet merely the Bodhisatta, not a fully self-awakened one'. The references are to this present life, at some time before the enlightenment when he became a Buddha, an Enlightened One, and so his career as Bodhisatta came to an end. Then the term Bodhisatta is used of Gotama from the moment of his conception, and in the Jātaka Tales of any of his more than five hundred previous births; e.g. 'in those days the Bodhisatta was born into a merchant's family'.[1]

In the Mahāpadāna Sutta the term Bodhisatta is extended from Gotama to previous Buddhas, and it refers back to the first one when 'as Bodhisatta, he ceased to belong to the hosts of the heaven of Delight, and descended into his mother's womb'. This is a natural development, for if there are other Buddhas then they too have passed through the stage of Bodhisatta before attaining supreme enlightenment. In Theravada usage the term Bodhisatta is generally confined to Gotama himself in his previous births, and up to his enlightenment, and to a limited number of similar Buddhas in preparation. The Mahāyāna usage will be considered in the next chapter, but it may be remarked that not only was the term Bodhisattva extended greatly in meaning by being used of supernatural beings, but it also designated learned teachers as 'a sort of degree in theology'.[2]

SEVEN BUDDHAS

The title of the Mahāpadāna Sutta means the 'Great Story' of Buddhas. It is a myth of former births and the deeds enacted in them, the story of Dhamma and its bearers and promulgators. It tells of six previous Buddhas, and of Gotama the seventh. Not here, but elsewhere in the Pāli canon, a Buddha to come is mentioned, Metteya (in Pāli; Maitreya in Sanskrit). So at least eight Buddhas were spoken of in the older texts, and a number more before the end of the Pāli canon. The seven Buddhas of this

[1] Majjhima Nikāya ii, 163; i, p. 22; Jātaka, 1.
[2] Dīgha Nikāya ii, 12f.

Sutta have been compared with seven sages of Hindu tradition, and even with the seven planets.

The Mahāpadāna Sutta begins with Gotama, the Exalted One, with clear and divine hearing, surpassing the hearing of men, asking his bhikkhus (monks) what they had been discussing, and offering them some religious talk 'on the subject of former lives'. He proceeds at once to list the six Buddhas before himself.

The first was Vipassi, who arose in the world ninety-one eons ago as Exalted One, Arahant, Buddha Supreme. He was followed at intervals by others, each one a Buddha Supreme, and the next five are named as Sikhi, Vessabhu, Kakusandha, Konāgamana, and Kassapa. The last three are all said to have arisen 'in this present eon'. And also in this eon 'I myself, an Arahant, Buddha Supreme, have arisen in the world'.[1]

On hearing this the disciples marvel at the great genius and master mind of the Tathāgata in remembering the Buddhas of old, with their ranks and personal and family names, the lengths of their lives, the trees under which they were enlightened, and the numbers of their disciples. These he gave in detail, with astronomical numbers of their spans of life and assemblies of Arahants. The Buddha admitted that he was able to remember all those facts by his discernment of the principle of truth, and also because *the gods have revealed* these matters to him and enabled him to remember them all. The commentators say that only religious teachers of karma and Buddhas can remember their previous lives.

Gotama then proceeds to list the lives and achievements of the Buddhas, and this becomes purely formal and repetitive, with practically the same words spoken about each of the Buddhas in turn. The Buddhas become types, or ideals, and therefore it is not strange, though perhaps deplorable, that there is much more detail given about the first Buddha than about Gotama himself. The monkish scribes tired of repeating everything and they gave most attention to the first, Vipassi.

When Vipassi ceased to belong as a Bodhisatta to the hosts of heaven, he descended into his mother's womb, mindful and self-possessed. But such is the rule for all Bodhisattas. 'It is the rule'

[1] Dīgha ii, 2.

that when he descends from heaven there is an infinite radiance, surpassing the glory of the gods, the Māras and Brahmās, manifested throughout the universe. 'It is the rule' that four sons of the gods go towards the four quarters announcing that nobody must harm the Bodhisatta and his mother. 'It is the rule' that the mother of the Bodhisatta is a virtuous woman, following the five rules of Buddhist morality; averse to stealing, unchastity, taking life, lying, and strong drink.

The attention that is given here to the mother of a Bodhisatta is important, not for the glorification of the mother, for that hardly happens, but because of the magical and Docetic elements that are introduced. There is an aversion to natural functions, even within marriage, through which the prejudices of the celibate monks appear. So 'it is the rule' that the mother has no mind for indulgence in the pleasures of sense with men when the Bodhisatta is descending into her womb, but she lives in the enjoyment of more spiritual things. No ailment befalls the mother, and she sees the Bodhisatta within her womb, as in a translucent gem, complete in all his limbs. To make sure that she remains immaculate, 'it is the rule' that on the seventh day after the birth of a Bodhisatta his mother dies and rises again to the heaven of Delight. The mother brings forth her child not after nine but ten months. She bears him not reclining but standing; the Jātaka introduction says the same, though as Foucher remarks, it is 'a position as uncomfortable as it is unusual'.[1] Although the child and his mother are perfect, and the birth is undefiled by any blood or uncleanness, yet to make sure two showers of hot and cold water fall from the sky to bathe the Bodhisatta and his mother.

'It is the rule' that gods receive the baby first and men afterward, and four sons of the gods present him to the mother saying, 'Rejoice, lady, for mighty is the son that is born to thee'. The infant Bodhisatta then stands firm on both feet, takes seven strides while a white canopy is held over him, and utters with the voice of a bull, 'I am Chief, Eldest, and Foremost in the world. This is the last birth. There is now no more coming to be.' Then infinite radiance is manifested throughout the universe, including the worlds of the gods, and the ten thousand worlds tremble.

[1] *The Life of the Buddha*, p. 30.

When Vipassi was born his rāja father sent for the Brahmin soothsayers, and they saw him to be endowed with the thirty-two marks of the Great Man, which are listed. He would either be a Lord of the Wheel, a righteous and universal king, or he would go forth into the homeless state and become a Supreme Buddha, rolling back the veil from the world. So he grew up a perfect young man, the darling of the people, living in palaces fitted for every kind of gratification of the senses.

After many thousands of years, for he lived eighty thousand years, Vipassi went out in a carriage and saw the Four Signs. First he saw an old man, learnt the fact of age, and returned to his rooms depressed by the thing called birth. Centuries later he saw a sick man and learnt of illness. Then he saw a corpse, and finally a monk in a yellow robe. Then Vipassi cut off his hair, donned a yellow robe, and went forth from the house into the homeless state. Many people followed him and did the same, till Vipassi escaped from the crowd and dwelt alone to meditate on the troubles of the world. Then to Vipassi the Bodhisatta a vision arose, knowledge, reason, wisdom and light arose; he won the way to enlightenment through insight, and being set free he became an Exalted One, Arahant, Buddha Supreme. He debated whether to teach the Truth, fearing that if men rejected it that would be hurtful to him. But one of the Great Brahmās came down and implored the Supreme Buddha to preach the Truth to beings that were perishing, and after three entreaties the Buddha looked over the world with a Buddha's eye in pitifulness. So he proclaimed to various hearers 'that Truth which the Buddhas alone have won'. The Great Brahmā also persuaded him to send out his disciples to preach Dhamma and he told them, 'Go not singly, go in pairs; teach the Truth, lovely in its origin, lovely in its progress, lovely in its consummation'. Then the Buddha gave them the monastic rule.

The Sutta ends with the present Buddha. Gotama was dwelling in solitary meditation beneath a giant tree, when he thought that there was one heaven that he had not dwelt in for a long time and so he went there. Then thousands of gods came and told him about Vipassi, that they had lived a holy life under him, and were reborn in an exalted heaven. Other gods told him of various Buddhas, down to himself, claiming to have been their followers. It was in this way that the Tathāgata could remember the Buddhas of old, with details of their families and disciples.

The Seven Buddhas are referred to also in the canonical Kindred Sayings. 'To Vipassi, Exalted One, Arahant, Buddha Supreme, before his enlightenment, while he was yet unenlightened and a Bodhisatta, there came this thought. . . . And to Sikhi, Kakusandha, Konāgamana, and Kassapa came this thought . . . And to me, before I was enlightened, while I was yet unenlightened and a Bodhisatta, there came this thought. . . . Alas, this world has fallen upon trouble.'[1]

That there were other Buddhas is assumed in a number of places, even when the superiority of Gotama is affirmed. In the Mahā Parinibbāna Sutta, the Book of the Great Decease, the venerable disciple Sāriputta says that he has such faith in the Exalted One that he thinks there never has been or ever will be any other greater or wiser than he is. But Gotama asks whether he has known all the Arahant Buddhas of the past, and whether he has perceived all of the future Buddhas, and whether indeed he penetrates the mind of the Buddha now alive. And later in the same Sutta it is said that far and few are the Arahant Buddhas who appear in this world, yet the present disciples will witness the passing away of a Tathāgata.[2]

The Questions of Milinda try to show that the Bodhisattas were not stereotypes, because there were differences between them. All Bodhisattas give away their wife and children, as illustrated by the Jātaka tales. But not all Bodhisattas practise austerities, which were performed by Gotama alone. Bodhisattas differ in four respects. There is a difference in the castes in which they become Buddhas; some are Brahmins, some Kshatriyas, but none of low caste. There is a difference in the length of time needed to practise the perfections so as to become a Buddha; Vipassi is said to have lived eighty thousand years and Gotama a hundred years. There is a difference in their heights.

But there is no difference among the Buddhas in moral habits, physical beauty, concentration, wisdom, the ten powers of a Tathāgata, the fourteen knowledges of a Buddha, the eighteen

[1] Samyutta Nikāya ii, 4f.   [2] Dīgha ii, 82, 108, 139.

Buddha-qualities, and the entire Buddha-nature (Buddha-dhamma). All Buddhas are exactly the same in their Buddha-nature, and they have unique knowledge of what goes on in the minds and senses of others, great compassion, all-pervading knowledge, and omniscience.

Gotama Buddha was the only one to practise austerities, which were testified by abundant tradition but might have seemed derogatory, because he renounced worldly life while his knowledge was immature and did this to bring it to maturity.[1]

The Abhidhamma texts of the Pāli canon also discuss the differences of the Buddhas, and hold that with the exception of differences in body, age and radiance, at any given time, Buddhas differ mutually in no other respect. Though it is admitted that some sects hold that they differ in other qualities in general. The sufferings of a Bodhisatta, notably Gotama, are considered from the point of view of freewill. Sufferings of other people are the result of their evil karma, but some teachers judged that the Bodhisatta decreed his own sufferings and freely performed difficult tasks through a specific power which was a virtual denial of karma.[2]

TWENTY-FIVE BUDDHAS

The Pāli schools agree on the names of the six previous Buddhas, but the names of other Buddhas which were added vary in the schools. Some of these Buddhas are mentioned in inscriptions, at Bharhut and Nigali-sāgar. The latter records how the emperor Aśoka, 'the beloved of the gods, when he had been consecrated fourteen years, increased the stūpa of Buddha Konākamana to double its former size . . . and came in person and worshipped'.[3] The Chinese traveller Hsüan Tsang said that he saw the pillar surmounted by a carved lion, but both the stūpa and the lion have disappeared, and the pillar is now in Nepal. Aśoka's inscription dates from about 250 B.C. and suggests that the doctrine of earlier Buddhas was established then, though how far it was integrated into any system cannot be said.

---

[1] Milinda's Questions, 284f.   [2] *Abhidhamma*, v, p. 354.
[3] R. Thapar, *Aśoka*, 1961, p. 261.

A long list of Buddhas is given in the Buddhavaṁsa, the 'History of the Buddhas', one of the latest works in the Pāli canon. In reply to a question by Sāriputta, Gotama gives a verse account of how he first formed the resolve of becoming a Buddha in the days of the first Buddha, who was Dīpankara. He was followed by twenty-three Buddhas, and the present Buddha is therefore the twenty-fifth. A similar list is given in the Introduction to the Jātakas, beginning with Dīpankara, and naming the twenty-four succeeding Buddhas including Gotama. The last six before him have the same names as in the earlier lists, beginning with Vipassi.[1]

The story of Gotama taking his vow to become a Buddha under Dīpankara, and then under each of the successive Buddhas, has entered into general tradition. At that time Gotama, a hundred thousand cycles ago, was a Brahmin named Sumedha, very wise and pondering already on the miseries of life. He heard that a mighty Buddha, Dīpankara, had appeared and went to seek him, lying on the ground before him and vowing to become a Buddha. Dīpankara foretold that he would achieve Buddhahood, predicted the names of his parents, his own future name Gotama, the names of his disciples and of his Bo-tree. So our present Buddha made his vow under twenty-four Buddhas including Dīpankara.

Lists of other Buddhas are given in the Mahāyāna and Sarvāsti-vādin texts. The Lalitavistara speaks of millions of Buddhas, and so does the Lotus Sūtra. While the Mahāvastu says that it knew three hundred million (*kotis*) Buddhas of the name of Śākyamuni. These astronomical figures may be based on notions of the numbers of stars, each of which was a world ruled by a Buddha, whereas the more modest enumeration of seven Buddhas may be from the analogy of the seven planets.[2]

The Buddhavaṁsa also gives some development of the Bodhi-satta doctrine. It is still applied only to Gotama, and is not an alternative to being an Arahant as in the Mahāyāna. And yet it seems as if the career of a Bodhisatta might be open to others, or that the more universal Mahāyāna idea developed from here. To

---

[1] Buddhavaṁsa; but this text mentions other Buddhas outside its list of twenty-five; there is Metteya to come, and contemporary with Dīpankara there were three other enlightened ones.

[2] Mahāvastu, 57.

become a Buddha, it is stated, the Bodhisatta must be a human being and male, he must be able to become an Arahant, must have made his vow before a previous Buddha, must not be a house-holder but a homeless one when making the vow. He must have five higher knowledges, eight attainments, and ten perfections. He must have great energy to obtain these qualities, and he must undertake to sacrifice his life for the Buddhas. These conditions are not far from those given to the Bodhisattvas in Mahāyāna writings.[1]

In the main, however, the Bodhisatta doctrines are not of much interest to Theravāda Buddhists, and the metaphysical Abhi-dhamma works hardly mention them. The fourth book in this final section of the Pāli canon is the Puggalapaññatti, the 'descrip-tion of individuals' according to their stages along the Noble Eightfold Path. The Bodhisattas are not found here, but in the classification of different types there is another kind of Buddha. This is the Pacceka-Buddha (Sanskrit, Pratyeka-Buddha), the individual, separate, private or hermit Buddha. This is a 'self-begotten' (*svayambhu*) Buddha, one who has attained enlighten-ment by his own efforts, and not through the teaching of another Buddha like most Arahants. But although he becomes a Buddha he differs from a complete Buddha (*sammāsambuddha*) in that he does not become omniscient and does not possess the fruits of full Buddhahood.

The Pacceka-Buddha does not preach like a full Buddha; he is said to have penetrated the flavour of enlightenment, but not the flavour of Dhamma. This is because he enjoys the solitary life and is often called 'a lonely rhinoceros'. Let him wander alone, like a rhinoceros, it is said, and it is this description of the Pacceka-Buddha that is most apt.[2] He lives as an island unto himself, taking no other refuge.

BUDDHA-TO-COME

Much more important is the Buddha to come, Metteya, who became very significant for the Mahāyāna but also plays an

[1] Buddhavaṁsa, ii, p. 59.
[2] Puggala-paññatti, i, 28f.; Milinda's Questions, 104.

Buddhas and Avatars

eschatological role in Theravāda. Yet he is rarely mentioned in the Pāli canon, and does not appear along with the list of the seven previous Buddhas.

The origins of belief in the coming Metteya are a matter for speculation. The similarity of the Sanskrit name Maitreya to the Vedic god Mitra, and the Persian Mithra, suggests a kinship with this deity who through the Romans spread across the world and had his temples in Britain. In the Pāli texts the names Metteya and Ajita, which are elsewhere combined into the double title Ajita Metteya, 'the invincible compassionate', appear as two of a group of sixteen disciples converted by Gotama. They are sent by an ascetic Bāvarī to the Master, and Metteya asks him: 'Who lives content? Who is a superman? Who treads the Middle Way?' And the Buddha replies that it is the man devoid of craving, always on his guard, his mind fixed and undefiled, who treads the Middle Way and is a superman. So Metteya and his companions become disciples.[1]

There is more detail about the future Buddha in the Wheel-turning Lion-roar Sutta. Gotama foretells a time when the celestial wheel, symbol of a wheel-turning king, slips from its place and then disappears. Thereupon poverty, stealing and violence increase. The span of life is shortened, the comeliness of men declines, and false opinions spread. There is a lack of filial piety, and little regard for authority. It is not surprising that many Buddhists identify this time with the present. But eventually people recognize that they have done wrong, and resolve to do good. By the efforts of self-salvation they increase in comeliness, prosperity and longevity. Then arises a wheel-turning king, righteous, with seven precious treasures, a thousand sons, and ruling from sea to sea in justice and not by the sword. At that period there will arise in the world an Exalted One named Metteya, an Arahant, a full Buddha.

Metteya is described in the usual formulas. He abounds in wisdom and goodness, he is unsurpassed as a guide for mortals, a teacher of gods and men, an Exalted One, a Buddha, 'even as I am now'. He, by himself, will know the universe, with its spirits and gods, Brahmins and princes, even as I now by myself thoroughly

[1] *Sutta Nipāta*, 1040, 1006. Thera-gāthā 20.

know and see them. He will proclaim the Dhamma, lovely in its
origin, progress and consummation, and make known the higher
life in all its purity and fullness. He will have thousands of disciples,
even as I do now.[1]

That is virtually all that the Pāli canon has about Metteya. But
Buddhaghosa in his commentary on the Abhidhamma speaks of
the path of Metteya, the future Buddha. He says that in the past
there was the Buddha Vipassi, and in future there will be Buddha
Metteya, and names his father as a Brahmin Subrahmā and his
mother as Brahmavatī. At the very end of his book he confesses
that he has come into Metteya's presence and is established in the
Refuges.[2]

In later Buddhism Metteya plays a larger role and, as Lamotte
says, his cult had a success that was as spectacular as it was unexpected. Buddhist literature devoted entire works to Metteya. In
the Mahāvastu it is said that Maitreya will be the last of these
Buddhas, and he is announced by Śākyamuni. But this is in a list
merely of groups of Buddhas; there have been plenty before, and
there will be plenty more. Dīpankara, who announced Śākyamuni
was himself the last of another succession. In the Lotus Sūtra
Maitreya plays a large part, which will be mentioned in the next
chapter.[3]

The Mahāyāna life of the Buddha, Lalita-vistara, says that when
the Bodhisattva Śākyamuni was about to leave the Tushita heaven
for his last birth on earth, all the sons of the gods fell to weeping
because heaven could not retain its brilliance without him. So the
Bodhisattva told the divine multitude that the Bodhisattva
Maitreya would teach them the Law, and taking off his crown he
placed it on the head of Maitreya and promised that he would be
the first after himself to attain supreme and perfect enlightenment.[4]

Even the Theravāda Buddhists cherish the hope of Metteya as
the Buddha to come; he is an object of aspiration in evil times and
it is hoped that he will restore the power of religion. When the
leaders of the five Theravāda countries celebrated the two
thousand five hundredth anniversary of the Parinirvāna of the

[1] Dīgha iii, 76.　　　　　　　　[2] Buddhaghosa's Atthasālinī 361, 414.
[3] Mahāvastu, 240.　　　　　　[4] Lalitavistara, trs. R. Mitra, 1881, pp. 73, 88n.

Buddha, at Rangoon in 1956, many people thought that a new era was now due, and that the new Buddha would soon appear.

It may be noted that the Buddhas are not identified with one another, in the texts that we have quoted. The descriptions of the previous Buddhas give them practically identical careers with Gotama, no doubt basing them upon his known life. Their similarity is forced home by saying that 'it is the rule' that many identical things happen to them. But though the Sutta on the other Buddhas is said to be about 'former lives' in fact there is no complete identification of each Buddha with the others. Gotama remembers the Buddhas of old, with the help of the gods, but he does not say 'I was that Buddha', as he does say 'I was that person' in speaking of his own previous births. This suggests an important difference, in the early stages, between the succession of Buddhas and the Hindu succession of Avatars, for the latter are clearly repeated incarnations of the same divine being, Vishnu or Krishna.

Similarly Gotama is not identified with Metteya, although the Buddha to come is his equal in nature and work, and is said repeatedly to be so 'even as I am'. The significance of Metteya is that the succession of Buddhas is not ended. He himself, of course, will not be the last. He expresses an eschatological hope, which is a common feature of belief in Avatars or Incarnation.[1] But in the Buddhist system, as in the Hindu, there is no real finality in the endless cycle of the universe.

INCARNATION AND REINCARNATION

If the successive Buddhas were not, at first, identified with Gotama he nevertheless came after a long succession of previous births. The idea of Incarnation, in India, is connected with the idea of Reincarnation. In the Christian context this is not so, and it is one of the major differences of doctrine. But in the Gītā when Krishna announced his own repeated births he declared that Arjuna also

---

[1] E. Abegg assimilates the 'Messianic' faith in Metteya Buddha to the similar eschatological hope for Kalkin, the future Avatar of Vishnu, and a comparable belief in the coming Soshyans among the Zoroastrians. See *Der Messiasglaube in Indien und Iran*, pp. 145ff.

had had many incarnations, the difference being that he did not remember them, whereas Krishna did.

The belief in reincarnation, which was established in Indian literature from the early Upanishads, and in popular belief no doubt long before, formed an important strand in the idea of the Buddhist succession. In Buddhism, however, in the absence of belief in a permanent soul, officially, it is rebirth rather than reincarnation. These births are recounted in the Jātakas, the 'birth stories' of the Buddha, which tell of his history down the ages in 547 tales.

The Upanishads do not speak of the memory of past lives as a proof of reincarnation, as modern apologists for the notion do. But the Laws of Manu say that by daily reciting the Vedas, and by harmlessness, purification and austerity, one obtains the faculty of remembering former births. And Buddhists have always taught that the Buddha could remember all his previous existences, since the canon said that at his enlightenment Gotama declared, 'I remembered a variety of former habitations; one birth, two births, three . . . a hundred . . . a hundred thousand births, and many an eon of integration and disintegration'.[1]

The Jātaka tales put this in story form, incorporating therein many popular fables, and at the end of each yarn the Buddha identifies himself with the principal character. The Jātakas begin with the Blessed One delivering a discourse of Dhamma in the great monastery at Jetavana, and other stories are located there or at different well known sites. The Master's face was glorious as the full moon, the marks of Buddahhood shone on him and light shone round about him to a fathom's length. He spoke in thunderous tones like a young lion, yet in a voice of eightfold perfection which ravished the ear. And dissident sects when they listened burst asunder other doctrines and betook themselves to the Buddha as their refuge.

The first story tells of a foolish and a wise merchant, and at the end they are named; the foolish one was the bad disciple Devadatta and the wise 'was myself'. The Bodhisatta is then identified with kings, Brahmins, ministers, hawkers, fairies, and even with monkeys, dogs, horses and bulls. So it goes on through more than

[1] The Laws of Manu, iv, 148; Majjhima Nikāya 1, 22.

547 births, since some tales are double and some repeated, and down to the last life when the Buddha is King Vessantara.

There is no clear order in the Jātakas, no progress or finality. In the tales themselves, apart from the scribal introduction, there is no mention of the ancient Buddha Dīpankara under whom Gotama was supposed to have made his first vow in an existence long ago, and there is no mention of the Buddha to come, Metteya. There is a slight reference to the previous Buddha Vipassi, who had sandal wood offered to him and was also known as Dasabala. And there is a hint of the Distant Epoch of the Buddha's existence, which commentators take to extend from the time of his first vow down to his last birth.[1]

Another late work of the Pāli canon, Cariyā-pitaka, 'the basket of comfort', gives thirty-five tales from the Jātakas in verse, indicating the conduct of the future Buddha in order to attain the ten perfections. A further work, the Apadāna, gives tales in verse of the former lives of monks and nuns. The doctrine of rebirth, then, was as deeply enrooted in Buddhism as in Hinduism, and may have come from a deep level of popular belief, however inconsistent it might appear to be with denial of a soul. The rebirths of a Buddha, and the succession of Buddhas, fitted into this pattern. They were glorified men, rather than Avatars of a supreme God. And yet there was a uniqueness about the Buddha that made him more than divine, in a transcendental sense.

UNIQUENESS

Theravāda Buddhism, despite its seven or twenty-five Buddhas, plus Metteya, tried to hold on to the uniqueness of Gotama Buddha. The Pāli texts agree that the Tathāgatas are plural, but few and far between. When Indra told their praises to the Vedic gods some said that if only four supreme Buddhas might teach Dhamma that would make for the welfare of many. Others replied that three supreme Buddhas would suffice, and others that two would do. Then Sakka replies firmly that at no time is it possible that in one and the same world-system two Arahant

[1] Jātaka, 547.

Supreme Buddhas should arise together, neither before nor after one another. This can in no wise be.[1]

Elsewhere Sāriputta declares that there was nobody in the past wiser than the Exalted One, nobody in the future, and nobody at present. There have been in the past and will be in the future, some who are equal to the Exalted One in enlightenment, but there is none now. For he has heard the Exalted One say that in times past there have been, and in future there will be, other Supreme Buddhas equal to himself in enlightenment. But it is impossible that there should arise two Arahant Supreme Buddhas in one and the same world-system.[2]

Milinda's Questions reaffirm this teaching and try to find reasons for it. If there were a second Buddha would not this world be all the more illumined by the light of them both? No, this is not possible, for this world-system can only sustain the special qualities of one Tathāgata. If there were a second Buddha the world would tremble, twist and disappear, like a single boat sinking under two passengers. Further, if there were two Perfect Buddhas at the same moment disputes would arise among their disciples, saying, 'your Buddha', and 'our Buddha'. And again, if there were two Perfect Buddhas at once the saying would be false which said that the Buddha is the foremost, the eldest, supreme, without equal. Other things that are mighty are unique, like the earth, the sea, space, Māra and Brahmā, and there is no occasion for a second. Therefore the Tathāgata, Arahant, the Perfect Buddha, is almighty and unique in the world.[3]

This assertion of the uniqueness of the Buddha in the present, very long, eon may have evolved in view of the teachings of northern schools which spoke of many Buddhas. The Theravādins are relatively modest. There have been Buddhas past, countless ages ago, and there will be Buddhas to come, in the far distant future. But for practical purposes there is only one Buddha and so Gotama, greatly glorified, keeps his eminence and uniqueness. He is *the* Buddha, after all, as far as we are concerned. His teachings

[1] Dīgha iii, 114.
[2] *ibid.*, ii. p. 108. This is despite another statement that four Buddhas arose in this present eon.
[3] Milinda's Questions, 237.

are true, and others are false; his scriptures are supreme. He alone is the fully enlightened, the Supreme Buddha, the teacher of gods and men.

The Avatars of Krishna in the Gītā are said to come age after age, and the implication is that there is only one at a time. This is reinforced by the teaching of the transcendence of Krishna as very God. In later Hindu usage the numbers of Avatars multiplied and the distinctions of ages became faint, and in loose popular talk today the word Avatar may be applied to many people. But in the cults it is either Krishna or Rāma that is supreme, and there is a uniqueness here.

In Buddhism something of the same process has been at work. There are many Buddhas in Mahāyāna belief, but their outlines are so blurred that they are much the same. In Theravāda belief there is only one Buddha, for the present eon. Although it is often held as an advantage against Christianity that Avatar or Buddha belief allows for many divine beings, in faith and practice there is a strong emphasis on singleness and uniqueness. It seems to be important for the strength of religion that the supreme object of worship and faith, whether Buddha or Avatar, should be transcendent and unique.

12

Developing Buddhology

Buddhist laymen demanded something more than a 'dead god', who only left 'relics' that could be venerated. They wanted a living God, a 'god superior to the gods' (*devātideva*), who continues among them his saving work, who can predict the future, work miracles, and whose cult (*pūjā*) is something more than a simple commemoration (*anusmriti*). So writes Lamotte, in his great history of Indian Buddhism.[1]

Many Mahāyāna texts stress the saving power of the Buddha. Nothing escapes the knowledge, sight, wisdom and perception of the blessed Buddhas. It is in fact a rule that the blessed Buddhas are endowed with great compassion and devoted to the service of the world. 'It is a rule' that three times at night and three times by day, they examine the world with the Buddha-eye. They ask themselves, 'Who is prospering? Who is in pain, danger, or torment? Whom can I save from evil destiny to place him in heaven and deliverance?' It may be that the sea, the abode of ocean monsters, could forget the time of the tide; the Buddha will never let the time pass for converting his cherished sons. This passage comes in fourteen stories of the Avadāna-śataka.

OTHER LIVES

We have tried to show already that the glorification of the Buddha developed from the earliest days. The Theravāda forms, as given in the Pāli canon, witness to this glorification, even though in its present state the canon was closed later than the beginning of the Christian era, and it is perilous to try to distinguish 'archaic' and 'original' elements.

[1] *Histoire du Bouddhisme indien*, p. 714.

There were numerous other Buddhist schools beside that which became the Theravāda. Some have vanished with no or little trace, and others like the Mahāsanghikas left texts some of which agree with the Theravāda and others differ considerably. Some of these, and of the later Mahāyāna, can be quoted to illustrate developments in Buddhology.

The Mahāvastu, 'the Great Story', says that it is based on the Vinaya monkish rules of a branch of the early schismatics, the Mahasānghikas. This branch is the Lokottaravādins, whose Docetic teaching said that the Buddha was supramundane (*lokottara*), though the theory is not much developed in this work, nor is there much about monastic discipline. The Mahāvastu is a collection in 'macaronic' Sanskrit of the history and legends of the Buddha which were current from about the second century A.D. to the fourth century. It is a valuable source of documentation for belief in Buddhas and Bodhisattvas.

The Mahāvastu begins with Gautama, whom it usually calls Śākyamuni, the 'sage of the Śākyas', but it refers back to the previous Buddhas in whose presence he first vowed to become a Buddha at some future time, and it pays homage to all Buddhas, past, future, and present (in the plural).

The virtues of a Buddha are said to be incomprehensible. Perfect Buddhas have five eyes: the eye of flesh, the eye of a god, of wisdom, of Dharma, and of a Buddha. These attributes are possessed only by perfect Buddhas, and not by Pratyeka-buddhas, arhats, disciples, or ignorant men. Although the Buddhas have physical powers, yet when they walk on the earth it rises and falls beneath their feet by magic power. Their Dharma-eye gives them ten powers, and the Buddha-eye eighteen special attributes. These powers belong to all Perfect Buddhas and are illustrated in Śākyamuni as a type.[1]

Therefore 'the Buddhas conform to the world's conditions, but in such a way that they also conform to the traits of transcendentalism'. They wash their feet, though no dust even clings to them, and 'this washing is mere conformity with the world'. The wind blows their clothes about but it does not harm them; they sit in the shade though the sun would not torment them. They eat and

[1] Mahāvastu, 158.

drink, but are never hungry or thirsty. They seem to become old, but there is no old age for them. They could suppress the working of karma, but for the sake of conformity with the world they conceal their powers and let karma become manifest. They have fathers and mothers, though their bodily existence is not due to the sexual union of parents. And the Buddha has a son, Rāhula, yet the Buddha was free from passion and this was 'mere conformity' with the world.[1]

The Mahāsanghika theologians based their teaching on the supramundane existence of the Buddha on a verse in the Kindred Sayings where it is stated that the Tathāgata is born in the world and grows in the world, but whether he walks or stands up he is not soiled by worldly Dhammas. So it was concluded that the worldly activities of the Buddha were fictional, and this Docetism is clearly formulated in the preface to the Mahāvastu and though this does not form the oldest part of the text, Docetic tendencies are present throughout.[2]

The Mahāvastu continues with the story of Dīpankara, which serves as a model for the lives of future Buddhas. His putative father was a universal king named Archimat, who had the seven treasures, a thousand sons, and ruled over the four continents not by the sword but by Dharma. Bodhisattvas are born in either noble or Brahmin families, ones that honour the gods and ancestors, and so the Buddha-to-be from the Tushita heaven chose Archimat as worthy to be his father. His mother was chosen similarly, and her end prescribed, for 'the mothers of all Bodhisattvas die seven days after the birth of the Supreme of Men'. This is explained as necessary, so that they should not afterwards indulge in love, for 'the Exalted One at all times proclaims the depravity of sensual desires'.[3] This increasingly Manichean tone is reinforced by the assertion that not only afterwards, but before the birth the queen asked her husband to abstain from sexual relations, and he allowed her to retire to a private mansion. So the conception of the Buddha is quite immaculate, and the father is eliminated. But this asceticism does not prevent the monkish writers from going into raptures over intimate details of the queen's body, 'whose belly with its bright streak of fair downy hair curves like the palm

---

[1] Mahāvastu, 168f. [2] Samyutta Nikāya, iii, 140. [3] Mahāvastu, 199.

of the hand'. Then the Bodhisattva actually enters her womb in the form of a snow-white elephant with six tusks.[1]

A Bodhisattva's mother is perfectly healthy and is attended by the gods. In her womb the babe sits on the right side with his legs crossed; he can see his mother, and she can see him like a body of pure gold. Gods come to visit him daily, and the unborn child raises his right hand to them in salutation and from the womb recounts the stories of his previous births. He is born in the tenth month, in the Lotus Grove. The mother stands under a tree, and the baby emerges from her side, as all the Supreme of Men are born. Her side is not rent by this kind of 'spontaneous Caesarean operation', because Tathāgatas are born with a body 'made of mind' (*manomaya*), a special tenet of the Lokottaravādins.[2]

The story continues on the pattern of the legends of Gautama's youth; but when Dīpankara lived in luxury, among women for diversion, their bodies made him think of cemeteries! The Four Signs are omitted, and the Bodhisattva immediately sat in a pond on a lotus flower, which closed up to form a peaked roof over him, and he proceeded to enlightenment.

The interest then turns to the professed aim of the story, how Gautama's vow to become a Buddha was made. Śākyamuni was at that time a young Brahmin named Megha, and hearing that the Buddha Dīpankara was near he brought some lotuses from a Brahmin girl, who was to be his wife in every birth thereafter. He threw the lotuses at Dīpankara and took the vow, 'I too will become a Buddha in the world. . . . Having thus crossed, may I lead others across . . . comforted, may I comfort others. . . . May I become this for the happiness and welfare of mankind, out of compassion for the world, for the sake of gods and men.' Dīpankara then assured Megha that after an immeasurable eon he would become a Buddha, of the name of Śākyamuni, in the city of Kapilavastu.[3]

The second and third parts of the Mahāvastu are devoted to the stories of Gautama and his later days. It is not a connected account, but tries to include every text that has a near or remote connection with the subject. The narrative follows roughly the life of Gautama

---

[1] *ibid.*, 203.   [2] *ibid.*, 218: Foucher, *Life of the Buddha*, p. 30.
[3] *ibid.*, 238.

given in the introduction to the Jātakas, and then takes in a number of stories from the Jātakas themselves of former lives of the Buddha. The account of his birth follows that of Dīpankara, which of course in turn was modelled on the traditions about Gautama. The Mahāvastu names thousands of other Buddhas, but says that in their succession Śākyamuni was the last, in the present cycle. Maitreya is named as the high-minded Buddha of a future age. The story ends with the conversion of King Bimbisāra, and there is no mention of the death of the Buddha.

Further Mahāyāna additions to the story of the Buddha are found in the popular Lalita-vistara, the 'account of the sports' of the Bodhisattva. His coronation of Maitreya in heaven in his place has already been mentioned (p. 160 above). When the Buddha was born, it is said, happiness came to the whole universe; all passion, hate, sorrow and selfishness disappeared, the mad became sane, the blind received sight and the deaf hearing.[1]

An interesting infancy story, which has been compared with Christian apocrypha, says that when the king took his infant Bodhisattva into the temple all the images of the gods, including Śiva, Śakra and Brahmā, rose up from their places and fell at his feet. They made manifest their respective shapes and recited verses in his honour. Then there is an extended version of the predictions of Asita, the so-called Buddhist Simeon, referred to in the Sutta Nipāta, but now shown as an ascetic who lived in the Himalasya and flew through the air to the royal palace.[2]

The story continues with the youth, marriage and four signs, and we cannot stay over the detail. As Foucher notes, the author of the Lalita-vistara was a mediocre novelist but an austere moralist. When the Bodhisattva was leaving his father's house it could not be admitted that he should disobey the paternal will. So as he left the palace it became ablaze with the light of his person and awoke his father, who pleaded with him to stay, but finally gave in since souls must be saved. Gautama returned to his chamber despite this secret interview, but was so disgusted at the sight of the sleeping people that he fled at once. 'For the monastic authors, this is too good an occasion to resist the temptation of gratifying their hatred of their most feared enemy-women. All the rage inspired by the

[1] Lalitavistara, p. 126.   [2] ibid., pp. 175, 138.

Developing Buddhology

fear of a temptation . . . is spread over the innocent group in the most abusive language.'[1]

The Lalita-vistara, like the Mahāvastu, carries the glorification of the Buddha to the most supernatural and improbable extremes. Yet like other writings of earlier schools of Buddhism they did not deliberately set out to invent new texts, only to improve them. But inventions, and quite new departures, were not long in coming.

THE LOTUS SUTRA

The scriptures of the Mahāyāna have a great deal that is foreign to the Pāli texts, and although discourses are introduced by the phrase 'thus have I heard', yet their subject matter diverges more and more from the old texts. One of the most important, formative, and still very popular Mahāyāna texts is the True-Doctrine Lotus (Sad-dharma-pundarīka) or Lotus of the Wonderful Law, preserved in Sanskrit and Chinese. Its early form may date from about A.D. 200 but the mythology may be earlier. It reveals the popular side of the doctrines of Buddhas and Bodhisattvas and is very significant for our purpose.

The Lotus begins, 'thus have I heard', and depicts the Lord staying on the Vulture Peak at Rājagriha, as often in the early texts. With him are thousands of arhats, monks, and nuns, including Śākyamuni's wife and son, Yaśodharā and Rāhula. There are eighty thousand Bodhisattvas, including Mañjuśrī, Avalokiteśvara and Maitreya. There are thousands of gods, including Īśvara (Śiva), Maheśvara (Vishnu?) and Brahmā, and myriads of demons. The Lord sat cross-legged on the seat of Dharma in deep meditation, and a ray issued from his forehead which illuminated thousands of Buddha-fields and revealed the Lord Buddhas teaching Dharma in all those fields.[2] So we now have many contemporary Buddhas in the vast Buddha-fields.

Then the Lord declares that Buddha-knowledge, the mystery of the Tathāgatas, is profound, and that Pratyeka-buddhas and disciples find it difficult to understand. Sāriputra implores him to

[1] ibid., pp. 280f.; Foucher, Life of the Buddha, p. 75.
[2] Saddharma-puṇḍarīka, I.

171

expound the mystery, but before he does so five thousand proud monks, nuns, and laymen leave the assembly. The Lord comments that his congregation is now free from the chaff, and that only by one vehicle, the Buddha-vehicle, does he teach Dharma. This is universal salvation, which is the purpose of the appearance of the Buddha in the world. The sole aim is to open the eyes of all creatures, by the Buddha-vehicle which finally leads to omniscience. He himself is at the present period a Tathāgata, for the welfare of many. If any arhats or Pratyeka-buddhas are conceited, and think they do not need this Buddha-vehicle, they should not be acknowledged as disciples. So the selfish aim of solitariness is rejected.[1]

On the other hand, those who do listen to Dharma, lead moral lives, or worship rightly, have attained enlightenment. Those who have worshipped relics, or erected stūpas, or even children at play who have dedicated stūpas to the Jinas, have all reached enlightenment. Even those who in front of relics said once, 'homage to Buddha', though with distracted thoughts, have gained superior enlightenment. This is the purest salvation by faith, and the doctrine is developed as the text continues.

The Tathāgatas are vowed to save by grace, for they all take the vow, 'Let me lead others to enlightenment'. And not only is the path of the Buddha opened to all but, even more significant, all men can become Buddhas. There is not now a tiny number of Buddhas, really different from the rest of men, but for the Mahāyāna the Buddhas are both transcendent objects of faith, and they offer the way to the deification of all men. There is no being who, after hearing the Dharma, shall not become a Buddha.[2]

Later the Lotus Sūtra develops the exaltation of the Buddha, employing titles which often parallel those used in Hinduism of Krishna-Vishnu. The Dharma has been discovered by the Highest Person (Purushottama), who is the King of Righteousness (Dharma-rāja), born into the world to destroy existence. He is the Jina (conqueror) who has appeared in the world like a cloud to refresh all beings, gods and men. He has no love or hatred to anyone, and proclaims Dharma to high and low, to wise and ignorant, without distinction. All his disciples shall become

[1] Saddharma-puṇḍarīka, pp. 38ff.   [2] *ibid.*, 2, 99.

Buddhas. The light of his doctrine shines like the sun upon the evil and the good, upon the Great Vehicle (Mahāyāna), or the vehicle of the Pratyeka-buddhas, or the vehicle of the disciples, for really there is only one vehicle. The Buddha is the Father of the World (Lokapitā) the Healer, the Protector of all creatures. He is 'God above the gods' (*devātideva*), who from the very beginning (*ādita eva*) had enlightened the Bodhisattvas.[1]

There is only slight reference to the historical circumstances of the life of Gautama, but it has an important result. The Bodhisattva Maitreya asks him about the duration of his life. He was born in Kapilavastu, a prince of the Śākyas, and reached enlightenment at the town of Gāya. That was only a short time ago, yet he has had countless followers for millions of ages. How could this be? So Arjuna had demanded how Krishna could have taught the sages of old before his birth. But Maitreya pushes the inquiry further. What happens when the Lord is extinct? Many Bodhisattvas fall into doubt about this, and will not believe after the extinction of the Tathāgata.

It is a tricky question, because while Krishna as God may be supposed to be eternal, and for the same reason to have no relics, yet the Buddha is believed to have died and his relics were divided among a number of stūpas. So the Buddha admits that people worship relics, in the opinion that his body is completely extinct. But in fact they do not see him, and the holy places are a device to educate them. Really he does not become extinct, for the Tathāgata is unlimited in the duration of his life. He taught the Bodhisattvas in the beginning, and he is everlasting; he lives for ever (*sadā sthitah*). He says that he was not completely extinct at that time, 'it was a device of mine'. Then, rather inconsistently, he adds like Krishna, 'I am repeatedly born in the world of the living'.[2]

That the Buddha never really died is the final stage of Docetism, and Suzuki says that it 'must have been a revolutionary teaching at the time'. Earlier texts, while surrounding the last days of the Tathāgata with celestial miracles, had clearly indicated his death, however briefly. All that now remained was his Dharma, and this

---

[1] *ibid.*, 7, 34; 14, 43; etc.
[2] *ibid.*, 15, 1f.

could be pointed to when the Buddha could no longer be indicated. But the Lotus Sūtra shows the Buddha living forever on the
Vulture Peak, offering his one Buddha-vehicle, that all beings
might be saved, and themselves become Buddhas. Its further
doctrines of Bodhisattvas need separate consideration.[1]

BODHISATTVAS AND BUDDHAS

It was said earlier (page 151) that in the Pāli texts the term Bodhisatta is applied to the Buddha before his enlightenment, and by
extension to the few other previous Buddhas before they arrived
at a similar state. The life of Gautama is the starting point of many
Buddhist theories, and so all Bodhisattas must live in the same
way, being particular instances of a general law.

The Mahāvastu agrees with this in the main, and while indicating four stages in the career of a Bodhisattva, it makes them the
same whether applying to Dīpankara or to Gautama. The four
stages or careers of a Bodhisattva are: his 'natural' career, when
he lives an ordinary life at home; his 'resolving' career, when he
vows to win enlightenment; his 'conforming' career, when he
lives in conformity with that vow; and his 'persevering' career,
when he is set on enlightenment without turning back.[2]

In the Lotus and general Mahāyāna teaching the Bodhisattva
develops into a being who not only seeks enlightenment for himself, but passes it on to others. The background of the saintly but
inactive monks, designated by the Pratyeka-buddhas and others,
helps to explain the growth of the Bodhisattva ideal, as a protest
against lack of spiritual and social fervour. Far from being a
choking weed, as Rhys-Davids described it, the Bodhisattva ideal
is claimed by Dayal as that which saved Buddhism from 'ship-
wreck by popularizing it and inventing compassionate Bodhisattvas as Buddhist counterparts to the Hindu deities and their
incarnations'. Further as Christianity naturalized its faith in pagan
Europe, by taking over local gods and shrines, giving them
Christian virtues and associations, so did Mahāyāna Buddhism
over much of central and northern Asia.[3]

[1] Laṅkāvatāra Sūtra, trs. D. T. Suzuki, 1932, p. xxxv.
[2] Mahāvastu, 1f.   [3] H. Dayal, *The Bodhisattva Doctrine*, 1932, p. 38.

The distinction of Bodhisattvas and Buddhas is not easy to maintain, and on one occasion in the Lotus Sūtra the Lord is asked why the different terms are used. He replies that as different pots are made of the same material, but contain different substances so it is with these noble ones, but in fact there is only one Buddha-vehicle. Further, although in theory Bodhisattvas are inferior to Buddhas, yet they are often spoken of in as exalted terms and, in practice, they are both supernatural beings who are gracious to their devotees.[1]

Numerous Bodhisattvas are named in the Lotus, and while they do not usually correspond by name to Hindu gods, yet they fulfil many of their roles. They often personify virtues or attributes that are seen in the Buddha himself. Maitreya may be the Vedic Mitra but he also typifies *maitri*, friendliness. Mañjuśrī personifies widsom (*prajñā*), and Avalokiteśvara personifies mercy (*karunā*).

One of the greatest Buddhas is Amitābha or Amitāyus (Amida), the Buddha of Infinite Light or Life, who rules in Sukhāvatī, the City of Bliss, the Western Paradise or Pure Land (the Shangri La of James Hilton). The Larger Sukhāvatī-vyūha text says that Amitābha is seen there visibly and is glorified and preached by the blessed Buddhas. And the Smaller text says that beings are not born in the Buddha-country of Amitābha as a reward of good works, but simply because they have heard his name and kept it in mind. Amitābha will stand before them at death and they will be reborn in his land of bliss.[2]

In the Lotus Sūtra this paradise has no women in it. Avalokiteśvara, the Bodhisattva, is chief minister, and though he is universal lord and king of kings, he stands fanning Amitābha on the right hand and left. However this is only a formal difference, and in much Mahāyāna devotion Avalokiteśvara is exalted to the supreme place, whether as Chinese Kwanyin, Japanese Kwannon, or Tibetan Chenresi, of whom the Dalai Lama is the incarnation. The Lotus has an important later chapter devoted to this Bodhisattva, which is cherished by millions of Buddhists, and constantly recited even by the anti-scriptural Zen monks.[3]

---

[1] Saddharma-puṇḍarīka, 5, 44.
[2] Sukhāvatī-vyūha, trs. F. M. Müller, 1894, pp. 45, 98.
[3] Saddharma-puṇḍarīka, 24, 29–31.

In the Lotus, when the Lord is asked why Avalokiteśvara is so named, 'the Lord who looks down', he sets him forth as an all-powerful being of grace. All the hundreds of thousands of creatures who suffer troubles will be released from their trials if they hear but his name. If in a ship at sea, tossed about by a gale, there is a single being who implores him, all will be saved. If a woman desirous of a male child adores him, she will get a beautiful son. Cherishing his name has equal merit with adoring Buddhas in number equal to sixty-two times the grains of sand of the river Ganges.[1]

Avalokiteśvara preaches Dharma in different forms, as a Bodhisattva, a Buddha, Brahmā or Indra. To those who are to be converted by Īśvara (Śiva) he preaches Dharma in the shape of Īśvara. It is not surprising that this syncretism swept across polytheistic Asia, taking in the Tibetan, Chinese and Japanese gods as aspects of the original Buddhas and protectors of the true Dharma. It became a fervent *bhakti* religion of adoration for the Buddhas and Bodhisattvas. Its sola-fideism was called by its enemies the 'short cut religion', and when the Jesuits reached Japan and found this teaching of salvation by faith alone they exclaimed in dismay, 'this is Lutheranism!'

The Lotus Sūtra is constantly concerned with universal salvation and in the Avataṁsaka Sūtra this became explicitly the task of the Bodhisattva. The Bodhisattva Samantabhadra took 'ten inexhaustible vows'. He would not enter nirvāṇa himself till all other beings were saved, and this meant not only men but the soul of every being, animate and inanimate. And the Laṅkāvatāra Sūtra confirms that Bodhisattvas do not enter nirvāna because of their inexhaustible vows.[2]

BUDDHA BODIES

The Mahāyāna writers rejected, or did not take up, the Hindu doctrine of Avatars, for it is scarcely comprehensible without a foundation of personal transcendental theism. Yet there was a parallel in the coming of the Buddha into the world to save beings, and he was also in some fashion transcendental. He was

[1] Saddharma-puṇḍarīka, 24. [2] Laṅkāvatāra Sūtra, 212.

not alone, however, in the work of salvation but was assisted by the Bodhisattvas, who were called 'sons' of the Buddha. Two major problems arose: the nature of the body of the Buddha, and the unity of the Buddhas. The Theravāda treatment of these problems, in some degree, has been mentioned previously.

The physical body (*rūpa-kāya*) was regarded as like the illusory shapes fabricated by a conjurer, and it was said that 'the *rūpa-kāya* is not the Buddha'. With the growing Docetism the visible body of the Buddha was considered as a 'device' to help the faithful, merely conjured up by the Dharma-body. Although there may seem to be some likeness between Buddhist beliefs and Hindu teachings of the manifest and unmanifest bodies of Krishna, yet the implications are different. And even more disparate are comparisons with Christianity. So Conze affirms that 'unlike official Christianity Buddhism is not a historical religion, and its message is valid independently of the historicity of any event in the life of the "founder", who did not found anything, but merely transmitted a Dharma pre-existing him since eternity'.[1] Not all Theravāda teachers today would agree with this dismissal of history, but it can hardly be denied of the Mahāyāna.

If the *rūpa-kāya* is not the real Buddha, then what is? In contradiction to it the Mahāyāna thinkers spoke of a *Dharma-kāya*, a Truth or Cosmic Body; for the Buddha both embodied Dharma and also was identical with the constituents of the universe, the same as absolute Reality (*Tathatā*). The emphasis on the Dharma revealed by the Buddha was based on the notion of a stable and fixed Dharma, whether there was a Tathāgata or not, and the Buddha became identified with Dharma rather than with any physical personality.

Later there was added the idea of a Body of Bliss or Community (*Sambhoga-kāya*), which was only visible to Bodhisattvas. This gave rise to a Three-body doctrine (*Tri-kāya*), sometimes compared with the Christian doctrine of the Trinity. But it formed part of the process of deification, and gave the Buddhas celestial bodies like the Hindu gods. The basic distinction was between the physical body and the Dharma-body, and it is these two that are usually compared and contrasted.

[1] *Buddhist Thought in India*, p. 232.

The Dharma-body implied the unity of all Buddhas, and so their identity. Therefore *the* Buddha was actually *all* the Buddhas of the past. And on the other hand, according to the Sarvāstivādins, since the Dharmas are identical in all the Buddhas, the faithful does not take refuge in the physical Buddha but in his Dharma. The corporeal life of a Buddha was illusory anyway, for 'it is a rule' that all Bodhisattvas do so and so, and therefore it could be deduced that none of this was done in the flesh.[1]

The Lankāvatāra Sūtra ('The Visit to Ceylon', Lankā) discusses the affirmation attributed to the Blessed One, 'I am all the Buddhas of the past'. This means that he had not only gone through a hundred thousand mortal births as men and animals, but also that he was previously the Buddhas Kāśyapa and others. The author distinguished four kinds of sameness in Buddhas. They are: (1) the sameness of letters, since his name B-u-d-d-h-a is used also for other Buddhas; (2) the sameness of words, in that he uses the sixty-four sounds of the Brahmin language like others; (3) the sameness of teachings, since all Tathāgatas know the teachings of thirty-seven branches of enlightenment; and (4) the sameness of body, in that all Tathāgatas are the same in their Dharma-body, with signs and perfections. There is no distinction among them, except that the Tathāgatas manifest varieties of forms to different beings.[2]

This means that all Buddhas have the same essence. But, when they wish to do so, they can appear in various forms to many beings. These are acts of grace, or perfection, and it is often stressed that there is no karma which forces a Buddha to be born. Karma, which determines the births of all other creatures, has been destroyed, or never really existed, in such a divine being, and he appears, or appears to appear, by his own choice and will. The one Buddha assumes many names, and these are not only personal designations, but also abstract titles such as No-birth, Emptiness, Suchness, Eternity, Cessation, Nirvāna.[3]

So the idea of Buddhahood was developed into a universal pantheism, or rather pan-Buddhism. Gautama was first of all made into a powerful and immortal being, the God above the

[1] Lamotte, *Histoire du Bouddhisme indien*, p. 689.
[2] Lankāvatāra Sūtra, 141. [3] *ibid.*, p. xiv.

178

gods. Then he was identified with everything and received the mystical attributes of the impersonal Brahman of the Upanishads. Finally, to complete the monistic process, not only are all Buddhas identical, but all creatures are this too. It becomes the goal of every being to become a Buddha, or realize its Buddha-nature. This is really the spreading weed, the monism which choked Vedāntic Hinduism. Unknown to Gautama, it gradually developed over the centuries to grip Mahāyāna philosophy. The popular religion, of course, continued gaily polytheistic.

BUDDHAS AND AVATARS

There are occasional close parallels in the Buddhist texts to the Hindu Avatar doctrines. The Lotus Sūtra itself speaks of the 'manifestations' of the Buddha as *vyūha*, a word used of the Avatars. The Lankāvatāra Sūtra has an interesting eschatological passage at the end. A hundred years after Śākyamuni's passing Vyāsa's Bhārata will appear, with the Pāndavas and Kauravas, Rāma and the Mauryas. Then will come an age of vice when the good Dharma will no more prevail. But after destruction the world will be reconstituted, and Vishnu and Maheśvara (Śiva) will teach about the creation of the world, and the Vedas, worship and charity will again prevail with the revival of Dharma.[1]

Some Buddhist teachers early pointed out the strange resemblance between the three bodies of the Buddha and Vaishnavite and Śaivite speculations about the three bodies of Īśvara. And there was occasional Buddhist reference to the authority of the Bhagavad Gītā to explain difficult questions.[2]

But these are only slight references and the idea of 'incarnation' is only present in Buddhist belief to the extent that it expresses the general belief in 'reincarnation' in successive existences on earth. Basically this is the same for all men, and the Buddha passing through more than 547 births did as any other man might do. He was a man, say the old texts, and this encouraged others to follow his example. On the other hand he chose his last birth, as Krishna always did, and was not forced to it by accumulated karma. And

[1] Laṅkāvatāra Sūtra, 264, 785f.
[2] *Histoire du Bouddhisme indien*, p. 437.

the Buddha alone, even above Pratyeka-buddhas, is fully conscious when he enters the womb, remains there, and leaves it. So in the Gītā Krishna had distinguished his births from Arjuna's because he knew them.

The Buddha is not an Incarnation or Avatar of God or any other superior being. He incarnates himself by himself. Yet there is a transcendental element, and the Buddha is a substitute-deity. The Buddha himself, or the reality behind all the Buddhas, or the Dharma-body, is ultimate and omnipotent. He is either utterly transcendent and absolute, like Brahman, or both transcendent and personal like Vishnu-Krishna.

In Mahāyāna teaching there are countless Buddhas and Bodhisattvas, yet as in Theravāda there is a determined move to show that fundamentally they are all one. This is not in the sense that there is only one Buddha at a time, to guarantee his supremacy, but there is a need to get beyond the bewildering multiplicity of Buddhas to their unity in the one Buddha or Dharma. The Buddha cannot be said to become incarnate 'once for all'; in Mahāyāna he hardly becomes incarnate at all. But the urge towards unity and uniqueness is important in its religious life.

13

Jinas and Avatars

The Jains are an ancient and important, but small, religious minority in India, now numbering about a million and a half followers. Western historians have spoken of their religion as 'founded' by Vardhamāna, Mahāvīra, an older contemporary of Gautama Buddha. But the Jains themselves regard Mahāvīra as the last of a long series of the Jinas of this era, of whom the first lived millions of years ago.

It is said that there are twenty-four Jinas, and there is an easy comparison with the twenty-five Buddhas of the late Pāli texts, and the twenty-two Avatars of the even later Bhāgavata Purāna. It seems likely that the Jain idea of twenty-four Jinas is the oldest, for it is common to their two major sects, the Digambara and the Śvetāmbara, which separated at least by the early centuries before Christ. Although the belief in successive Jinas is closer to the Buddhist idea of successive Buddhas than to Hindu doctrines of Avatars, yet there are some interesting links with Hindu myths, particularly the Krishna cycle.

LIVES OF THE TWENTY-FOUR JINAS

The Jain saints are called Jinas, 'conquerors', or Tīrthankaras, 'ford-finders' or 'crossing-makers', those who have made a crossing over the waters of transmigration to find salvation in Nirvāna.

The earliest Jina was Rishabha of Kośalā, who lived millions of years ago. His story is pure myth, and he is credited with famous teachings and inventions. Rishabha lived two million years as a prince and six millions as a king; he was the first king, the first Jina, the first Tīrthankara, and he also has the title Ādinātha, the 'first protector'. For the benefit of his people he taught the seventy-two sciences, of which writing is the first and arithmetic the most important, the hundred arts and the knowledge of omens. He taught men agriculture and trade, as well as the arts of painting, pottery, smithery and weaving; and he taught women dancing, singing, and the arts of love, which commentators on the sūtras give in detail comparable to the Hindu Kāma Sūtra.[1]

Rishabha is mentioned in some Hindu texts. The Vishnu Purānā says that he was a magnanimous king who, having ruled in equity and celebrated many sacrifices, adopted the life of an anchorite until emaciated by his austerities he put a pebble in his mouth, and naked went the way of all flesh. The Bhāgavata Purāna with more sectarian prejudice says that Rishabha will wander about naked in the dark Kali age so that men in great numbers will desert the proper rituals, revile Brahmins and the Vedas, and worship some of the Jain Arhats as divinities.[2]

Twenty-three Jinas follow Rishabha in Jain tradition, and their names and details are recorded in the texts: their fathers and mothers, birthplaces, heights, colours, ages, emblems, places of Nirvāna, and the interval elapsing before the next Jina. Like the successive Buddhas, they are much of a muchness.[3]

Heinrich Zimmer, in his study of the 'Philosophies of India', gave special attention to Pārśva, the last Jina before Mahāvīra. Since he lived a modest two hundred and fifty years before Mahāvīra, and died at the age of a hundred, it is reasonable to suppose that Pārśva may have been a historical personage. If traditional dating is accepted then he attained Nirvāna in 772 B.C. But the story of his life, apart from different parentage, is too closely modelled on that of Mahāvīra to detain us here. As with the Buddhas, it is the life of the last in the series that serves as a model for the predecessors and has the most likelihood of containing historical elements.

The life of Mahāvīra is sketched in the Āchāra-anga Sūtra, the first of the Angas, the sacred books of the Śvetāmbara Jains, and in more detail in the later Kalpa Sūtra. Mahāvīra came down from

[1] Kalpa Sūtra, 210ff.; A. Guérinot, *La Religion Djaïna*, 1926, pp. 100f.
[2] Vishnu Purāna, 2, 1.
[3] See the table of Jinas in J. Jaini, *Outlines of Jainism*, 1940, facing p. 6

the great Vimāna heaven, which is like the lotus among flowers
and like the swastika among celestial regions. He had lived there
many years till the end of his allotted existence among the gods.
He knew that he was to descend, and that he had descended, but
he knew not as a child when he was descending. His father was a
Brahmin named Rishabha-datta ('gift of Rishabha'), and his
mother Devānandā ('divine bliss'). Mahāvīra entered as an embryo into her womb, when the stars were in an auspicious con-
junction. His mother saw fourteen lucky signs in her dream, and
when she woke up she asked her husband what they could por-
tend. He determined that she would bear a son, after nine months
and seven and a half days. He would be a lovely boy, and would
know the four Vedas and the Angas. The mother-to-be accepted
this, and with her husband enjoyed 'the noble permitted pleasures
of human nature'. So there is no virgin birth, immaculate conception, or aversion to sensual pleasure.[1]

Then comes a strange interlude. Śakra (Indra), the chief of the
gods, was 'enjoying the permitted pleasures of divine nature,
under the great din of uninterrupted story-telling', and looking
down on the continent of India he saw Mahāvīra taking the form
of an embryo in the womb of Devānandā. The god rose up hastily
in confusion, took off his shoes, threw his seamless robe over his
left shoulder, and knelt on his right knee before the Jina. He
revered the Tīrthankaras, the lights of the world, the givers of life
and knowledge, the liberated liberators, who have reached Nirvāna, and Mahāvīra the last of them who was predicted by the
former Tīrthankaras. Śakra thought that Arhats should not be
born in low or poor or Brahminical families, but in noble families
like those of Ikshvāku or Hari (names found in the Gītā). So he
sent a soldier to remove the embryo and place it in the womb of
a Kshatriya woman called Triśalā, wife of Siddhartha (also the
name of Gautama Buddha). This was done while both women
were asleep, unclean particles were removed, and the embryo
was carried in the soldier's hands without harm. This curious story
gives preference to the Kshatriyas over Brahmins, for both the
Buddha and Mahāvīra were Kshatriyas who had numerous disputes with the Hindu Brahmins. Some writers, like Zimmer,

[1] Kalpa Sūtra, 1ff.

183

think that both Jainism and Buddhism represent a resurgence of old non-Aryan religious. But it will be remembered that later Krishna stories said that the baby was exchanged for a girl, to save him from the demon king Kaṁsa; but this was to put him among the cowherds and the whole context is different. (See page 73 above.)

The Kshatriya mother Triśalā then sees fourteen lucky signs in dreams, of which the first is a white elephant with four tusks, and the fourth is the beautiful goddess Śrī, whose lovely body is described by the monkish writers at greatest length and with an attention to detail that even surpasses the Mahāvastu description of Buddha's mother, and is more reminiscent of the Song of Solomon. It is said that every mother of a Tīrthankara sees these fourteen dreams, in the night in which the famous Arhat enters her womb. And when her husband calls the dream-interpreters they declare that when mothers have these fourteen great dreams their boy will be either a universal monarch, or a Jina who rules universally by Dharma. There are close parallels with Buddhist ideas.[1]

The baby Mahāvīra did not move in his mother's womb, but when this stillness alarmed her he quivered a little. In the night of his birth there was a divine lustre, caused by many gods and goddesses descending and ascending. He was born at a fixed auspicious time, a perfectly healthy boy, and the mother perfectly healthy herself. His parents called him Vardhamāna, but the gods gave him the name of Mahāvīra, 'great Hero'.

The Ācāraṅga Sūtra says that Mahāvīra's parents were worshippers of the previous Jina, Pārśva, and although they were Kshatriyas they were not rulers. For many years they followed the ascetic way, and finally rejected all food and fasted to death, thus getting rid of karma. They were reborn as gods and will eventually attain final Nirvāṇa. Mahāvīra adopted the life of a householder, married Yaśodā (Buddha's wife was Yaśodharā), and had a daughter. The Kalpa Sūtra says that while still in the womb Mahāvīra had vowed not to undertake the ascetic life during the life of his parents. But when they had gone to the world of the gods, with the permission of his elder brother and

---

[1] Kalpa Sūtra, 46, 73f.

the authorities of the kingdom, he made the great renunciation. The gods praised him, saying: 'Best of Kshatriyas, establish the religion of Dharma, which benefits all living beings in the whole universe.' Śakra, king of the gods, produced by magic a gorgeous palanquin with a costly throne, and sat Mahāvīra in it while circumambulating him three times, and Śakra and Īśāna fanned him. Mahāvīra was carried to a park, and there under an aśoka tree he put off all his clothes except one garment, and plucked out his hair in five handfuls, which Śakra caught in a diamond cup and carried to the Milk Ocean.

For a year after his renunciation Mahāvīra wore one robe, and after that he walked about naked. The two chief Jain sects are the Digambaras, 'sky-clad', whose monks are naked, and the Śvetāmbaras, 'white-clad', whose monks wear white robes and are found mainly in the colder northern parts of India. The alienation between the two sects goes back to the early days and is centred on the extremes of asceticism. The Digambara hold the uncompromising ideal of the Kevalin, the 'isolated' monk. Not only do they reject the scriptures of their opponents, but they deny that Mahāvīra was married or was born by some divine gynaecology. Mahāvīra did not even eat or drink, and his body was simply kept alive by an influx of material particles.[1]

The Śvetāmbara agree that for twelve years Mahāvīra neglected his body, and suffered hardships from nature and men with equanimity, exerting himself for the suppression of the defilements of karma. Some of the older texts tell of the many sorts of living beings which crawled about on his body causing pain. He meditated and did not answer those who saluted him, and so was beaten with sticks by sinful people. He saw women as 'the cause of all wicked acts'. He never washed or cleaned his teeth, and sometimes slept in gardens and sometimes in cemeteries. Dogs bit him and few people protected him, but in all things Mahāvīra sought to meditate, even if badly treated. So he committed no sin, nor consented to the sins of others. Killing no creatures, he begged his food.[2]

In the thirteenth year, on a river bank, under a Sal tree near an

[1] W. Schubring, *The Doctrine of the Jainas*, trs. W. Beurlen, 1962, p. 61.
[2] Ācārāṅga Sūtra 8, 1f.

old temple (like the Buddha), after fasting two and a half days without drinking water, Mahāvīra attained the highest knowledge called Kevala (isolation or integration). He reached Nirvāna, complete and free, and became a Jina and an Arhat. He was omniscient and understood all things. He saw all the conditions of the world, of gods and men and demons; where they come from and where they go to, the thoughts of their minds and their secret deeds, their births and rebirths as gods and demons. He taught Dharma, first to the gods and afterwards to men. Mahāvīra gathered around him many disciples, and at his death it is said, no doubt with pardonable exaggeration, that there were fourteen thousand monks, thirty-six thousand nuns, one hundred and fifty-nine thousand lay votaries, and many more females, sages, professors and mighty ones. Mahāvīra lived seventy-two years in all, and when his karma was exhausted he died, freed from all pains.

The death of Mahāvīra is clearly stated a number of times. In the town of Pāpā, near Patna, he quitted the world, cut asunder the ties of birth, age and death. He became a Siddha (perfect), a Buddha, a Mukta (liberated), a maker of the end to all misery, free from all pains, and so he died. The night in which he died was lit up by many ascending and descending gods, and there was great confusion and noise.

KRISHNA PARALLELS

The story of Mahāvīra has been considered in some detail for its general interest for religious thought, its pattern for the lives of other Jinas, and some of its parallels to the Krishna and Buddha stories. Some of the names are practically identical with some in the Buddha stories, and no doubt there was borrowing between these two powerful and contemporary religious movements. On the other hand there were many Indian ascetics and the patterns of their lives often had much in common.

Among the lists of Jinas there are several names that appear in the Krishna tradition. The twenty-second Jina, the one before Pārśva, called Arishtanemi (or Neminātha), is described as the first cousin of Krishna, his father having been brother to Vasudeva, the father of Krishna. This Jina, like Krishna, is always represented as black, and his emblem is the Vishnuite conch shell. But the Jains claim that he was superior to Krishna, physically and intellectually, and his rejection of luxury and adoption of asceticism show him to have been the opposite of Krishna, as least as depicted in the Purānas. However, he must be mythical, if one accepts the interval of eighty-four thousand years, which is supposed to separate him from the next Jina, Pārśva.

The Krishna mythology is particularly influential in Jain ideas of the cosmos. After the Jinas there are the temporal heroes, whose names and status often link up with non-Jain originals. There are world-emperors (*chakravartin*), and two heroic figures, half-brothers, Vāsudeva and Baladeva, who have been made into types. In the Kalpa Sūtra the dream-interpreters tell the king that the mothers of Jinas or world-emperors wake up after seeing fourteen great dreams of conception, the mothers of Vāsudevas awake after seeing seven great dreams, and the mothers of Baladevas awake after seeing four great dreams.

In the Jain system of the ever-revolving wheel of time, in each half-circle there arise twenty-four Jinas, twelve world-emperors, nine Vāsudevas, nine Baladevas, and smaller numbers of legislators. These appear in the continent of India, though it is assumed that a corresponding number also appears in the northern continent, and during the cycle of time the world either deteriorates or improves. The Vāsudevas, like Krishna, are dressed in yellow, have the sacred bird Garuda of Vishnu on their banners, and carry Vishnu's symbols of conch-shell, discus, club and sword. The Baladevas are dressed in dark robes, have the palm tree as emblem and carry clubs, arrows and plowshares.[1]

The names of these heroes are recounted, and their names in previous lives, with those of their fathers and mothers, their teachers, their opponents, and the towns where they first resolved to enter on their present form of existence. These are given in popular verses, and show knowledge of the Mahābhārata, as well as Jain invention. In the present series of these heroes the Vāsudevas include the names of Nārāyana (Vishnu), Puroshottama (Great Person), and Svayambhū (self-born). The Baladevas

[1] *The Doctrine of the Jainas*, pp. 18f.

include Rāma, who is probably the Balarāma, brother of Krishna, and Pauma who is Rāma-chandra, the hero-avatar of the Rāmā-yana. The opponents include Rāvana, the demon enemy of the avatar Rāma. The Epic story of Draupadī and her five Pāndava husbands also occurs in the Jain Angas, and when she was abducted Vāsudeva defeated her captor and restored her to her husbands.

In the cycle of ages the present period (Dushama) is evil and began three years after Mahāvīra reached Nirvāna. No other Jina will appear in this epoch, and no Jain disciple can attain Nirvāna now without at least one rebirth. But things will get worse and religion will disappear. An even more horrible period will follow in which the universe will be devastated, and would disappear but for the fact that it is eternal. But at last the wheel will turn and an upward revolution will begin, heralded by seven kinds of rain which will make seeds grow again on the earth. Then a new age will come, in which twenty-four new Tīrthankaras will appear. So in fact the twenty-four Tīrthankaras of our era are only a small part of an endless cycle of these exalted ones, who appear at irregular intervals to establish Dharma. This eschatology corresponds to Hindu and Buddhist ideas of the future.

In predictions of the future Jinas there are several more names from the Krishna mythology. The first ten Jinas are named and the eleventh will be Devakī, the mother of Krishna, who at present is working out her karma in the eighth world of the gods. The twelfth future Jina will be Krishna himself, under the name of Amama. The fourteenth Jina will be Krishna's brother, Baladeva, and the sixteenth is Krishna's stepmother, Rohinī, the mother of Baladeva. The twentieth Jina will be another relative of Krishna, Kunika.[1]

These references, and others, in recorded accounts of the mythology, show the great popularity of the Krishna cult, not only among Hindus but among Jains at the time when their scriptures were being compiled, in the early Christian centuries. There is no rejection of Hindu myth, and the Avatars are adapted in some degree to the succession of Jinas.

The Jinas are not only spiritual pioneers, but, like Avatars and Buddhas, they have become objects of devotion. Although in

[1] S. Stevenson, *The Heart of Jainism*, 1915, pp. 276f.

theory the Jinas have passed beyond worldly concerns and cares
for mortal beings, there are texts which show the religious impulse overcoming doctrine. In the lives of sixty-three famous
men, by the great Jain teacher Hemachandra (died A.D. 1172),
there are praises of the twenty-four Jinas by name and appeals are
made for their help. 'May the blessed Abhinanda give great joy.
... May the blessed Lord Sumati grant your desires. ... May the
Jina Śitala protect you. ... May Śreyamsa, the sight of whom is
a physician for creatures, be for your emancipation. ... May the
blessed Lord Arishtanemi destroy your misfortunes. May the
Lord Pārśvanatha be for your emancipation. May there be good
fortune from Holy Vīra's eyes, whose pupils are wide with compassion even for sinful people, moist with a trace of tears.' The
last clause refers especially to Mahāvīra's known compassion,
illustrated in a story of him taking pity on a god who had tried
in vain to distract the Jina from meditation.

There are further praises of the Tīrthankaras, and prayers:
'Purify us, protect me, prepare liberation for us quickly, spread
endless happiness. ... Mahāvīra is one to be worshipped by the
whole world; set my mind on Dharma, give me strength for the
crossing of existence. Homage to you, compassionate one.'[1]

JINAS AND AVATARS

A further Indian sect, contemporary with Jainism and Buddhism was that of the Ājīvikas, whose history and doctrines have
been pieced together by A. L. Basham. Much of what is known
about them comes from Jain and Buddhist sources, which combated them as deterministic and extremely ascetic. Buddhist
descriptions place three Ājīvikas in the highest rank, but according to the Jain Bhagavatī Sūtra the Ājīvikas believed in twenty-
four Tīrthankaras, of whom their current teacher Gosāla was the
last. It seems unlikely that the Ājīvikas, who believed in im-
mensely long cycles of ages, would be content with only three
Tīrthankaras, and since their origins were close to the Jains they
probably shared their belief in twenty-four.[2]

[1] Trishastiśalākā-purushacaritra, trs. H. M. Johnson, 1931, pp. 1f. See my
Worship in the World's Religions, 1961, pp. 66ff.
[2] A. L. Basham, *History and Doctrines of the Ājīvikas*, 1951, pp. 275f.

Mahāvīra among the Jains, and Gautama among the Buddhists, were the last of a long series. This showed that the Dharma was eternal, not invented by anybody. But in practice it was the present Jina and Buddha who was the pattern for all the rest, and so there is a unity under the apparent diversity, and a virtual uniqueness. So for the Ājīvikas Gosāla was treated with the greatest respect and was considered omniscient, and Basham speaks of his 'divine status' and the application to him of the word *tēvan*, 'the God'. Yet their Tīrthankaras were not so far removed from the Ājīvikas as they were to the Jains; they appeared from time to time, as unexpectedly as the rainbow, and were believed to return to earth when their doctrine was in danger. It seems that at least one school of the Ājīvikas believed in occasional Avatars, brilliant and sudden theophanies of a god, and they had an elaborate worship with costly ceremonies. The eventual decline and disappearance of the sect may have been due to the attraction of a number of its followers into the worship of Krishna.

The Tīrthankaras of Jainism were not Avatars in the sense of incarnations of God in the world, as in Vaishnavism. The theory of a succession of twenty-four Jinas is parallel and perhaps previous to that of Avatāras, but its basic assumptions are different. The parallel is really with the twenty-four Buddhas before Gautama, and Jainism probably provided the pattern for this late Buddhist theory, which, as we have seen, was first propounded as comprising seven Buddhas.

Jainism is not humanistic, any more than Buddhism is. It does not teach self-salvation, but dependence upon a supernatural truth revealed by omniscient and adorable transcendent beings. However, this could not guarantee long popular appeal. The Jains had considerable following for a time, and rich and powerful patrons, but Hinduism won back most of its converts by attacks on the intellectual and religious planes. Śankara attacked the Jain doctrine of the non-universality of the Self, and Rāmānuja disputed the error of supposing that Being can originate from Non-being, quoting the Upanishads in his support. He criticized both Jains and Buddhists for refusing to philosophize and taking refuge in ambiguity, saying 'May be it is. May be it is not. May be it is and is not.'[1]

[1] *Vedānta-Sūtras, with the Commentary of Rāmānuja*, pp. 514f.

But the most serious opposition to Jainism and Buddhism in India came from the theistic religions, both Vaishnavite and Śaivite. One of the great Śaivite teachers of south India, Sampantar, was said to have been born in answer to the prayer of his parents that he might win back those who had abandoned theism for Jainism and Buddhism, and sons of his followers call him an Avatar of one of the sons of Śiva. Sampantar won back the king of his country to Śaivism, and with his younger contemporary Appar aroused many people in Tamil country to *bhakti* devotion. At the same time the Vaishnavite poets, singing of the love manifested in the Avatars of Vishnu, reinforced the popular appeal of theism even further. Eventually Buddhism almost disappeared from India, and Jainism shrank to a mere million or so adherents, before the powerful Hindu Avatar faith and theism.

14

Incarnation in Islam?

THE QUR'ĀN

Aldous Huxley said that the doctrine that God can be incarnated in human form is also found in the Mohammedanism of the Sūfīs, and this claim must be considered briefly although it will soon be apparent that there is little, if any, relationship to the Avatar beliefs. To turn from Hinduism and Buddhism to Islam is to enter a new world of thought, yet Islam went to India and there were some mutual influences and both Hinduism and Islam faced the problems of the relationship of God to man. The question of Incarnation is further complicated by the fact that Islam arose six centuries after the beginnings of Christianity. Muslim theologians knew of the doctrine of Incarnation in some form, yet they seem to have rejected it almost to a man.

There is no mention of the Incarnation, as such, in the Qur'ān, and no use there of a later Islamic term, *hulūl*, for Incarnation. Jesus is referred to as 'a word from God', and 'his Word which he committed to Mary', but the reference is to the manner of his birth and not to any Christian Logos doctrine. Although the Trinity is formally denied in the Qur'ān it is misunderstood, or only heretical versions of the doctrine are controverted, and the Christian doctrine of the Incarnation of Christ is not considered in relationship to the Trinity. The meanings of the terms 'Son of God' and 'Trinity' in the Muslim scripture have been discussed at length in my book *Jesus in the Qur'ān* and need not be considered again here.[1]

[1] *Jesus in the Qur'ān*, 1965, pp. 126ff.

Incarnation in Islam?

In the development of Islamic theology the idea of Incarnation was sometimes discussed and condemned. The idea was found in the term *hulūl*, 'settling in' or 'contained in', derived from *halla*, to 'alight' or 'settle'. This was applied both to the relationship of the soul to the body and to the idea that a divine spirit could enter in man. The second notion was rejected as dividing the divine essence. The Christian doctrine of Incarnation was denied, and extreme sects which taught *hulūl* were excommunicated on the same grounds as Christians.

Al-Ghazālī (1058–1111) has been called the greatest of Muslim theologians. He has been congenial to some western scholars, though certain of his doctrines are strange to Christianity even where they are not direct attacks on Christian theology. He strongly condemned belief in Incarnation, saying that God 'is not *hulūl* in anything and nothing is *hulūl* in him'. There is some ambiguity in his mystical writings, but formally he condemned the idea of divine indwelling, and in his *Deliverance from Error* he declared that some conceive of mystical nearness to God as 'inherence' (*hulūl*), and some as 'union' (*ittihād*), but 'all that is erroneous'. In the literal sense God and man cannot become one, either by the mystic losing his humanity in God, or by a third unity being formed of God and man as Christians believe.[1]

Ghazālī's criticisms of the Christian doctrine of the Incarnation are typical of Muslim opinion, and they are set out in his book *The Excellent Refutation of the Divinity of Jesus Christ according to the Gospels*.[2] Here Ghazālī demonstrates the wide knowledge that many Muslim scholars had of the Bible, using it both to extend their commentaries on parallel passages in the Qur'ān and to condemn Christian and Jewish teachings from their own scriptures. Yet, as a Muslim writer remarks, although Ghazālī shows a commendable knowledge of the Bible yet, like other Islamic theologians, he does not show a 'feel' for the Christian position.[3] In this no doubt he is like many Christian writers, who have discussed

[1] W. M. Watt, *The Faith and Practice of Al-Ghazālī*, 1953, p. 61.
[2] *Réfutation Excellente de la Divinité de Jésus Christ d'apres les Evangiles*, trs. R. Chidiac, 1939; F. E. Wilms, *Al-Ghazālīs Schrift wider die Gottheit Jesu*, 1966.
[3] F. Shehadi, *Ghazālī's Unique Unknowable God*, 1964, p. 26n.

'Mahomet' and 'the Alcoran' in scornfully critical terms, without realizing that these are holy to Muslims and that scorn effectively prevents any religious dialogue. In Ghazālī's case, with all his learning, he often misses the point in Christian belief.

Ghazālī begins by noting that he has found Christians weak and uneasy in their beliefs. The vulgar have no knowledge of theology, and the more learned justify their belief in the Incarnation on the authority of Aristotle on divine union, comparing it with the entry of the soul into the body. From these he turns to the Gospels and discusses passages, especially from St John, which speak of the unity of God and Christ: 'I and the Father are one', 'that they may be one like us', and so on. The belief in unity is compared to the error of a man who looks in a mirror reflecting a coloured object, and thinks that the reflection is the form of the mirror which in itself has no colour. So the Christians think of Christ, when they see the radiance of the divine light shining within him. But they are mistaken in imagining that the nature of God could be made one with the nature of man.

Ghazālī explains the Gospel verses as metaphorical. When Jesus prayed that the disciples might be one 'like us', he rejected the proper sense of the words in favour of metaphor. The proof of this is shown in that Jesus prayed to God for his disciples, whereas if his unity with God gave him the right to divinity it would follow that he would have asked for his disciples to be gods. But the very thought of this is shameful.

Then Ghazālī turns to Biblical passages which clearly show the humanity of Jesus. He was a person of evident human nature, who underwent hunger, thirst, fatigue and sleep. Jesus even suffered, 'at least according to what they maintain', in the Crucifixion, where he said, 'My God, why hast thou forsaken me?'. Like some other theologians Ghazālī tried to have it both ways, since Islamic orthodoxy denied the Crucifixion, but Christian belief in it might be used against them. He proceeds to instance the limitations of Jesus: in cursing the fig tree, admitting his ignorance of the day and hour, and his statement, 'Me, a man that told you the truth' (John 8, 40). Only a Docetist need disagree.

Ghazālī then discusses the meaning of the word *hulūl*, and any divine privileges that might be claimed for Jesus. This is metaphorical language; the term *hulūl* and the expression 'I and my Father are one' were not given to the founder of our revealed law, Muhammad, nor to anyone else among the Muslims. But Jesus also was the founder of a revealed law, and so when he used the above terms he was making a comparison, without any suggestion that they should be taken in a literal sense.

The terms 'fatherhood' and 'sonship' can also be justified in the Christian context as metaphorical expressions. The Torah had spoken of 'Israel my eldest son', and Jesus spoke of 'My Father and your Father, my God and your God'. Similarly the word Lord (*Rabb*) is used of God, but also of human owners of things, and it may be used of Christ. Ghazālī quotes with approval Paul's verse, 'There is one God, the Father . . . and one Lord, Jesus Christ' (1 Cor. 8, 6). He declares that this 'demonstration is truly admirable'. Such a tribute to the apostle of the Gentiles is rare among non-Christian writers.

In a brief treatment of the Prologue of the Fourth Gospel, Ghazālī says that the title 'Word' has no relationship to the divinity of Christ, but it reveals the essence of the Creator and his different aspects. When he comes to the critical verse, 'the Word was made flesh', he prefers a Coptic version which, he says, runs, 'the Word was made a body'. If this suggests that God was made Jesus it is ludicrous. Equally metaphorical are the words that Christ existed before Abraham, and that he who has seen him has seen the Father.

Ghazālī was aware of some of the Christological differences of Christian sects, and criticized them in turn. The Jacobites taught that God created the humanity of Jesus and then united himself with it. The result was a third reality, which was unlike either of its component parts, for it had all the attributes of divinity, as well as all the attributes of humanity. But a thing that has human attributes is human, and cannot also be something else. This is unintelligent, like talking of cock's eggs.

The Melkites were worse than the Jacobites, for they taught that there were two distinct natures in Jesus, and spoke of the union of God with universal Man. This is as fabulous as the griffin. The Nestorians in their turn spoke of a union of will between God and man. Ghazālī is kinder to them, but refuses to grant anything more than a metaphorical union.

Basic to Ghazālī's view of the Incarnation is his doctrine of the divine nature. Anything that is incompatible with or derogatory to divinity must be wrong; this is unexceptionable. A perfect God cannot be in the position that his existence depends in any way on something else, and the combined reality, God-in-Christ, would seem to depend on the existence of its component parts, and so could not be truly divine. But underlying this criticism is the more fundamental principle that God cannot share his nature with any thing or person. The Hindu 'thou art that', and the Christian aspiration to be 'partakers of the divine nature', are equally abhorrent.

Logically Ghazālī is opposed to all forms of mysticism, though his logic failed when it came to the point. God is unique, and that means, in Ghazālī's doctrine, that God is never literally *one with* any person, and further that he is not even *like* any person. This seemed to cut the ground from under the Christian doctrine of the Incarnation, and also from mystical teachings of union with God[1]. God is both unique and unknowable. It may be commented that if God was ever dead, this was the place. If God is unknowable there can be no Incarnation; but if he can be incarnate then he is known as never before.

SHĪ'AS AND OTHERS

The great majority of Muslims are Sunni, followers of 'tradition'. The Shī'a, 'followers' of 'Alī, though a minority, comprise many different sects, and are particularly important for our purpose since ideas of divine indwelling or similar beliefs, often occur. In Shī'ism belief was placed in divine manifestations. The Qur'ān had spoken of revelations and mediations between God and man, but the true Word or revelation was the Qur'ān. The Shī'a added the idea of the Imām, the human manifestation of the divine and the leader of salvation. The term Imām is used several times in the Qur'ān, for a sign, model and leader. The earliest Shī'a development identified the Imām with 'Alī, and his sons Hasan and Husain stressing their flawless genealogy and limiting the manifestation of God in the Imāms to 'right guidance'. This view is still held by the Zaidīs, who are nearest to the Sunnis.

[1] *Ghazālī's Unique Unknowable God*, p. 27.

With the passing centuries Greek philosophy was studied throughout Islam and adapted to particular needs. Beliefs in prophets and Imāms developed into ideas of cosmic powers. A new theory of the Imām was that the cosmic force, the eternal instrument of creation, was borne by the Imāms, who came one after another in a series, like Avatars. One Imām is always present in the world, which would perish if the Imām disappeared. This has been described as a series of 'missionary campaigns' of the Deity, launched for preaching the eternal religion.[1]

In a kind of Neo-Gnosticism the relationship between the Imām and God was spoken about in a way not unlike that between Christ and God in Christian theology, and many mystical allegories were made of their communion. Although most theologians did not accept this it became powerful among the masses, especially in Persia, and influenced both Sūfīs and Ismā'īlīs. But most of the Shī'a rejected the notions of transmigration (*tanāsukh*) of the Imāms, their rebirth and incarnations. Rather, it was thought that the divine light shone upon the Imām, who was otherwise an ordinary mortal, like Muhammad who had said, 'I am a man like yourselves'. The soul and body of the Imām existed independently of the eternal light of the Imām.

To extremists there was complete *hulūl*, the divine light dwelt fully in the Imām bodily, the mortal part of him was completely absorbed, and finally he was identical with God. Both the Zaidīs and the middle of the road Imāmīs combated this doctrine, as bringing Shī'ism into disrepute.

The orthodox Ismā'īlīs reject both Incarnation and transmigration, but such ideas are held by 'ultras' (*Ghulāt*) who believe that God became incarnate by indwelling (*hulūl*) in 'Alī. Both Twelver and Sevener (Ismā'īlī) Shī'a excommunicate the extremists, Nusairīs, Druzes, and the like, calling them *hulūlīya* like the Christians.

The Nusairīs hold that spiritual beings emanate from the ineffable deity in a hierarchy of Name (*ism*), Door (*bāb*), and other classes. Five names include 'Alī, though sometimes he has been placed above them all. The 'Men of God' (Ahl-i Haqq) believe in seven successive manifestations of God, coming to dwell 'in a

[1] *Shorter Encyclopaedia of Islam*, pp. 166f.

garment', accompanied by four angels. His first appearance was in the Creator, the second in 'Alī, and the third in leaders of the Men of God. There is belief also in a thousand and one reincarnations of men.

The Druzes (Durūz), founded by Darazī among others, are now regarded as a separate religion from Islam, but call themselves Unitarians. They believe that the Fātimid Caliph and Imām Hākim, 'Our Lord', held a position comparable to the cosmic intellect and was the last incarnation of God. As an embodiment of the Godhead he was above 'Alī, and so Ismā'īlism was superseded. He was also beyond good and evil and this explains away symbolically the cruelties of the wicked Caliph. When Hākim died it was said that he was hidden, like the 'hidden Imām' of the Shī'a, but he will appear at the end of time to establish justice in the world. The Druzes have different Pillars of Faith from orthodox Islam, to the number of seven, and including acceptance of the unity of Our Lord. They believe not only in Incarnation, or emanation, but also in the transmigration of souls, of which there is a fixed number who are reborn immediately after death, until they are perfected and ascend to the stars.

SŪFĪ BELIEFS

Sūfī mystical teachings on unity have an important bearing on belief in Incarnation. From the fourth Islamic century there came ideas from late Greek philosophy, and particularly the Plotinian doctrine of emanations from God. Mystics came to speak of union with God as the result of divine emanation, or as due to the divine spark in man which revived under the effect of illumination, or as the result of consciousness of undifferentiated existence wherein the soul realized its oneness with God. Since Islam went to India early and over the years became increasingly involved in Indian ideas there were probably Hindu influences also upon the later Sūfīs, though this was in a pantheistic and not an Avatar direction. The stark contrast of God and man, which is found in the Qur'ān and orthodox Islamic theology, seems to be quite irreconcilable with the claims of some Sūfīs not only to be united with God but to 'be God'. But this is quite natural on Hindu monistic terms although, as has been remarked earlier, monism does not lead towards the Avatar doctrine but rather against it.[1]

In fact nearly all the Sūfīs rejected the use of the term *hulūl* 'indwelling' or 'incarnation', because this word had Christian undertones. To speak of a place for incarnation, a point of impact for immaterial realities, was regarded as an attempt at materializing them. Sūfī writers warned their followers of the dangers of heresy and wrote special chapters in their manuals listing the dangers to which mystics might be exposed, and in these books *hulūl* appears regularly. The term *ittihād*, 'becoming one', was preferred by Sūfīs to describe the mystical union in which the creature becomes one with the Creator. To some mystics this suggested that there are two beings who become one, and to others human individuality was only a phase which passes away in the divine reality.[2]

The teaching of the great Persian mystic Husain b. Mansūr al-Hallāj is important in this context and disputed. Junayd, who has been called 'the Crown of the Mystics' said that he saw much folly and nonsense in the words of Hallāj and he rejected the notion of incarnation.[3] Hallāj was executed for heresy (A.D. 922). His most famous and offensive saying was *Anā 'l-Haqq*, 'I am Reality', or 'My "I" is the Creative Truth'. This was an apparent identification of himself with God, by assuming a title used of God in the Qur'ān, but it arose from the most intimate communion and its progress can be traced in his *Dīwān* ('collection'). God is here called Lord, Friend, and Lover. Man is his intimate and chosen one, and asks him, 'Say to me, "I have redeemed thee"' God is even spoken of as Father, a title very rare in Islam: 'For me, the orphan, I have a Father, in whom I take refuge.'[4]

Little by little the closeness of man and God grows. 'Between myself and God there is no longer any intermediary explanation, demonstration, or miracle to bring conviction.' The proof is God himself, towards him, in him. But the mingling of divine and human becomes virtual identification. 'Thy spirit mingled little

[1] R. C. Zaehner, *Hindu and Muslim Mysticism*, 1960, pp. 86ff.

[2] L. Massignon, *Essai sur les Origines du Lexique Technique de la Mystique Musulmane*, 1954, pp. 21, 84.

[3] A. H. Abdel-Kader, *The Life, Personality and Writings of al-Junayd*, 1962, pp. 31f.

[4] *Le Dīwān d'al-Hallāj*, trs. L. Massignon, 1955, p. 17.

by little with my spirit, and now I am thyself; thy existence is mine and it is also my will.' This is a union of will and spirit: 'His spirit is my spirit, and my spirit is his spirit; what he wishes, I wish; and what I wish, he wishes.' But it is more, for when man calls to God, it is in fact God who calls to himself. And 'when I saw the Lord with the eye of the heart and asked him, "Where art thou?" then he replied, "thyself".'

So Hallāj arrived at undifferentiated unity of God and man. 'I said to him, "Where is the road that leads to God?" He replied, "There is only a road between two, and here, with me, there is nobody else".' The unity is affirmed in order to deny duality in God 'Is it I, is it thee? That would make two gods. Far be from me the thought of affirming "Two".' So comes the most famous verse of Hallāj

> *I have become he whom I love, and he whom I love has become myself.*
> *We are two spirits infused into one body;*
> *So to see me is to see him, and to see him is to see us'.*[1]

Trouble arose because the word 'infused' (*halalnā*) is related to *hulūl*, and other mystics took pains to refute it. The immediate disciples of Hallāj accepted it, but most later Sūfīs, while honouring him as a martyr, deny that Hallāj taught *hulūl*, and they interpret his saying, 'I am the Real', in a monistic but not an incarnational sense. Yet the influence of Christianity on Hallāj was marked. Two other verses say:

> *Praise be to him whose humanity manifested [to the angels] the mystery of his radiant divinity,*
> *And who later showed himself to his [human] creatures openly, in the form of one 'who eats and drinks'.*[2]

The first lines are said to refer to Adam, whom God showed to the angels, according to the Qur'ān. The second part refers to Jesus, of whom the Qur'ān said that he 'ate food'. But Jesus is not merely a divine manifestation in the sense of a creation, for he shows the divine nature since the terms used, 'humanity' (*nāsūt*)

---

[1] *Le Dīwān d'al-Hallāj*, p. 93.   [2] *ibid.*, p. 41.

and 'divinity' (*lāhūt*) were borrowed from Syrian Christian usage for denoting the two natures of Christ. The Manichees also used these terms, but Hallāj is a rare Muslim writer to employ them and they were later condemned.[1]

Hallāj said that he would die in the religion (*dīn*) or 'confession' of the Cross, and he was literally crucified. It was in Jesus, rather than Muhammad, that he saw the perfect man who represents God by revealing the creative Truth from within himself. Yet despite the attractiveness of Hallāj, especially for Christians but also for many Muslims, there is an underlying monism in his teachings that is inconsistent with orthodox mysticism, Christian or Islamic.

Another famous Persian mystic, Jalāl ud-Dīn Rūmī, (d. 1273), often spoke of Jesus but blamed the apostles for perverting the unity of his way into different sects. He says that the distorters had no scent of the 'unicolority' of Jesus, nor a disposition imbued with the tincture from the dyeing-vat of Jesus.[2]

Rūmī expounds the belief that in every era there is a new manifestation of God; 'every instant the Loved One assumes a new garment, now of age, now of youth'. First the Spirit plunged like a diver into the clay of Adam and appeared in the world, then he became Noah and entered the ark, he became Abraham and was preserved from the fire, he became Jesus and went up to heaven to glorify God. In every generation he was coming and going, until at last he appeared in Muhammad and ruled the world and he became 'Alī with his sword. It was even 'he in human shape' that cried 'I am the Truth', for the one on the scaffold was not Hallāj as the foolish thought.[3]

However, Rūmī makes clear that this is not the transmigration of individual souls, but it is the doctrine of pure unity, monism. Following Shī'a teaching he declares that in every age after Muhammad there is a saint who acts as his representative. In every epoch there is a living Imām, whether he descends from 'Alī, as the Shī'a think, or from 'Umar as the Sunni hold. This is the Mahdī, the one guided by God, and the Hādī, the Guide, a title of God himself. He is both hidden and present, he is the Light of

[1] *Essai sur les Origines du Lexique Technique*, p. 42.
[2] *The Mathnawī of Jalālu'ddīn Rūmī*, trs. R. A. Nicholson, 1960, ii, p. 30.
[3] *Dīwān*, trs. R. A. Nicholson, in *Rūmī, Poet and Mystic*, 1950, pp. 142f.

Muhammad, and he is the lamp of lesser saints who receive light from him.[1]

Again, the divine unity is original. Where were Adam and Eve before creation? Where were Moses and Jesus when the Divine Sun was rising? It is assumed that they were yet undifferentiated, but divine. Jesus arose in his turn; 'he was the soul of Moses, and Moses the soul of him'. Later Balaam, the son of Beor, was like the Jesus of his time. Then Muhammad (Mustafā), the chief of the prophets and the sea of purity, was named in the Gospel; his characteristics and appearance, his warring and fasting, were mentioned.[2]

The birth of Jesus, recognized as miraculous in the Qur'ān, is described by Rūmī as due to the contact of the Universal Soul with the partial individual soul, which received from the Universal a pearl which was put into its bosom. Being so touched on its bosom the individual soul became pregnant, like Mary, 'with a heart-beguiling Messiah'. But there is a difference between a human Messiah who travelled on land and water, and the Messiah who is beyond the limitations of spatial measurement.[3]

Rūmī mentions Jesus many other times. He is a guide and giver of health; he was an ascetic at whose cell all the sick would gather and were healed by his breath. He was taught by God and came speaking into the world, in his cradle. Jesus was intoxicated with God; his human form was angelic and he ascended to heaven. being carried by Gabriel, the celestial bird. Jesus raised the dead by pronouncing the name 'He' (*Hū*, God). But basically, whether it is Jesus or Muhammad, or any other prophet or Imām, they are all emanations of the divine unity. There is no real Incarnation, and Rūmī would have rejected such a materialistic doctrine. Therefore he does not treat Jesus as a real man; he is a sort of angel, and 'Jesus, in the form of man, was really homogeneous with the angels'.[4]

In Spain, at the other end of the Islamic world, lived Ibn 'Arabī (d. 1240), who is often taken as the most extreme monist, teacher of the heretical doctrine of 'identification' if not 'incarnation'. Ibn

---

[1] *The Mathnawī*, ii, p. 263.
[2] *ibid.*, ii, p. 21.
[3] *ibid.*, p. 282.   [4] *ibid.*, vi, p. 422.

'Arabī criticized Christian belief in Incarnation, and misunderstood it as most Muslim writers have done. He agreed that it is
true to say that Christ is divine, but in the sense in which everything else is divine. It is true also that Christ was the Son of Mary,
that good Quranic title. But it is to be an infidel to maintain that
God is me alone, or you alone, or Christ alone. God cannot be
limited in any form, even in thought.[1]

Ibn 'Arabī taught that 'there is nothing but God'. God is not a
creator, nor one who incarnates, but he manifests himself in
countless forms. Therefore God is his creatures, and the creatures
are himself, for all proceed from the single essence. Man unites in
himself the form of God and also the form of the universe. He
manifests the divine essence, with its names and attributes. He is
the mirror by which God is revealed to himself, and so is the final
cause of creation; man is necessary to God, so that he may be
manifested to himself.[2]

With God there is no time, plurality or unity. He is the one
without oneness, the single without singleness. There is no other
than he and no existence but his existence. The Prophet had
declared that God said to Moses: 'I was sick and thou didst not
visit me, I asked help and thou didst not give it to me.' It is strange
that Ghazālī also attributed this to Moses, though of course it is
from the Gospel, where it has anything but a pantheistic meaning.
Ibn 'Arabī interpreted this Gospel saying to fit his own theory.
The existence of the beggar is the existence of God, and the
existence of the sick is his existence; both accidents and substance of all created things are the existence of God. There is
nothing but the face of God, which is found wherever we turn.
Wheresoever his camels turn, there is he.' It follows that 'you are
no other than God'. In place of your own essence and qualities
there are the attributes of God, for you are one and the same
with him.[3]

Despite this plain monism, Ibn 'Arabī has his own doctrine of
the Logos (*kalima*), starting however from Plotinus and not from
the Gospel. For him the Logos is the creative principle, the inward

[1] E. A. Affifi, *The Mystical Philosophy of Muḥyid dīn ibnul 'Arabī*, 1939, p. 20.
[2] *Shorter Encyclopaedia of Islam*, pp. 170f.
[3] R. Landau, *The Philosophy of Ibn 'Arabī*, 1959, p. 83.

aspect of the Deity, through which God becomes conscious of himself and produces the world. There are twenty-two terms used by Ibn 'Arabī to designate the Logos, for he drew his material from many sources and used any name for the one reality. He spoke of it, for example, as the Reality of Muhammad, the Spirit of Muhammad, the Real Adam, the Perfect Man. In his interpretation of the manifested Logos he gives it a specifically Islamic interpretation, yet with his own twist. Other Sūfīs, like Hallāj, had identified the divine principle with Muhammad, but they did not give it such an abstract form.

In the thought of Ibn 'Arabī the manifested Logos is not the Word made flesh in any Christian sense. Nor is it Muhammad the prophet from Mecca, whose form is identified with the Word. But it is the Reality (*haqīqa*) of Muhammad, the active principle of divine knowledge, the spiritual but not the phenomenal head of the saints. There is a hierarchy of prophets or Words. Each prophet is *a* Logos (*kalima*), but not *the* Logos, which is Muhammad alone, his Reality. All other prophets and saints derive their knowledge from the Seal of the Prophets, namely Muhammad. Even when a saint receives knowledge from Jesus, this comes from the Light of Muhammad, for he is the unique and unparalleled being in existence.[1]

It must be emphasized that the Logos is here identified only with the Spirit of Muhammad, and not with his earthly person. It is said that all the prophets, Moses, Jesus and Muhammad, were born and died in time, but the Spirit of Muhammad is eternal. It is both the union of all the Words, and identical with the divine Spirit.

There are similarities between these teachings and some Christian doctrines, and clear differences. The Reality of Muhammad is spoken of as threefold: 'my Beloved is three, although he is One'. This is a Trinity of aspects but not of persons. Then Muhammad is elevated to a place resembling that of Christ in Christian Logos doctrine, but he is not a second person in the Godhead. Further, there is not only one Logos, but many Logoi, everything is a Logos. The Reality of Muhammad, is both the rational principle in the prophets and saints and also the indwelling principle in all things.

[1] *The Mystical Philosophy of Muhyid dīn ibnul 'Arabī*, pp. 72f.

Incarnation in Islam?

In Christian belief God *is* spirit, *is* love. But Ibn 'Arabi's One is a transcendent and attributeless Being, who is known only through what is called the Spirit of Muhammad. In Christian faith God has many attributes, and yet comes in a real Incarnation. Ibn 'Arabi's God is pure essence and unapproachable, acting only through an agent that is not human at all. Whatever may be thought of his doctrine of God, Ibn 'Arabi's doctrine of man is negligible, and perhaps the two go together.[1]

There are countless other Sūfīs, whose beliefs ranged from extreme monism to near-orthodox dualism. But to both wings, and those in between, the doctrine of Incarnation was hardly, if ever, understood in the Christian sense. Emanations from God, or identification with God, were acceptable and this harmonized with Indian monism and no doubt was partly produced by it. Some influence of Indian Avatar theory might be found in the notion of successive emanations, but the tendency is away from the strong personal theism of Vaishnavism and Śaivism and towards the monism of non-dualistic Vedāntism. The Muslim Sūfīs, then, do not illustrate a universal tendency towards belief in Incarnation but they rather show the binding hold of monism.

[1] *ibid.*, pp. 87f.

PART III

CHRISTIAN AND OTHER BELIEFS

15

Incarnation and Avatars

In the interpretation of Christology in our times account must be taken of the claims and practices of other religions which were unknown to Christendom in earlier centuries. Today discussion of beliefs has also to be conducted against the background of an egalitarianism which sees all religious leaders as the same and proclaiming an identical message, a 'perennial philosophy'. So having considered Avatars and Buddhas, it is time to mention some of the basic elements in Christian doctrine in the light of comparable, if different, beliefs in Indian and other Asian religions.

BIBLICAL DOCTRINE OF INCARNATION

The classic statement of Christian faith in the Incarnation is in the Prologue to the Fourth Gospel, 'the Word became flesh' (John 1, 14). Both the divine and the human reference to Christ are here, for the 'Word was God' and also 'dwelt among us'. There are Jewish and Greek backgrounds to this Prologue, and in speaking of the Word (Logos) without explanation John used a term with which his readers must have had some acquaintance. The synthesis of Platonic and Stoic ideas which was popular in the first century B.C. sought to reconcile Platonic beliefs in a transcendent God with the pantheism of the Stoics. For the Stoics the Logos was divine, expressed in the universe, and man was a spark of the universal Logos. But the attractive parallels of this pantheism with the Brahman–Atman equation in Hinduism break down if applied to John's Gospel. Christ is the Logos, which lightens every man, yet when he comes to 'his own' they do not receive him. Men become true children of God through faith in him, and the

Logos dwells as really in 'flesh' as Moses did when he brought the Law.[1]

The Jewish philosopher Philo tried to spread the Stoic-Platonic Logos idea, but his thought is far from consistent, and his Logos roughly takes the place of the divine Wisdom which Hellenistic Judaism had stressed. Already in the Old Testament Wisdom was spoken of as having an independent existence in the divine presence, as a 'master workman' with God (Prov. 8). The rabbis later developed the figure of Wisdom in personal expressions about the Law (Torah).

John makes a synthesis of Jewish and Greek words and beliefs, based upon the Christian story and experience. The Logos is the divine speech but also the divine action. 'In the beginning was the Logos' refers back to the creation in Genesis 1, and probably also to Proverbs 8, 22: 'The Lord possessed me in the beginning of his way, before his works of old. I was set up from everlasting, from the beginning, or ever the earth was.' The Christian message is not just an ethic, or a proclamation, but it is an act. It is not simply knowledge, *gnosis*, which might be acceptable to Brahmins with their comparable stress on knowledge, *jñāna*. It is Christ, in act, become flesh. John found that preaching Christ implied a cosmogony, as Paul and the epistle to the Hebrews had done before him. The doctrine of the Incarnation was the inevitable expression of the belief that 'God was in Christ'.

Ancient Near Eastern religions had long believed in manifestations of gods among men. The Greeks held that the gods came down from Mount Olympus for a variety of reasons, chiefly to sport with the daughters of men or spend a night or two with their devotees. But although they had innumerable children by human mothers the Greek gods never became men, and there is a world of difference from Greek myth in the firm emphasis of John on the Logos becoming 'flesh'. In the Mysteries divine beings died and rose again or, more correctly, they descended into the underworld and emerged again. But the dying Adonis, Tammuz, Osiris, and the like, were vegetation deities concerned with the crops and magical immortality, going into the ground and shooting up like plants. They were never human beings who were

[1] C. K. Barrett, *The Gospel according to St. John*, 1956, pp. 28f., 127f.

hungry and tired like Jesus, weeping at the death of his friends, sweating in Gethsemane, bleeding on the Cross and buried in a grave.

There is no evidence from the New Testament that the Incarnation, death and resurrection of Jesus had anything to do with the seasons of the year or with fertility cults. The Jews naturally rejected such cults, and their exclusiveness was invaluable. The early Christians were Jews, the Cross and Resurrection formed the core of the first preaching of the Church, and they were centred on a historical figure, a man known to everybody, friend and foe alike. There is at least this resemblance to Indian belief, that there also the Avatar faith flourished without the help of dying and rising vegetation spirits.

The first three Gospels, the Synoptics, no doubt keep more closely to the history of Jesus, without such long discourses and reflections which form much of John. Yet each evangelist deliberately sets his narrative in a theological framework. The Gospel according to Mark begins, as we have it, with the introduction of 'the Gospel of Jesus Christ, the Son of God', and it puts the work of Jesus against the preparatory mission of John the Baptist. Matthew and Luke start with the birth narratives, giving both the Virgin Birth and the genealogies of Jesus through Joseph to Abraham and Adam. The Incarnation of the Logos is not taught in the Synoptics as in John, or as implied by Paul, but faith in the divinely sent Christ is present throughout and the Gospels demonstrate his life in full humanity but with divine power. While John expressed the coming of the Logos by this philosophical term, Matthew and Luke used popular stories to expound a similar faith. How far the Virgin Birth narratives have been shaped by Hellenistic ideas is much debated, and B. H. Streeter explained them by the use of the Buddhist term *hormon*, 'accommodation' to a mythopoeic tendency which nevertheless formed an idea substantially the same as that of the Logos.[1] Clearly different concepts from the Christian stories appear in the narratives of the birth of Avatars and Buddhas in the round of transmigration. Yet there are dangers of Docetism in all these miraculous stories and Emil Brunner said that 'the majestic wonder of the Incarnation

[1] B. H. Streeter, *The Buddha and the Christ*, 1932, p. 129n.

of the Son of God is not made greater but smaller by the biological theory of the procreation through one sex alone'.[1]

Before the Gospels were composed, as we have them, came the work of Paul whose writings are the earliest that have survived. Although apparently Paul had never seen Jesus he wrote of him in his human life as 'born of the seed of David' and 'declared to be the Son of God with power . . . by his resurrection from the dead' (Romans 1, 3–4). This verse has been compared with the so-called Adoptionism of Acts, 'God has made him both Lord and Christ, this Jesus whom you crucified' (Acts 2, 36). The Pauline writings contain teachings on Incarnation, not only in the frequent use of terms like Son of God, but in what have been named the 'Christological Hymns' (Phil. 2, 6–11; Col. 1, 15–20; and 1 Tim. 3, 16, which may be 'Pauline' though not all by Paul. John 1, 1–14, not of course by Paul, has been also considered as such a hymn). In Philippians it is said that Christ Jesus was in the 'form' (μορφή) of God, but 'emptied' (ἐκένωσεν) himself and took the 'form' (μορφή) of a servant. A possible Docetism in the phrase 'being made in the likeness of men' is countered by the assertion that Christ 'became obedient unto death, even the death of the cross.' In Colossians the Son is called the image (εἰκών) of the invisible God, the firstborn (πρωτότοκος) of all creation, and in him all the fullness (πλήρωμα) of God was pleased to dwell. Yet he made peace 'through the blood of his cross'.

The critical opinion that Paul wrote all of Philippians, if not Colossians, has been challenged by the view that these passages were 'Christological hymns', independent and 'Hellenistic'. But since it is usually thought that Paul adopted them, if he did not compose them, the question in either case is, what did they mean to Paul? Further, the early Hellenists, like Paul, were Jews and it was these Jewish missionaries who expressed the faith in terms understandable to their converts, rather than the converts imposing their own terms on the missionaries.[2] Paul, apparently, had not seen Jesus but he developed a Christology of which part, at least, was current among earlier Christians who tried to explain the significance for themselves of the historical and exalted Jesus.

[1] E. Brunner, *The Mediator*, E.T. 1934, p. 325.
[2] R. H. Fuller, *The Foundations of New Testament Christology*, 1965, pp. 230ff.

Paul spoke of Christ as the 'last Adam' and the 'second *man*' (1 Cor. 15, 45f.), though in this passage Christ is rather a celestial and idealized figure. Paul also said that he did not know Christ 'after the flesh', though he agrees that once Christ had been so known (2 Cor. 5, 16). But he refers even more clearly to the human Jesus as 'born of a woman, born under the law', and in his death he 'became a curse for us' by being hanged on a tree (Gal. 4, 4; 3, 13).

CRUCIFIXION

The fact of the Crucifixion of Jesus dominates the writings of Paul. So in all other New Testament books, hymns and fragments, the Cross assures the historicity of the Lord. The centrality of the Cross in Christian history and worship, which some Hindu and Buddhist critics regard as morbid, shows at least that the roots of Christianity are in fact. Compared with Avatar beliefs, Christian faith in the Incarnation is not simply guaranteed by birth but by death, by the whole of human life, and this makes for its distinctiveness.

There are already signs in the New Testament of that Docetism which was to dog Christology, and of which there are parallels in other religions. That Christ only 'seemed' to live appeared to glorify him, yet this suggestion destroyed the basis of Christian faith in a true Incarnation. Opposition to Docetism may be noted in the assertions, found significantly in the late Fourth Gospel, that blood and water came out of the side of the dead Jesus, and that at his resurrection Thomas was invited to put his hands into his Master's side. No doubt for a similar purpose Luke says that the risen Christ was not 'a spirit', and that the disciples were invited to touch his hands and feet, though it is not stated that they did so.

The canonical New Testament, and this was doubtless one reason for it being established as a canon, insists on the historicity, the true birth, life and death of Jesus. But some early Christian circles had a growing desire to play down or deny the sufferings of their Lord. Ignatius, about A.D. 115, said that certain people believed that Jesus 'suffered in semblance'. Later in the second century the apocryphal Gospel of Peter declared that on the Cross Jesus not only refused a drug but 'was silent, since he felt no pain'. And that most dreadful of all cries of dereliction, 'My God, my God, why hast thou forsaken me?' was perverted into a lament, 'My power, why have you left me? And when he had so spoken he was taken up'. This suggests that he went up to heaven without really dying. About the middle of the second century the apocryphal Acts of John affirmed that during the Crucifixion Jesus appeared to John in a cave, saying to him, 'John, unto the multitude below in Jerusalem I am being crucified and pierced . . . but unto thee I speak'. And later he says, 'Nothing therefore of the things which they will say of me have I suffered. . . . I was pierced yet I was not smitten; hanged, and I was not hanged; that blood flowed from me, and it flowed not.'[1]

Paul spoke of the 'scandal' of Christ crucified to the Jews, for how could the Messiah of God be killed? And it was 'foolishness' to the Greeks, for the gods could not die (1 Cor. 1, 23). Modern writers from other religions have often felt sympathy with these Jews and Greeks. A Buddhist writer speaks of the revulsion that he feels on going into a Christian church and seeing an image of a naked man bleeding and dead on a Cross. 'I cannot help thinking of the gap that lies deep between Christianity and Buddhism.' The symbol of Crucifixion is one of the most difficult things to comprehend. 'The crucified Christ is a terrible sight and I cannot help associating it with the sadistic impulse of a psychically affected, brain.' How can such an object of devotion conduce to calm and spiritual elevation? This is called a morbid preoccupation with death, which makes Christians negative and neurotic, instead of finding the detached calm that comes from discovering that there is no self and following the Middle Way between extremes.[2]

It can be agreed that there has sometimes been too great an emphasis on the dead Christ, to the neglect of the living Christ, yet depreciation of the harsh reality of the Crucifixion and its centrality to Christian faith may be linked with an under-

[1] M. R. James, *The Apocryphal New Testament*, 1924, pp. 91, 245f. Such beliefs adversely affected the Islamic understanding of Jesus also, see *Jesus in the Qur'ān*, ch. 11.
[2] D. T. Suzuki, *Mysticism Christian and Buddhist*, 1957, pp. 129, 136f.

estimate of the reality and power of evil in the world. With the terrible wickednesses of this century, in wars and concentration camps, the evil that is in man can hardly be overlooked. Yet during a visit to Japan Arthur Koestler found it impossible to convince traditional religious leaders there of the wickedness of Nazi concentration camps; such things were foolish and stupid, they said, but not sinful or wicked.[1]

Others have wondered whether the Cross is necessarily central to Christianity, and it is peculiarly difficult for Muslims whose Qur'ān appears formally to deny the Crucifixion. Kamel Hussein, in his sympathetic historical novel about Good Friday, seems to feel that the passivity of the first disciples in accepting the Cross has affected Christianity ever since. 'From them came that sadness which is a ruling element in the character of the greatest adherents of Christianity, their fear of sin, their love of self-reproach and abasement, their sense of the importance of the sin of Adam and their belief that it had to do with the anguish that Christ underwent that mankind might be saved from its consequences.' And he speaks again of the result of the anguish of the disciples. 'Such a psychological stress could not be without effect on their psyche. Is it not just possible that such effects can be inherited? The best Christian in his most sublime moments is a sad man.'[2]

Is that how others see us? How different things look from the inside, for many Christians would not regard their fellows in the faith as sad people, oppressed by a sense of sin and revelling in self-abasement. It is true that there have been powerful beliefs in Original Sin, and even in Total Depravity, and popular religion has sung about this world as a 'vale of tears'. Yet many would now argue that these are aberrations, with little basis in the Bible. Dr. Hussein, as an Egyptian Muslim, would be thinking especially of Coptic Christians and others who have been persecuted minorities. In conversation he admitted to me that he had in mind particularly the monastic element in Christianity, which originated in Egypt and still has its black-clothed monks there.

The centrality of the cross is hardly diminished in modern

[1] *The Lotus and the Robot*, 1960, p. 274.
[2] *City of Wrong*, E.T. 1959, pp. 120, 224.

western Christian theology, though its meaning is interpreted in different ways from the past. Theories of the Atonement as Dramatic, Penal or Moral have been discussed incessantly. But behind all modern debates there have remained convictions of the historicity and focal importance of the Cross. Undoubtedly Jesus died, that death was the result of human sin, and this demands some doctrinal explanation. Aulén, in his small but valuable study, emphasized the inseparable connection of the Incarnation and the Atonement in classical doctrines. The Incarnation is not a mere appearance of God, a theophany, but it is part of the redemptive work of Christ, as a man, but in whom God operates. For 'God was in Christ, reconciling the world unto himself' (2 Cor. 5, 19).[1]

RESURRECTION

Christian incarnational beliefs are distinctive not only in affirming the coming of Christ as a man, and his true death on the Cross, but also in declaring faith in his Resurrection. This was basic to early Christian preaching. The apostles claimed to be witnesses of the resurrection of Christ, and Paul carried this into the scheme of salvation by saying that 'if Christ has not been raised, then our preaching is vain, and your faith also is vain' (1 Cor. 15, 14).

This is not easy to accept, though the evidence is clear that it was the unquestioned faith of the early Church and has remained so down the ages. To the first Christians trust in God implied that his Christ should not be abandoned to death, 'because it was not possible that he should be held by it' (Acts 2, 24). Perhaps it is this conviction that is echoed in the Qur'ān where, having asserted that the Jews could not crucify the Messiah, it is then said, 'Nay, God raised him to himself' (Sūra 4, 156). In this verse there is an Ascension without a Crucifixion.

The Biblical stories of the Resurrection of Christ, however, have been criticized and defended in modern times differently from past ages. The Empty Tomb, described in different ways in the four Gospels, but absent from the sole account in Paul (1 Cor. 15), has been said by some writers to be an unnecessary addition

[1] G. Aulén, *Christus Victor*, 1931.

to the primitive faith. It has been called Docetic, in implying that
Jesus did not die like other men after all or his body did not
decay; or it is called anti-Docetic in stressing a physical resurrection. Some regard it as natural, if paranormal, and others insist
that it was supernatural.[1] Yet that the apostles believed they had
seen Jesus alive again after death can hardly be denied, from
the many references in the New Testament, and the faith of the
early Church was insistent on this fact.

It is possible to over-emphasize the latter point, or press it to
illegitimate conclusions. J. Knox says, quite properly, that the first
Christians declared that they saw the risen Jesus, and there is no
doubt that they believed this, but they did not see the manner of
his actual rising. He says again that the Church cannot be said to
remember the 'rising' of Christ; it does not 'remember' his
Resurrection, but it 'knows' the Resurrection. It is not a memo-
rial, but a faith in the living Christ present now. Knox seeks to
justify his argument, unnecessarily, by asking, 'how could Jesus,
who was crucified, the remembered One, have become Christ,
the living Lord, except through the interposition of some objective occurrence? And how can this "objective occurrence" be
described otherwise than as a "rising from the dead"?'[2]

This appears to resemble the argument that the proof of the
Resurrection is not in any appearances of the risen Christ, but in
the existence of the Church, with its membership raised from
eleven scattered men on Good Friday to three thousand en-
thusiastic believers at Pentecost. This could not have happened, it
is said, without a Resurrection, of some kind, and this is the real
proof and meaning of the risen Christ. It is not too great a step
from here to hold that Christ existed, somehow, in the Church
and this is the Resurrection.

But here the comparative study of religions can reveal a weakness in the argument. For other religious leaders died, and yet
their religions spread rapidly, without experiences of resurrection
as such. When Muhammad died, at the early age of sixty-two
and after only a short illness, his followers could hardly credit the
catastrophe. 'Umar, who was to be the second caliph, asserted, 'By

[1] See H. W. Montefiore in *Christ for Us Today*, 1968, p. 106.
[2] J. Knox, *The Humanity and Divinity of Christ*, 1967, p. 78n.

God he is not dead: he has gone to his Lord as Moses went and was hidden from his people for forty days, returning to them after it was said that he had died. By God, the apostle will return as Moses returned.' But Abū Bakr, the first caliph, an older man and the Peter of the movement in devotion to his master, un-covered the face of the dead Prophet and kissed him. Then he went out to the people and said, 'O men, if anyone worships Muhammad, Muhammad is dead: if anyone worships God, God is alive, immortal'.[1] The Prophet was then buried and there was no question of resurrection. But the faith of Islam spread rapidly and with unparalleled success, so that just a hundred years after the death of Muhammad his armies were found from China to the heart of France.

It may be objected that this was a faith in God and not in Muhammad, but success of the religion and glorification of the founder, without doctrines of resurrection, are phenomena seen in many religions, for example those of the Buddhists, Jains, Zoroastrians, Confucians and Sikhs. It could be claimed that Jesus 'became Christ, the living Lord' through an objective occurrence, and Muhammad remains a man because there was no such event. But this would misunderstand Islam and the essential place of Muhammad in it, which is so generally under-estimated in the West and which will be discussed later.

Make no mistake, this is not an argument against the Resurrec-tion, which is fundamental to Christianity. But it seems that some modern expositions of this faith tend to found it upon shaky grounds, and since these can be seriously criticized by compara-tive religion there is a danger of weakening the basic faith. Christ-ian history is different from that of other religions. Jesus had been crucified, and his disciples were disillusioned and broken. To these men the risen Christ restored faith and zeal. But they were convinced by objective evidence, and not just by their own reflections which could be dismissed as wishful thinking.

Some other writers hold that the Resurrection was the sole distinctive faith of the early Christians and the only explanation for the rise of the Church. There was no ideology to proclaim, such as Islam had with its passionate monotheism, no fixed

[1] *The Life of Muhammad*, trs. A. Guillaume, 1955, pp. 682f.

teaching as given by the disciples of the Rabbis, no new legisla-
tion. Perhaps this goes too far, since faith in Jesus as the Messiah
and in his Parousia (appearing) were potent doctrines in the early
Church. Yet these would hardly have been possible without the
Resurrection, and the birth of the Church remains '*an unsolved
enigma for any historian who refuses to take seriously the only explanation offered by the Church itself.*'[1]

The Resurrection and the Crucifixion complete the incarnational faith, as the work of God in face of evil in the world, going
down before it but not defeated by it. Kamel Hussein, from an
enlightened Muslim viewpoint, appears to feel this, accept part of
it, and yet be unable to follow to the conclusion, because a vague
Ascension rather than Resurrection is what the Qur'ān taught.
One of his discussions centres round the dilemma of the disciples,
whether to fight to liberate Jesus or let him be killed unresistingly.
They followed the words of their Master on non-violence; he was
killed, they waited in grief for three days, and 'to the present
day Christianity has not freed itself, and perhaps never will, from
the entail of that sorrow and regret which haunted the souls of
the disciples because . . . they held back from saving him. They
have been destined to bear the reproach of the great sin – the sin
of abandoning Christ to his foes.' So Christians are called sad and
have no way of atoning for what happened.

A corresponding event happened in early Islam which worked
out differently. After moving to Medina Muhammad planned to
waylay a Meccan caravan, but his three hundred men were met by
a thousand of the bravest Meccans. Supposing that the Muslims
had 'let their Prophet die at the hands of the Quraish without
striking a blow for his safety'. That might have been the end of
Islam. As it was, they routed the Meccans, and 'Islam came into
the open and developed high-handedly with a good deal of
pride'.[2]

But Dr. Hussein finds it impossible to believe that surrender
could have been the end of Islam, and he feels that 'the history of

[1] C. F. D. Moule, *The Phenomenon of the New Testament*, 1967, p. 13; see
H. Grass, *Ostergeschenen und Osterberichte*, 1962, p. 243, 'we are concerned with
God's action in them and not merely with the products of their own imagina-
tion or reflection.'

[2] *City of Wrong*, p. 224.

Islam would probably have been identical with the history of Christianity, growing through submission, humility and heroic resistance to persecution.' Perhaps it would have been better that way, and Islam would have been freed from its Holy Wars. Dr. Hussein declares, despite other arguments, that 'there can be no doubt that the decision of the [Christian] disciples was the right one, by the criteria of revelation and religion. . . . Nor is there any doubt that they were mistaken in fearing the collapse of the Christian religion when their master was no more with them.'[1]

It is just at this point that the absence of belief in the Resurrection, or lack of understanding of its power, makes itself felt. For while it is admitted that the success of Christianity, despite the Cross, is due to 'things that transcend the capacity of the human mind fully to understand', yet this is not attributed clearly enough to the power of God, nor to the fact of the Resurrection. The evidence for the risen Christ is not simply the existence of the Church. The Resurrection was the act of God, but the fact that the Church progressed despite great opposition was due both to the experiences of the apostles and to the continuing power of the risen Lord among them.

The Church worships a living and not a dead Lord. This is where there is some truth in the objection to morbid attachment to images of a dead man, and why an empty cross is preferred by many Christians to a crucifix. In the eastern Churches the glorified Christ holds the central place in many paintings and mosaics, from St. Mark's in Venice to Hagia Sophia in Istanbul and beyond. Christ in glory, with his hand raised in blessing, or seated with his hand lifted up for teaching, recalls many pictures and images of the blessing and teaching Buddha. Christ is Holy Wisdom in Istanbul, as he was in the Parthenon in Athens when it was a church. Yet this Christ is not only a teacher, or a Logos, his hands and feet bear the 'tokens of his passion', and the Gospels that he carries are open at verses such as 'Come unto Me' or 'I am the Light of the World'. The Christian faith is in Christ crucified, but also risen and alive for evermore, and both of these beliefs are essential to the doctrine of the Incarnation.

[1] *City of Wrong*, p. 119.

UNIQUENESS AND ESCHATOLOGY

The uniqueness of Christ has always been part of the belief of traditional Christian theology. It is expressed by the epistle to the Hebrews in saying that Christ 'has been manifested now once, at the end of the ages' (9, 26). But the context here is that of the Cross, for he offered up himself 'once for all'. The uniqueness of Christ is seen first in his singularity as an individual historical man; much more in his identification with the sole Messiah who plays the central role in the establishment of the kingdom of God; but chiefly in his Death and Resurrection. In these latter ways Christ is quite different from any other religious figure.

The uniqueness of Christ has been stressed by Barthians who insist on the once-for-all-ness, *einmaligkeit*, the 'scandal of particularity', the breaking of the divine Word into history. Curiously enough while they are insistent upon the particularity of Christ, writers of this kind often repudiate attempts to establish the historical facts of the life of Jesus, and some of them are extreme Form Critics who almost deny that it is possible to have any historical knowledge of Jesus at all.

Emil Brunner, however, while he agrees that all Christian credal affirmations are 'mythological' in the sense that they must be inadequate descriptions of divine activity, yet speaks of the 'myth' of the Christian revelation as a unique and decisive event. He claims to accept the full historical personality of Jesus of Nazareth, and speaks of his gradual growth and development and his human limitations. This was in fact the way of the early Church, for precisely the men who knew the historical Jesus better than we can do were those who first came to worship him as Lord. It was these first Christians who spoke of the uniqueness of the Christ and his death 'once for all'.[1]

It is better to start with the human life and death of Christ in considering, as we shall do later, his relationship to other religious leaders who are also called unique. More general arguments for the uniqueness of Jesus are sometimes made, such as the one that instances his 'openness to every situation'.[2] But followers of the Buddha or Muhammad would claim this for their leaders, and

[1] *The Mediator*, pp. 328, 377.
[2] F. W. Dillistone in *Christ for Us Today*, p. 96.

221

they might well assert that they were open to some situations that Jesus never had to face.

More important is the claim that Christ is unique because of the eschatological context of his life and work. He came in the 'fulness of time', to inaugurate the 'last time', the *eschaton*, and so he must necessarily be unique. The claim is true, for Christian faith, but similar statements are made about other religious leaders. Krishna came in the last Kali age and, in another context, Muhammad was the Seal of the Prophets, the last and best Apostle.

Moreover, eschatology has implied a coming figure, who will destroy evil and establish righteousness. Krishna is to be followed by Kalkī, an apocalyptic figure bearing a flaming sword and riding a white horse. The Buddha of this era is to be succeeded by Maitreya, the expected bringer of fortune and right. Islam awaits the coming of the Mahdī or Messiah, or both. How different are these from the age-old Christian expectation of the Second Advent of Christ? And if Christ is to come again was his first coming unique? Or can it be assimilated to the theory of successive Avatars or Incarnations?

Such questions are strange to traditional Christology, but they are asked today in the light of new knowledge of the teachings of other religions. What think ye of Christ? means to many people, What think ye of Krishna and Buddha as well? Even when Christian faith accepts the uniqueness of Christ, that need not imply a lack of relationship to Avatars and Buddhas. In fact the relationship of Christianity to the other religions of the world is largely the relationship of Christ to other teachers. Are they all simply men, with particular religious and moral exhortations? At least this is not how their followers have seen them down the ages. And a denial of any 'religious' value to these figures might lead to a denial of Christian faith as well.

What is the relationship of Christ to other religions? Are they all, in their cultural contexts, preparations for the Gospel? Is Christ the 'Crown of Hinduism', to use the description popularized by J. N. Farquhar in 1913? Does he complete that religion, and in what ways? Or is he 'the Unknown Christ of Hinduism', as Fr. Panikkar said in 1964? What then of Krishna and his followers, and Buddha, and Muhammad? These are a few of the questions that demand consideration and that will be discussed in the following chapters.

16

Theophany:
Differences between Krishna and Christ

REPEATED AVATARS

In a previous chapter twelve characteristics were listed of classical Hindu beliefs about Avatars (page 120). Perhaps they were credited with too much but many modern Indian writers would claim all this, philosophers like Dasgupta and Radhakrishnan. Nearly all these characteristics might be held in some degree of the Christian Incarnation. Two great exceptions are the animal Avatars and, related to them, the repeated and successive Avatars. The theory of repeated Avatars must be looked at more closely now.

In the classical text in the Bhagavad-Gītā it is said clearly: 'I come into being age after age' (4, 8). This repeated Avatar seems to be quite different from the Incarnation and death of Christ 'once for all'. Zimmer says that the Avatar is not a unique, astounding entrance of the divine into mundane affairs, 'but a rhythmical event, conforming to the beat of the world ages. The saviour descends as a counterweight to the forces of evil during the course of every cyclic decline of mundane affairs, and his work is accomplished in a spirit of imperturbable indifference. The periodic incarnation of the Holy Power is a sort of solemn leitmotiv in the interminable opera of the cosmic process . . . to silence the disharmonies and to state again the triumphant themes of the moral order.'[1]

It is sometimes said in depreciation of Christianity that it teaches only one Incarnation, with a fierce exclusiveness that led

[1] H. Zimmer, *Philosophies of India*, 1951, p. 390.

to Inquisitions and wars, whereas Hinduism and Buddhism believe in many Avatars and Buddhas, in many great men, with a broad tolerance.[1] But it is not as simple as that, and it could be held that the difference is not so great as it appears, at least in the classical Indian doctrine. For while Krishna comes 'age after age' (*yuge-yuge*), yet these ages are separated by many thousands of years, so that the Avatar is *the* Incarnation for the present world era. And in the Gītā there is no suggestion that the Avatars are any other than the one Krishna. Further, Hindu devotees worship Krishna, or Rāma, or another, and many hold that their own special Avatar is the supreme divinity, as he is regarded in practised worship.

Similar belief and practice may be seen in Buddhism, at least in the Theravāda forms. There have been Buddhas in the past, and there will be Buddhas to come, of whom the eschatological figure Metteya is particularly favoured. But the Pāli texts affirm strongly that there is only one Buddha now, for this very long world eon. If there were two Buddhas the world could not support them, their followers would split into rival camps, and that would detract from the supremacy of the one Buddha who is sole teacher of gods and men.

It has been noted previously that uniqueness is a common claim of religious faith, perhaps an essential claim. This is found in religions that have no belief in Incarnation; it is in orthodox Judaism which holds that Moses was 'the chief of the prophets', and even more in Islam which regards Muhammad as 'the Seal of the Prophets', 'second only God', sinless and intercessor with God. This comparison is not meant to denigrate the importance of uniqueness for Christian faith, but rather to suggest its necessity for all faith. Uniqueness is a frequent phenomenon, if that is not an Irishism.

INCARNATION AND REINCARNATION

The Bhagavad-Gītā is the classical text for teaching the supremacy and uniqueness of Krishna. He is the Purushottama, the Supreme Spirit, manifested but identical with the eternal Brahman. Yet he

---

[1] See A. Huxley, quoted on p. 13.

appears in different ages, to restore order and harmony, and to bestow grace on his devotees. And the repeated Avatars are set in the context of the doctrine of reincarnation, for that is clearly stated.

> *Many births have passed for Me,*
> *And for you also, Arjuna:*
> *I know all of these*
> *But you do not know them.*   (4, 5)

The divine manifestation appears to be the same as that of men, in happening many times; the difference is that Krishna knows the details of all his previous births which the man Arjuna did not. Similarly at his enlightenment the Buddha looked back over his early lives, having now achieved perfect and more than divine knowledge. It might be concluded that God and man are basically identical, and that when Arjuna's ignorance is dispelled he will realize that he is the same as God. This conclusion would be natural to a monist, but the Gītā never says that Arjuna is God. It toys with monistic phrases and in one verse it even says that Krishna is Arjuna (Dhanamjaya, 10, 37), which is logical if he is all beings, but the reverse is never stated. Not only the terrible transcendental Vision (ch. 11), but also many exhortations to devotion and emphasis on 'coming to Me' show that religiously the Gītā is not fully monistic, and that there is an abiding difference between God and man, and this is not merely a matter of the present limited knowledge of Arjuna. Belief in reincarnation, which runs through the Gītā, does not fit easily into this theism, and it has affected the doctrine of Avatars.

Belief in reincarnation or transmigration (*samsāra*) was unknown to the Aryan priests of the Rig Vedic hymns, and when it appeared in the Upanishads it was clearly a new doctrine to the Brahmins. Yet such a belief is profoundly rooted in India, and writers like Zimmer consider that it formed part of the Indus Valley or non-Aryan level of religious thought, and was preserved in Jainism and Buddhism as well as entering Hinduism.[1]

The Gītā links the many births of Krishna with those of Arjuna. Yet there can be no power of Karma to bring the deity again into

[1] *Philosophies of India*, p. 184n.

the world. As Krishna says elsewhere, he continues 'in action' (*karmani*) but he is required to do nothing, and has nothing un-attained to gain, yet he continues to work to sustain the universe and to give an example of work to others (3, 22f.). So in the incarnational verses Krishna says that though he is unborn, and his self is eternal, yet he comes into being by his own mysterious power (4, 6). But Krishna is not bound by his earthly actions, for he sits as indifferent ('sitting in as sitting out'), unattached to actions. Fools that despise him in his human form do not know his higher state, as the great Lord of beings (9, 9f).

Theism modifies reincarnational theory, and this is further affected by the purpose of the Avatars. This purpose is to main-tain Dharma, uphold harmony, put down evil and restore good. So Krishna sends himself forth, 'whenever Right is languishing', apparently in any age and many times (4, 7). He is in his nature the divine being, not held by the wheel of reincarnation, and not determined by Karma. His incarnations have the purpose of world salvation, and they are different from those of Arjuna, not only by knowledge but by purpose and his very nature.

Avatar and Theophany

The successive Avatars of Hinduism are theophanies, manifesta-tions of the divine in visible form. Compared with the Christian Incarnation the Hindu Avatar doctrine has different presupposi-tions. The Avatar appears and disappears calmly and impassively. When he has subdued the forces of evil, says Zimmer, he 'with-draws from the phenomenal sphere as calmly, solemnly, and willingly as he descended. He never becomes the seeming tem-porary victim of the demon powers (as did Christ nailed to the Cross), but is triumphant in his passage, from beginning to end. The Godhead, in its very aloofness, does not in the least mind assuming temporarily an active role on the phenomenal plane of ever-active Nature.'[1]

In humanity and historicity the Avatar doctrines are weak. In the story of the Mahābhārata the gods went to Vishnu to plead that the earth might be freed from oppression, and so the god

[1] *Philosophies of India*, p. 390.

sent a portion (*aṁśa*) of himself, without diminishing his infinite essence. The same theme appears in the Rāmāyana. There may have been human chiefs called Krishna and Rāma, but the legends are so worked into the pattern of theophany that their lives really begin in heaven. They live and act on earth, but 'heaven is their home'. Krishna has some human traits, and many more appear in the Purānas, but even in the Gītā he has four arms (11, 16), and in the later myths he is a bewildering mixture of playboy and super-man. Rāma, too, while he grows from childhood to manhood, every so often reveals his divine majesty, and even when he bears suffering he does so with supernatural detachment.

There is never any suggestion that Krishna was *a man* among men, for he could not really divest himself of divine power. But Christian faith began with Jesus as a man, and we shall have to look further at this point. It can be remarked now that theologies which speak of Jesus as 'man', normal or typical man, but not 'a man', a historical individual, may well guarantee his divinity as an Avatar yet they appear to weaken the doctrine of Incarnation in the flesh.

An Indian Christian writer, V. Chakkarai, who has written of *Jesus the Avatar* says that Christian theory and experience of the Incarnation 'differ in essential respects from the Hindu'. For the 'avatars are phenomena of recurring nature, and the periodicity and multiplicity of these divine self-manifestations, if we may so call them, are their striking characteristics'. Yet he finds the real difference from Christian belief in this, that Rāma and Krishna were temporary and passed away; having done their duties they left this world, the one through entering a river and the other being killed by a hunter. The Avatars come and go, from time to time, but there is no abiding and permanent presence among men, whereas 'the Spirit of Jesus is incarnated again and again in human hearts.'[1] There is truth in this, but there is danger also of obscuring the faith in the 'once for all' work of Christ, so that he also becomes a theophany or a series of appearances or presences. This writer prefers the term Avatar to Incarnation and historicity, for the latter have a material and unique character that does not apply to Avatars.

[1] V. Chakkarai, *Jesus the Avatār*, 1930, pp. 136f.

In the classical Hindu epics of the Mahābhārata and Rāmāyana there is little that can safely be taken as historical. Neither of them has the life history of a real man, comparable with that given in the Synoptic Gospels. It is true that the later Purānas are full of details of the wondrous works of the infant prodigy Krishna and his other heroic and amorous adventures, and these tales are dwelt upon with loving care by countless Hindus. There is a living Krishna here, but the narratives compare with the early church apocrypha rather than with the Gospels, and the inventiveness of the stories testifies to the poetic imagination of their authors rather than to the life and death of a real man.

THEOPHANY AND INCARNATION

Christian tradition does not exclude theophanies, for there are many manifestations of God in the Old and New Testaments, through angelic messengers and divine visions. But none of these is an Incarnation, historical and in 'flesh'. The Avatar doctrines, it has been seen, begin from above, with the god who comes down to make brief appearances on earth, age after age. But Christian doctrine did not begin there; it started from the historical Jesus, and because every individual is unique the doctrine of the uniqueness of Jesus is grounded in this particular humanity, though it goes far beyond it when considering his work and the final significance of his person.

No doubt to the thought of many previous ages the Incarnation began in heaven, like the Avatars, and such a faith has often been expressed in verse. Milton in *Paradise Lost* depicted the heavenly Christ offering himself to his Father in place of Adam, even before Adam's sin:

> *Behold me then, me for him, life for life*
> *I offer, on me let thine anger fall;*
> *Account me Man: I for his sake will leave*
> *Thy bosom, and this glory next to thee*
> *Freely put off.* (3, 236f.)

In the olden days the proof of the Incarnation and the heavenly origin of Christ would have been taken as evident from the

Gospels, particularly John. Jesus taught that he was God, it was said, and had come down from heaven. But many people would now dispute whether the Bible ever baldly calls Jesus God, or even puts the title Son of God on his lips. The difference between the Fourth Gospel and the Synoptics, however much it may be played down, is crucial here.

With the much greater study of the historical Jesus in modern times, it is perhaps easier to approach the Gospel story and see the human Jesus than at any time since the first century. This brings us closer to the viewpoint of the disciples, who saw Jesus first as a man but came to believe in him as the exalted Lord at the Resurrection. So some modern non-Barthian Christology makes an approach 'from below', beginning with the historical man Jesus and proceeding to show grounds for faith in his divinity. No doubt God was in Christ 'from above to below', but to understand where faith started we must begin 'below', where we are, in the world in which Jesus lived as a man. Christology did not commence with a story of an Incarnation from heaven, but that background was assumed later when interpretations were made of the 'flesh' of Jesus among men.[1]

The first disciples, who knew Jesus as a man, had no knowledge of his pre-existence and such a belief was not necessary to their faith, or to the salvation of the people who were healed in body and soul by him. Later in the development of doctrine the pre-existence of Christ was thought to be almost as important as his post-existence. Yet the Church never taught that the *humanity* of Jesus had any pre-existence in heaven or that it was co-eternal with God. His humanity is what Jesus shared with us, consubstantial with ourselves, and belonging to the created order of things. It was a real and limited humanity, and therefore it can hardly be said that there was any 'conscious continuity of life and memory between Jesus of Nazareth and the pre-existent Son'.[2]

There is a great difference here from the Avatars. In the Gītā Krishna says that he knows every one of his previous births, and in Tulsī Dās's *Holy Lake of the Acts of Rāma* the child Avatar

[1] See G. G. O'Collins, 'The Christology of Wolfhart Pannenberg', in *Religious Studies*, 1967, pp. 369ff.

[2] D. M. Baillie, *God was in Christ*, p. 150.

displayed his wondrous form to his mother, with a myriad universes in every hair of his body, making her realize that the Father of the world had become her son.

MAN-GOD

If Christology needs to begin from below, with the historical Jesus, and the earliest Christian faith arose gradually in this way, can the same be said of the Avatars of Hinduism? Or is faith in Christ more akin to that which is accorded to the Buddha, or even to Muhammad? These were no doubt historical persons, who will be discussed later with the faith related to them, but for the moment the Avatars will be considered.

It is a modern Hindu belief that the Avatars are outstanding human beings, or manifestations of God in them. Rāmakrishna said that 'they are human beings with extraordinary original powers and entrusted with a Divine commission. Being heirs of Divine powers and glories, they form a class of their own. To this class belong the Incarnation of God like Christ, Krishna, Buddha, and Chaitanya and their devotees of the highest order.'[1] And Vivekānanda said that 'in the history of mankind there come these Messengers, and from their very birth their mission is found and formed. The whole plan is there, laid down, and you see them swerving not one inch from that. . . . Do you not remember in your own scriptures the authority with which Jesus speaks.'[2]

If the Avatars are only men then their numbers might be legion, and any outstanding religious personality could be conscripted into their ranks. So Rāmakrishna said again, 'An Avatara is a human messenger of God . . . whenever there is any waning of religion in any part of the world, God sends his Avatara there to guard virtue and foster its growth. . . . So when a Saviour incarnates, innumerable are the men who find salvation by taking refuge in him.'[3]

Despite superficial resemblances to and borrowings from the Gītā, this point of view is fundamentally opposed to that of the

[1] *The Gospel of Ramakrishna*, 1947 edn., p. 300.
[2] *Complete Works of Swami Vivekananda*, 1931, iv, p. 118.
[3] *Sayings of Sri Ramakrishna*, 1925, pp. 135ff.

scripture. For Krishna is not a 'human messenger', and his successive appearances are not human geniuses but divine theophanies. Moreover in the Gītā other traditional Avatars which are
mentioned elsewhere in the Mahābhārata, such as Rāma, are not
named as such. It is the Blessed Lord, Krishna, who comes from
age to age, because he is the Supreme Eternal Person and highest
Brahman. So his Avatars are divine and not human.

Of course there is no reason why the Avatar title should not be
applied to human beings, provided that a new theory is worked
out for them, but it would be better to use another name. It
should be quite clear that the 'human messenger' is not the Avatar
of the Epics or Purānas, and a limitless multiplicity of Avatars
would tend to destroy whatever there is of value in the doctrine.
Ninian Smart, who is one of the few writers to discuss Incarnation in the framework of the comparative study of religions,
takes the concept of *avatāra* to be that of a descending Deity who
has his proper abode beyond the manifested world. But he then
considers that 'feature of many religions' which holds certain
human beings or beings of human appearance to be divine. And
the argument goes on to examine the claims for deified men, or
men who are 'candidates for divinity', remarking on characteristics of holy men which tend to assimilate them to the divine.
These criteria are applied to the Incarnation, and to some degree
to Buddhist belief, but while they may be suitable for modern
Hinduism we have seen that they do not properly apply to the
classical Avatars.[1]

Swami Akhilananda, a modern Indian writer who presents
what he calls a *Hindu View of Christ*, begins with a chapter on
'Christ, an Incarnation'. The indefinite article is significant. He
opens with statements from Rāmakrishna and Vivekānanda about
Avatars as human beings, but then hovers between humanity and
divinity in confusing ways. Incarnation is used interchangeably
with Avatar, as though the two terms meant the same thing. Incarnations have 'a little trace of human characteristics', but 'at the
same time their divinity shines forth like the midday sun'. They
'assume human forms', and live in the midst of men who are
steeped in ignorance and are unaware of their true relationship to

[1] *Reasons and Faiths*, 1958, pp. 108f.

God, while the incarnations 'are fully aware of their divinity from the time of their birth'. They know that they have a purpose to fulfil and it will be accomplished 'no matter what people do to them'.[1]

According to this writer the difference between divine incarnations and ordinary saints is that the latter are 'at first bound souls and then they become illumined', whereas incarnations are the true embodiment of divine light and power from the beginning of their lives. Incarnations are conscious of God without any struggle, though it is an effort for them to bring their minds down to this plane and teach others how to attain superconsciousness, yet they sacrifice themselves lovingly to achieve this goal. Because of human involvement in ignorance, and inordinate affections, misunderstandings arise and 'when incarnations come antagonism and disharmony can be observed in families'.

Incarnations again, it is said, because they have 'a little touch of the human element' may have 'a kind of desire or longing in them', but as they are free souls they are not bound by desires and can give them up at any moment. 'When they depart from the world, they feel no pain or agony because they are leaving it; there is no feeling of separation.' This statement is followed by a discussion of whether Jesus fulfilled his purpose or felt disappointment, and the conclusion is reached that 'divine incarnations, such as Jesus, are not frustrated when they see no immediate results of their work'.

It is a small step from here to say that 'as an incarnation, God sees the past, present, and future. . . . Does anyone think that Jesus did not know the world's future?' He must have known what was going to happen, since he had perfect knowledge and lived in the superconsciousness of God. So Jesus was never disappointed, for he came to show how man can become God-conscious and his purpose was fulfilled when even a small number of people were inspired by him.

This writer concludes that his Hindu view is nearer to Christian orthodoxy than to liberalism, though it may be doubted whether he either understands Christian orthodoxy or represents Hindu orthodoxy. He holds that Christ was 'unique in comparison with

[1] *Hindu View of Christ*, 1949, pp. 24ff.

ordinary men', as against those liberals who think that all men are divine, but he claims that there are 'many special revelations and special manifestations in the form of divine incarnations'. The distinctions between revelations and manifestations are not discussed.

There is no doubt that many modern Hindus, differing from the exclusiveness of classical writers and Brahmins on the unique authority of their own scriptures, are willing to recognize the divine inspiration of other sacred books and the divine natures of founders of other religions. Christ and Buddha, and to a lesser degree Muhammad and others, find themselves brought into the scope of an all-embracing Hinduism. The Avatar faith seems ideally suited to include these teachers, who have come age after age, to different peoples and countries. But it is an Avatar faith approached from the human end, and almost as misunderstood as the Incarnation. The Man-God is acceptable, but not the God-man. The Oriental Christ, it has been said, is the Christ of human love and grace, and not the western Christ of dogma and formalism. There is good here, but another doctrine keeps coming in. 'Dogma apart', says another, Hindus today would agree that Jesus was an ideal man in almost every respect. He is the wise man who knows things as they really are, he is in the perfect relationship of superconsciousness to God, he was indifferent to success and undisturbed by the Crucifixion(!). He was always composed like the true Yogi portrayed in the Gītā as unperturbed in joy or sorrow, the same to foe and friend, indifferent to results. There is plenty of dogma here, even if it is not the same as that of orthodoxy.

When one protests that this indifferent yogic Christ is a radical distortion of the Gospel picture, and that the particular elements of the life of Jesus should guarantee him some kind of uniqueness, one is met with a sweeping claim, such as that made by Vivekānanda, which in effect set up another intransigent dogmatism. In his famous address to the Parliament of Religions in Chicago in 1893 he said, 'Vedānta alone, under some form or another, is fit to become the universal religion of man. For, while all the other great religions of the world are based on the lives of their founders, Vedānta alone is based on principles. It is absolutely impersonal.

Its authority is not affected by the historicity of any particular man.' But perhaps that impersonality and lack of historicity are its most serious weaknesses, and principles are open to the most subjective interpretations. In any case, this is an admission of the radical cleavage between unhistorical religion and the Incarnation.

KRISHNA AND CHRIST

Vedānta is impersonal and based on monistic principles that logically deny the possibility of a subject–object relationship between God and man. In reaction against this the Śvetāśvatara Upanishad, the Epics, the Purānas, medieval mystics, Śaivism and Śaktism, all testified in India to the need for faith and devotion centred round the gracious activities of personal gods and Avatars. Hindu religion, as distinct from some of its philosophy, experienced the same necessity for personal faith that was felt in Buddhism, Islam and Christianity.

But are the personal Avatars so different in their nature and context as to forbid comparison with the Incarnation? Has Christ no point of contact with Krishna, so that once the differences have been established there is no more to say?

Belief in both Avatars and Incarnation arose in theistic contexts, so that they reveal God. In this they are different from Buddhism, which ignores God, and from Islam which denies Incarnation. That God has personal relationships with man, and appears in the world through a human form, is common ground to Hinduism and Christianity, and here at least they are closer to each other than to other religions. It is the theistic background that has made it possible for Krishna to be loosely called an Incarnation, and Christ an Avatar, however inadequately.

The God that is revealed is both transcendent and manifested, great and gracious. He is not the impersonal divine principle that can only be indicated by negatives, nor the Wholly Other that cannot be compared with anything else. By their nature and lives the Avatars and the Incarnation reveal the nature of God who, although he is 'unmanifest beyond the manifest', yet appears in a human body careless of the scorn of fools. Therefore the man who loves the manifested God is dear to him, 'dear beyond measure', and the highest bliss is found in coming to God and in union with him.

Some moral distinctions can be made between Christ and Krishna. They may seem important to those who have been trained in Biblical morality, and though in the past it has not often been argued that a high moral character is evidence for Incarnation, yet such an approach would not be unacceptable today, and there may be more in it than appears at first sight. Here the Christ of the Gospels seems far superior to the Krishna of the popular Purānas. But in the Bhagavad-Gītā the lofty character of Krishna is always in evidence; he is the supreme Yogi, the sustainer of Right, indifferent to the rewards of actions, yet loving his devotee. The Krishna of the Gītā, at least, is God speaking to man, in long dispassionate dialogue, so as to bring him to the supreme knowledge that will set him free from the illusions and defilements of this world.

This high moral note was blurred in some later devotion, which became ecstatic and erotic, and by its excesses it alienated thoughtful modern writers like Tagore, so that they repudiated Avatar doctrine while holding to the grace and personal revelation of God. At the same time the Gītā has had a renewed popularity among Indian intellectuals, partly due to the influence of Gāndhi, and its strong ethical notes, proceeding from the Avatar Krishna, have been influential in modern times.

The moral character of Christ is different from that of Krishna, and it is one of the most attractive elements of the Gospel. Yet while the ethical principles of the Sermon on the Mount remain a great challenge to mankind, these are not the whole Gospel. Nor is Christ simply a revelation of a moral Deity, for if this were so perhaps a theophany would suffice, or even if revelation demanded a real Incarnation yet its meaning might consist only in moral attitudes.

The difference between Christ and Krishna has been seen by various writers to lie in the distinctive histories of Avatar and Incarnation. J. N. Farquhar, who was one of the most influential apologists for Christianity in India in the earlier years of this century, said bluntly that 'the Krishna of the Gītā is a myth, but

Jesus Christ is a historical person'. And he added that 'he is a historical person; and he is the only man who ever actually claimed to be the God-man. He called himself the Son of Man and the Son of God, and he was crucified because he would not give up the claim.' Farquhar paid tribute to the Gītā, but said that it was purely imaginative, and its appeal lay in the fact that 'man needs an incarnate Saviour'. Elsewhere he said that 'Jesus is the reality of which the Gītā gives an imaginative picture', and that 'the author of the Gītā would have been a Christian, had he known Jesus'.[1]

Modern critical study of the Gospels makes it much less easy to make the confident assertion that the Gospels are historical while the Gītā is not. The Gospels, even conservatives admit, are documents of faith and opinions differ widely as to their reliability as historical material. That Jesus called himself Son of God, and even more that he was crucified because he held to the claim to be God-man, would be severely criticized today.[2]

A foundation of Gospel history, without holding to every detail, is maintained by theologians who accept the legitimacy of literary criticism and build on moderate conclusions. Tillich makes his affirmation of the uniqueness of Jesus, compared with other religious figures, as that of a historical event. 'The biblical picture of Jesus is that of a unique event. Jesus appears as an individual beside others, but unique in his destiny, in every single trait of his character, and in his historical setting. It was just this concreteness and incomparable uniqueness of the "real" picture which gave Christianity its superiority over mystery cults and Gnostic visions. A real, individual life shines through all his utterances and actions. In comparison, the divine figures of the mystery cults remain abstract, without the fresh colours of a life really lived.'[3]

There is a good deal of truth in this, in the individuality of the words and deeds of Jesus, and they are clearly superior to those of the leading figures in most mystery cults of the ancient world. But when we come to Krishna it is not so easy. It is true that

[1] *Permanent Lessons of the Gītā*, 1912, p. 31; and E. J. Sharpe, *Not to Destroy but to Fulfil*, 1965, p. 200.
[2] *God was in Christ*, pp. 57f.; but see C. F. D. Moule on the importance of the Gospels as narratives, in *The Phenomenon of the New Testament*, pp. 100f.
[3] *Systematic Theology*, ii, p. 174.

Theophany: Differences between Krishna and Christ

Krishna in the Gītā may be regarded as a myth, or at most a theophany. Krishna speaks, but he does very little else, apart from transfiguring himself into terrifying cosmic forms. But the Krishna cult as it became popular in India depended far more upon the Purānas, and especially the Bhāgavata Purāna, for its knowledge of Krishna. And here there are many details which are cherished, so that the god appears as a human hero, sometimes all too human.

In the popular Krishna legends there is a constant mingling of human and divine. When the baby Krishna was laid to sleep he cried and kicked his feet, but these tiny feet, soft like sprouts, capsized a cart and broke its shafts. One day when his mother placed the baby on the ground a huge demon carried him away in a whirlwind, but the child caught the monster by the neck and throttled it. When Krishna's companions said that he had been eating mud, he denied it and told his mother to look into his mouth; there she saw the universe, earth and air and sky, moving and unmoving. Then Krishna stole the butter, and in guilt his eyes seemed to tremble in fear so that his mother tried to bind him with a rope 'like an ordinary person', but the rope was always too short till the god in pity for her allowed himself to be bound, and then he pulled down two trees to free himself.

These legends cannot be history, yet they are treasured by millions of believers, who dwell with love on every detail and consider them to have happened 'historically'. Apocrypha may be history in the eyes of faith, and comparable stories that are told about the Buddha and Muhammad demonstrate the importance of story to religion, which is not satisfied with abstract principles.

For Tillich it is not mere stories that are significant but the 'unique event' of Christ. The Gospel has 'the fresh colours of a life really lived', but it demonstrates in that life his 'historical destiny and the tensions of finite freedom'. So the New Testament is not concerned simply to tell 'the story of a uniquely interesting man', and the Gospels are not mere biographies. The picture they give is that of 'the one who is the Christ and who, for this reason, has universal significance'. The individual characteristics of the historical Jesus are not hidden, but they are related to his nature as the Christ'.[1]

[1] ibid., ii, pp. 174f.

Tillich affirms that 'Christology is a function of soteriology', for Christ cannot be understood apart from his work as Saviour. This is rooted in history, but it is not mere story or morality. The problem of salvation raises the question of the nature of Christ and gives guidance to the answer. Christ cannot be understood apart from his work, and on the other hand that work is not 'a kind of priestly technique' complete apart from his person.

A similar point was made by Otto in his specific comparison of the Indian and Christian religions of grace. Christ is called the Mediator between God and man, in revealing the transcendent Deity, but such a function of mediation is found in many religions, both historical and unhistorical. 'But that Christ was a "propitiator" is the profoundest meaning of his coming, and all speculative doctrines about his person derive their special meaning and the theological criterion of their validity from this fact.'[1]

Belief in a 'propitiator' involves the concepts of human sin and divine forgiveness. The idea of sin or evil (*pāpa*) is present in Hinduism, as it probably is in all personal theisms, and it appears even in Buddhism when relationships to the original or eternal Buddha are sufficiently personalized. Salvation or liberation (*moksha*) is not only release from the troubles of temporal existence but from the 'knots of the heart', which bind man to evil but can be unbound by grace. So there are conversions from evil living to the life of detachment or devotion.

Yet the sense of sin rarely has the same weight in India as in Christianity. This can be exaggerated, but the hard facts of evil must be faced. To Hindus sin too easily means trouble (*kleśa*) or pain, and not the guilt of cruel or wicked action. Repentance brings calm detachment rather than reconciliation with God and man. The power of Karma is a chain which must be broken, but it is not a 'fall' which is a perversion or defilement of the inner nature, and a helplessness which demands a Saviour.

Therefore Indian ideas of a Saviour differ too. The Lord, Krishna or Śiva, may 'forgive' men who come for refuge, but this is done by overlooking their faults, in leniency or indulgence. The Lord has compassion on his devotees, and he is sorry for the sufferings that they endure in the round of transmigration or

[1] *India's Religion of Grace*, 105f.

through their own foolishness. In the Gītā Krishna says that even if you are the worst of sinners you can cross over the sea of evil by the ship of wisdom. And, more personally, that he is the Saviour from the sea of transmigration for all those who cast their actions on to him and meditate on him with unswerving Yoga (4, 36; 12, 7).

In Christian faith God so loved the world that he sent his Son to save us. God was in Christ, and while we were yet sinners Christ died for us. It is the death of Christ that is the final act, the revelation that is more than a principle but is a unique event, the reconciliation that is the act of God himself. The life of Krishna ended with a mistaken shot by a hunter, or a bolt from old age. The human life of Christ not only ended on the Cross, but it is in the light of the Crucifixion that all the life before it takes on new meaning.

17

Docetism, in Buddhology and Christology

BUDDHAS AND AVATARS

The Avatar beliefs of Hinduism have apparent parallels in Jainism and Buddhism, at least in the later stages of the development of these beliefs. The twenty-two Avatars of the Bhāgavata Purāna compare with the twenty-four Jinas and twenty-five Buddhas. Yet the latter two lists are compiled on the principles of successive sages or superhuman enlightened ones, rather than the theistic theme of continuing appearances of the divinity on earth. Jainism and Buddhism have been called 'transtheistic', but this term would more properly be applied to Upanishadic monism which transcended personal theism. In Jainism and Buddhism there is no 'theos' to transcend, at least in the singular. There are plenty of gods about, and the Buddha is 'god above the gods', but these divinities play no significant role in the way to enlightenment; they are angels or 'gentlemen', but not saviours.

Yet although the theory may be weak, the function of a Buddha is similar to that of an Avatar. Just because he is above the gods, the Buddha takes the place of a supreme Deity in the affections of his followers. To these faithful ones there are numerous Buddhas, but in practice among the Theravāda it is the sole Buddha of this present world eon that is significant. And while the Mahāyāna have far more Buddhas and Bodhisattvas than even the widest Avatar lists, yet by a principle of economy or henotheism there may be a concentration upon one particular object of worship.

Although the basis of Buddhism is not theistic, in the strict sense, yet some parallels with the Christian doctrine of Incarnation have often been suggested. This is because Gautama Buddha, far more than Krishna, can be claimed as a historical figure. Round his person multitudes of legends gathered, and Docetism flourished in the most extravagant forms. Yet there was a basic history, and this gave Buddhism a concern with history that is lacking in ancient Hinduism. It is often said that ancient India was not interested in history, and it contrasts strongly with ancient Israel, Greece or China. But it is not surprising that interest in history was shown by the monks of Jainism and Buddhism. The Mahāparinirvāna Sūtra may claim to be at least partly historical. and the Pāli Chronicles of Ceylon may be even more so. The Jains and Buddhists had two principal motives for recording history; the first motive was the earthly life of their teachers and the second was the universal mission which provided a purpose to history. They accepted history, not as a cycle of endless and almost meaningless occurrences, but rather as a succession of waves in the progress of the doctrine. So there was an interest in the past and a purpose for the present and future. In this respect they are closer to Christianity than some aspects of Hinduism.

BIBLICAL PARALLELS

Possible Buddhist influence upon the story of Christ has often been suggested, and at least it may be possible in the Christian apocrypha, among the Gnostics and especially Basilides. Whether there was a Buddhist colony in Alexandria has at least 'not yet been finally disproved.'[1] It was in Alexandria that the first awareness of Buddhism appeared in Christian literature. Clement of Alexandria, at the end of the second century, wrote of 'those of the Indians who obey the precepts of Boutta, whom through exaggeration of his dignity they honour as a god'. Clement also referred to the Brahmins, and to the relic stūpas and celibacy of the Gymnosophists, a title probably indicating the naked Jain monks whom, he said, 'know not marriage nor the begetting of children'. Origen made several references that suggest Buddhist influences, which will be considered later.[2]

[1] H. de Lubac, *Aspects of Buddhism*, E.T. 1953, p. 87.
[2] *Stromata* I, 15, 71; 3, 7. See E. Benz, 'Indische Einflüsse auf die frühchristliche Theologie', in *Abhandlungen der Akademie der Wissenschaften*, etc., no. 3, 1951.

Jerome in the fourth century supported his contention that virginity was a higher state than marriage, by the rather dubious expedient of showing that virginity was so well esteemed among the heathen that some of them believed in virgin births. He said that there was a belief 'among the Gymnosophists of India that the Buddha, founder of their doctrine, was born of a virgin and emerged from her side'.[1] We have seen earlier (p. 135) that in some of the Theravāda stories the Buddha's mother, a married queen, simply had a dream of a white elephant and gave birth after ten months to the child while she was standing under a tree. Then in the Mahāyāna she was secluded from her husband and later gave birth from her side. Even here she was not a virgin, and although some, but not all, of the stories may be pre-Christian there is little likelihood of any connection with the Gospels or even with the apocrypha. And the real Gymnosophists, the Jains, are even less likely to be the source for belief in a virgin birth (see pp. 183f.).

Some other Buddhist stories seem to have closer resemblances to Christianity, and of these the most striking is that of the old sage Asita, the 'Buddhist Simeon'. Admittedly there is some parallel in the situations of Simeon and Asita; in both instances predictions are made by an old man of the marvellous future of the the new-born child. Yet the differences are far more notable. Asita was an old *rishi* who lived on the side of a peak in the Himalayas and his practice of Yoga had given him miraculous powers, so that he heard the gods announcing the birth of the Buddha. With his divine eye he saw all India and the baby Bodhisattva in his father's house, bearing the thirty-two marks of great men. Asita flew through the air to the palace, circumambulated the child, and declared that he would either become a universal monarch or a Buddha. Then he burst into tears because he would be too old to witness the future illumination of the child, who would in fact become a Buddha. After being gratified with food, he took the air journey back home. The setting in the Gospel is quite different. Simeon lived in Jerusalem, and went to the temple by divine guidance when Jesus was carried there. He took the baby in his arms and blessed God that he could now die

---

[1] *Contra Joviniam* 1, 42.

in peace, for he had seen the salvation which had been prepared before all peoples.

The Buddha was not taken to a temple, in the canonical texts. But in the late Legend of Aśoka the young Bodhisattva was carried into a temple of the gods, at which all of them fell down at his feet so that the child received the title of Devātideva, 'god superior to the gods'. And in the Mahāvastu when the child was taken to bow his head in the temple of the goddess Abhayā, he presented only his feet while the goddess herself bowed down to the child. Some writers have compared this story with the apocryphal tale of Pseudo-Matthew, a Latin compilation perhaps of the eighth century, wherein Mary and Jesus on the flight to Egypt lodged in a temple which had three hundred and sixty-five gods, and all the idols fell to the ground before him, fulfilling the prophecy of Isaiah that all the idols of Egypt would be moved at the presence of the Lord. But the purpose of the Buddhist story is quite different; far from wishing to overthrow the gods the Buddha wanted to teach them and bring them to take refuge in himself.[1]

The Buddha was tempted by Māra on various occasions, and so it has seemed easy to describe him as fasting in the wilderness, defeating his tempter, and receiving the ministries of angels, like Jesus in the Gospels. But the Buddha was not in the wilderness. The Bo-tree was in a pleasant spot near a river and adjacent to the famous Vaishnavite shrine of Gāyā. The demonic Māra tried to persuade the Buddha to renounce his austerities, failed, returned again with his daughters to stop him preaching to mankind, and after further defeat reappeared at intervals till the end of his life. It was the creator god Brahmā himself who came from heaven to implore the Buddha to preach. In contrast, the Gospel story gives three temptations from Satan, each of which was defeated by a verse from scripture.

Some of the stories in Christian and Buddhist traditions have been explained as borrowings, and as Buddhism was earlier by four or five centuries, the assumption was that Christianity was influenced by it. Estimates of the number of Buddhist-Christian parallels have varied, from fifty to one, the favourite survivor

[1] E. Lamotte, *Histoire du Bouddhisme indien*, p. 741.

being the Asita-Simeon analogy. But, as Thomas remarks, 'in proportion to the investigator's direct knowledge of the Buddhist sources the number seems to decrease'.[1] Whether there are any links or not, the chief events of the lives of Christ and the Buddha, birth, vocation and death, the very items that would be affected by comparison, disappear from the list of possible influences altogether.

Some writers explain similarities by what Martin Dibelius called '*a law of biographical analogy*'. He says that at bottom there is 'a fixed idea of the life of a holy man; such a man may neither be born nor die without the significance of the event being proclaimed from heaven. ... Divine powers are always ready to help him in stress and to proclaim his merits. Many points of agreement between Buddha-legends and the Jesus-legends . . . arise, not from borrowing, but from this law of biographical analogy.'[2]

It is difficult to see why such analogy should be dignified with the title of 'law'. It need not be denied that there have been tendencies to glorify great men, but what is important is to affirm that under later interpretations there are real historical figures. Then the different contexts must be examined, and the characteristics of the figures brought out, without reference to analogy or borrowings. Foucher, who does not hesitate to dissect the narratives critically, says, 'if instead of reasoning in the abstract, you confront the corresponding passages . . . you will see that, under the apparent conformity of preoccupations or of situations, neither the letter nor (what is more important) the spirit of the two texts, once placed side by side, resemble each other the least in the world.'[3]

DOCETISM

Buddhism is full of Docetic ideas and the significance of the attitude behind them will be considered again in the closing chapter. If they did not influence the Gospels the possibility that Buddhist ideas may have affected later Christian thought cannot be ruled

[1] E. J. Thomas, *The Life of Buddha*, p. 248.
[2] M. Dibelius, *From Tradition to Gospel*, E.T. 1934, pp. 108f.
[3] A. Foucher, *La Vie du Bouddha*, 1949, p. 21, these lines are absent from the English translation of Foucher's book.

out. There is the extraordinary fact that the Christian saints Bar-
laam and Josaphat, never officially canonized but commemorated
in the calendar, were Buddhist originals, Josaphat being Bodhisattva or Buddha.[1] Before that, Docetic ideas may have come
from the east into the Acts of John of the second century where
a disciple said that he often desired to witness the footprint of
Jesus 'whether it appeared on the earth: for I saw him as it were
lifting up himself from the earth'. Similarly the Mahāyāna
Buddhists had said that the Supreme of Men always walked without touching the ground, for mountains rose and subsided as he
walked over them and the soles of his feet were not stained by dust.[2]

However, a fundamental difference emerges between Christian
and Buddhist Docetism, as these and other possible parallels are
studied. It is that whereas in Christianity Docetism was regarded
as heretical and gradually weakened, though it did not die out
completely, in Buddhism it increased and remained acceptable to
a large body of orthodox Buddhists of all schools. In the early
stories of the birth of the future Buddha his married mother had
a dream of an elephant, which her husband interpreted symbolically, but later texts made this into a general law by which all
Buddhas of past and future enter their mothers' wombs in the
form of a white elephant. We have seen (pp. 136f.) that the Pāli
texts retain human traits of the historical Buddha. Ānanda took
pity on his master's infirmities and ministered to him; but in later
tradition Ānanda was accused of slander for imagining that the
Tathāgata's body could suffer, for it was a body of diamonds.
Before his enlightenment, it was said, the Buddha had a human
body which could be fed, could change and die, but before his
Nirvāna his body was made of diamonds, it had no passions, no
birth and no death.[3] The Lotus Sūtra declares that the Buddha did
not die, 'it was a device of mine'. The objection that men revered
the relics of his body is overruled as an 'opinion', a right aspiration, but based on ignorance of his true nature. Like the Avatars,
'repeatedly am I born in the land of the living'.[4] Later idealists

[1] See D. M. Lang. *The Wisdom of Balahvar*, 1957.
[2] M. R. James, *The Apocryphal New Testament*, pp. 252f.; Mahāvastu, 168.
[3] H. de Lubac, *Aspects of Buddhism*, pp. 119, 177.
[4] Saddharma-Puṇḍarīka, 15, 7f.

said that the Buddha might appear as a man but his body surpassed all the worlds. That which appeared on earth was the *nirmāna-kāya*, a fictitious body, and the conclusion was reached that the Buddha never came into the world, and never taught Dharma, for there were no beings to be taught.

In contrast to this massive Docetism in Buddhism, the parallel tendency in Christianity was diffused and condemned by the councils of the Church. The establishment of the canon of the New Testament enabled men to distinguish broadly between the historical basis and later apocryphal and magical tales. Officially the Church rejected Docetism and this affected even the propagators of such a view. The heretic Marcion thought that the body of Christ was pure appearance, but his followers had to admit that it was a real body though composed especially from cosmic elements. The church councils regularly affirmed the humanity of Christ, as well as his divinity. No doubt a good deal of popular Docetism remained, and it tainted theology and devotion all down history. Popular writers and artists explained the supremacy of Christ by treating his life as that of a god in a human body, rather than a really human life with limitations of growth and ignorance, temptation and struggle. Perhaps it is only today that theologians can confidently speak of 'the end of Docetism', and claim that practically all modern thinkers take the full humanity of Jesus more seriously than has been done since the first century.

Yet it seems that the Buddha was a historical figure, and much is made of this fact by modern apologists who say that Gautama was a man, with nothing supernatural about him, and his teaching was a simple ethic which should be acceptable to the rationalistic western world. The trouble is that this is not how the Buddha is viewed, or ever has been viewed, in any of the eastern schools of traditional Buddhism, Theravāda or Mahāyāna. The Buddha is not a god, a *deva*, but he is superior to all exalted human and divine beings, and is called the super-god (*atideva*), and the god beyond the gods (*devātideva*). He has all the qualities that go with divinity and supremacy, but he is not the originator of the universe, for such an idea does not appear in the theory of cyclic rounds of emergence and dissolution.

The Buddha is not an Avatar, in the sense of a theophany or

incarnation of a deity upon the earth. Yet there is a belief in re-incarnation which is close to incarnation. All Buddhists believe that the Buddha became such after more than five hundred previous lives on earth. From his bliss in the Tushita heaven he looked down to the earth and decided to be born for the last time, and many legends were told of his voluntary incarnation which is regarded as a great act of renunciation. The Mahāparinirvāna Sūtra says that he consciously and deliberately left his form 'in the heaven of delight and descended into his mother's womb', whereupon the earth shook and trembled violently. This has been compared with Christian story: the heavenly preparations for descent to earth, the choice and purity of the mother, marvels that happened at the time of birth, the superhuman incarnate life, and so on. But even if one grants the human incarnation of the Buddha, there is no God manifest in him. If Nirvāna is the Buddhist goal and divine substitute, he is hardly Nirvāna-become-flesh. Perhaps he does incarnate Dharma and is closely identified with it. But there is a wide difference between this and the Christian faith in God who so loves the world that he comes in person to seek and save the lost.[1]

The Buddha was not a god, but was he regarded as a man by Buddhists? There is a Pāli dialogue which has been translated, 'are you a god? are you a man?' and giving a negative reply each time. But this is seen now as a mistranslation, for the future tense is used, 'will you become?' (*bhavissati*). So the Buddha does not reply 'I am not' (these things), but 'I shall not become them'. This clearly means that 'he will not again "become" any of these creatures, having destroyed the basis of rebirth'.[2]

PERSON AND WORK

The Buddha may be compared with Christ not only, and perhaps very little, in historical life and work, but more importantly in glorification and religious functions. In the Lotus Sūtra the Buddha is called the Great Lord (*Maheśvara*), Ruler of Right (*Dharmarāja*), and chief among the rulers of the world. He

[1] Dīgha Nikāya ii, 108; see W. L. King, *Buddhism and Christianity*, 1963, p. 58.
[2] *Gradual Sayings*, trs. F. L. Woodward, 1933, ii, p. 44.

'created all' from the moment when he began preaching the doctrine, and other lords are derived from him. Although he arrived at perfect enlightenment at the town of Gayā, the truth is that he attained enlightenment myriads of ages ago. The Buddha is 'born into this world to lead to beatitude', and he appears 'in this world to save'. The one who is 'the father of the world' and full of compassion 'appears in this triple world . . . in order to deliver from affection, hatred and delusion the beings subject to birth, old age, disease' and so on. So the Buddha is supreme, manifested, and Saviour.[1]

This Buddhology has been compared with developing Christology, as shown for example in the epistle to the Colossians.[2] There it is said of Christ that 'in him all things were created . . . and in him all things subsist'. But the context is that of divine creation, and the agency of the Logos or Wisdom in it. The incarnate Christ here is 'the image of the invisible God', and 'the son of his love'. It is through the incarnate Christ that God 'reconciles all things to himself', and he makes 'peace through the blood of his cross'. Although Christ reveals God this is not his only work, which is to save and reconcile men to God and, despite the cosmic background to the divine plan in this passage, the physical reality of the Incarnation is stressed in the 'blood'.

There are some writers who object that not only is the Mahāyānist glorification a departure from original Buddhism, but that the notion of a Buddha saving men is also an intrusion. Such objections are heard in the western world and on the fringes of Buddhism, from westernized Japanese or Ceylonese. The Buddha is represented as a humanist, a Socratic, almost a scientific figure, and he is not called Saviour except in the sense that he discovered and showed the path to liberation. But in all traditional schools and scriptures the Buddha is regarded as supreme, he has numinous qualities, and not only his teaching but his presence and protection are sought, daily and in the cults of relics and holy places.

It is not surprising that the Lotus Sūtra makes the Buddha declare that as father of all beings, 'I must save them from this

[1] Saddharma Puṇḍarīka 4, 60; 5, 19, etc.
[2] I. A. Sparks, 'Buddha and Christ; a Functional Analysis', in *Numen*, 1966, pp. 190f.

mass of evil'. Yet the meaning and purpose of salvation differ in Buddhist and Christian contexts. In Theravāda teaching salvation is the removal of ignorance rather than forgiveness of sins, and because there is no righteous God there is no reconciliation with him. Māra was defeated by the Buddha through his superior knowledge, and a similar process is seen in the Buddhist disciple. The Noble Eightfold Path is sometimes called the way of deliverance from Māra, but it begins with 'right view' and continues with right behaviour. So the realm of Māra is transcended by the one who sees the emptiness of the world, and the falsity of popular opinions about the self.[1]

Even in the more personal teaching of salvation in Mahāyāna, where the example of the Buddhas is stressed, knowledge is one of their chief characteristics. They seek to bring all beings to the same knowledge, and the self-sacrifice of monks tends to be diverted into meritorious works comprising chanting of texts. Compassion is exercised through 'religious' action, rather than in care for the sick and outcast, because the material world is undervalued.

Christian emphasis upon the Crucifixion and the 'blood' is distasteful to some Buddhists. D. T. Suzuki significantly objects to the Christian emphasis upon 'the corporeality of our existence'. He considers that the idea of self-denial is wrong. 'As there is no self, no crucifixion is needed, no sadism is to be practised, no shocking sight is to be displayed by the roadside.' He contrasts the crucifixion-image of Christ with the 'picture of Buddha lying on a bed surrounded by his disciples and other beings non-human as well as human'.[2] In a romantic interpretation he speaks of these 'other beings' as animals which came together to mourn the death of the Buddha, though the texts call them gods. Once they were gods, then gentlemen, now animals! It is undeniable that crucifixion was a horrible punishment, but it was decreed by Pilate, and not by the 'sadism' of Christians. At least Christianity looks plainly at the facts of life, its sufferings and cruelty as well as hope and joy. The danger is that the Buddhist should think that there is no world, no evil but rather ignorance or foolishness, no Nazi

[1] T. O. Ling, *Buddhism and the Mythology of Evil*, 1962, pp. 62f.
[2] D. T. Suzuki, *Mysticism, Christian and Buddhist*, pp. 136f.

concentration camps, no Japanese tortures, no war in Vietnam.

Yet the Buddha himself, despite some of the interpretations of certain of his followers, was not a colourless individual, sitting forever impassively under the Bo-tree. It was the sight of suffering, in the Four Signs of age, disease, death and asceticism, that drove Gautama away from home to find solutions for the troubles of life. His analysis of the cause of suffering as being in desire can be criticized, but it was not simply pessimistic. It led to the cure, and the prescription of the path away from sorrow to peace. This is different from the Christian teaching of the reconciliation of sinful men with God through the Cross. Yet Buddhism is attractive because, despite differences from Christianity, there are similarly unselfish purposes. Whether one may speak of an Unknown Christ of Buddhism or not, there are some common motives as well as diverse particulars between these two religions.

18

Adoptionism: Christ and Muhammad

GLORIFICATION

In some modern Christological studies it is said that Adoptionism was 'the original Christology', this led 'inevitably' to belief in the pre-existence of Christ, and only two further possibilities remained, Docetism and Kenoticism (self-emptying).[1] But the comparative study of religions shows examples of religious leaders where a similar process of glorification took place, yet without the same conclusion. Of the great religious figures of the world who are central to their faith Muhammad even more than the Buddha can be studied historically. The Prophet of Mecca was undoubtedly a man and the Qur'ān insists that he 'ate food', like Jesus and Mary. The Qur'ān rejects the Docetic notion that other messengers, such as Jesus, were 'a bodily appearance not eating food, nor were they immortal'. But Muhammad himself performed no miracles, he claimed to be 'nothing but a human being', though at the same time he was prophet and the Apostle of God (sūras 21, 7; 17, 95).

The persons of Christ and Muhammad have often been compared, but are there valid parallels between them? W. C. Smith suggests that Christians and Muslims have even been partly alienated, because they have misunderstood each other's faith by trying to fit it into their own patterns. The commonest error, on both sides, he says, is to suppose that the roles of Christ in Christianity and that of Muhammad in Islam are comparable. Smith suggests, on the contrary, that the role of Muhammad is more like that of Paul. Both were apostles, bringing a message. But Paul's message was Christ, the Word made flesh. Muhammad preached the Word made Book, the Qur'ān. For Christians the Word of

[1] J. Knox, *The Humanity and Divinity of Christ*, pp. 95f.

God is not the Bible, though it is often taken to be this, yet according to the Fourth Gospel the Word of God is Christ. So in comparing these two great religions, says Smith, the Word of God is Christ compared with the Qur'ān, rather than with Muhammad. The Bible corresponds more to the Ḥadīth, the Traditions of Islam, and that is why Biblical criticism can be compared with Ḥadīth criticism. Muslims object to criticism of the Qur'ān as strongly as Christians object to criticism of Christ. Both are objects of faith and subjects of divine revelation.[1]

This objection would be justified if the study of Muhammad was restricted to the man who appears in the Qur'ān, considered by modern critical methods. But it needs much modification when discussing how Islam developed particular attitudes towards Muhammad, as it did with growing fervour. Western scholars tend to isolate Muhammad from the later glorification of his person. They study the historical man, 'warts and all', but often give inadequate attention to his position at the heart of faith. Yet Constance Padwick, in her beautiful study of Muslim devotions, drawn from ordinary prayer books in use today throughout the Islamic world, says this: 'No one can estimate the power of Islam as a religion who does not take into account the love at the heart of it for this figure [Muhammad]. It is here that human emotion, repressed at some points by the austerity of the doctrine of God as developed in theology, has its full outlet – a warm human emotion which the peasant can share with the mystic. The love of this figure is perhaps the strongest binding force in a religion which has so marked a binding power.'[2] And Annemarie Schimmel, writing of Islamic devotional poetry in India, stresses this love for Muhammad. 'It is a love which has been reflected in the numberless blessings, expressed every day by millions of faithful Muslims over the name of him who was "only a slave to whom it was revealed"'; it is reflected in the poems setting forth, in terms of the profoundest devotion, the praise of Muhammad, which precede every poetical composition in the Islamic countries'.[3]

[1] W. C. Smith, *Islam in Modern History*, 1957, 17n.

[2] C. E. Padwick, *Muslim Devotions*, 1961, p. 145.

[3] 'The Veneration of the Prophet Muhammad, as reflected in Sindhi poetry', in the symposium *The Saviour God*, 1963, p. 129.

GROWTH OF DEVOTION TO MUHAMMAD

Although convinced of his own subordination to God as recipient of the divine message, yet its heavenly origin gave Muhammad particular importance from the outset. He was sent as a 'warner' to a people to whom no prophet had been sent before. Jews and Christians had their sacred books and prophets, which he recognized, but now Muhammad came with 'a Book whose signs have been made distinct as an Arabic Qur'ān' (12, 2, etc.). There is a sacred history, in the election of the Arab people, and in this the Arab prophet is central.

As time progressed, and the religion spread and strengthened, the later sūras of the Qur'ān gave growing importance to the person of Muhammad. Those who swore allegiance to him were said to swear allegiance to God. God was his patron, and Gabriel and the angels supported him. Men were told to lower their voices in the presence of the messenger of God, and not to put him on the same footing as others, not to insult him or enter his house without permission. In an important verse Muhammad is called 'the Seal' of the prophets (*khatam*; 33, 40). No explanation is given of this term, but tradition soon assumed that Muhammad sealed and closed the line of prophets, though the Qur'ān does not say so. Therefore he would be the last, and greatest, prophet, and none would appear after him, a belief that gave difficulty at times. The profession of faith (*shahāda*, testimony) testifies that 'there is no god but God; Muhammad is the Apostle of God'. This is the first of the five pillars of religion, which soon developed, though it is not in the Qur'ān in this form, and which makes a Muslim distinctive from a Jew or Christian by professing faith in Muhammad's special position.

Very quickly veneration of the person of Muhammad arose. In the standard biography, about a hundred years after his death, earlier verses are quoted which say of Muhammad, 'he was the light and brilliance that we followed, after God, and he was our sight and hearing'. And again, 'no woman ever conceived or gave birth to any like the Apostle'; he was a blessed guiding light to illumine the world, and the 'best of creation'.[1] Very early the

---

[1] A. Guillaume, *The Life of Muhammad*, 1955, p. 690; W. N. Arafat, 'The Elegies on the Prophet in their Historical Perspective', in *Journal of the Royal Asiatic Society*, 1967, pp. 15ff.

sinlessness of Muhammad and all the prophets was accepted throughout Islam, and he was looked upon as the great intercessor. Popular faith has long held that Muhammad will intercede for his followers on the day of judgement. God gathers together the believers and they turn to Adam for his intercession. But he reminds them of his sin and refers them to Noah, who passes them on to Abraham. All the apostles are appealed to, until at last Jesus advises them to seek the help of Muhammad. Having girded himself the Apostle falls before God, who tells him to arise since intercession is granted to him. Muhammad prostrates himself for numbers of people, till finally only those are left who are to suffer eternally.[1] Many Muslims believe in the intercession of Muhammad on other occasions, and that of other prophets and saints, though the modern Wahhābī of Arabia hold only to the intercession of Muhammad at the judgement.

In the development of Islamic mysticism Christian influence was strong in the first centuries, and the adaptation of Christian works would be the source of many words attributed to Jesus in Sūfī writings. The poverty and simplicity of Jesus are often mentioned, in a kind of Ebionite manner, and there are exhortations to 'take Jesus as your pattern' and a declaration that 'Jesus is the Seal of the saints'. In time, however, Muhammad became the supreme example of mystical life and an object of devotion. R. A. Nicholson remarks that in medieval Islam the Prophet took on some of the attributes of Christ shown in the writings of Paul and John. It might seem that in modern western Christianity the reverse process is at work, and Jesus is divested of divinity and presented more like the early Muhammad, 'only a man'. Perhaps this is due to a decline in Christian mysticism.[2]

In popular religion although there are many other saints it is Muhammad above all who is cherished, invoked and followed. The commonest phrase on Muslim lips, and in books where some form of it follows every mention of the Prophet, is the 'blessing' (*tasliya*): 'May God call down blessing on our Lord Muhammad, and on the family of our Lord Muhammad, and greet them with peace.' This is essential to devotion, whole books have been

[1] *Shorter Encyclopaedia of Islam*, p. 512.
[2] R. A. Nicholson, *The Idea of Personality in Sūfism*, 1923, p. 43.

written on it, and it is regarded as bringing rewards and the for-giveness of sins.[1]

All the details of the person and life of Muhammad are trea-sured. He is called the best of mankind, the man of power, the hero of the sword, the rider of the Night Ascent (to heaven from Jerusalem), for whom the palm trees wept and the stones did homage, the brilliant dawn and the light of lights. Miracles and visions of the Prophet are related for which there is no canonical authority, but which are precious to devotion. Further, as there are litanies on the Beautiful Names of God, so there are litanies on the Names of Muhammad. Sometimes the titles are interchange-able: Light of lights, Friend of strangers, Companion of the lonely, are used of God and Muhammad.

There is no doubt that Muhammad has a cosmic position, not only in mystical philosophy but in popular faith, and failure to realize this is one of the chief causes of western misunderstanding of Islam. It is said that Muhammad told his followers not to praise him as the Christians praised Jesus, but in fact they have done almost that. In many mosques today the name of Allāh is written on one side of the wall by the prayer niche, and the name of Muhammad on the other. This can be seen both in the former cathedral of Hagia Sophia in Istanbul, and in the adjoining Blue Mosque which is used for Islamic daily prayers.

Several major processes took place within Islam. Conservative orthodox theology tended towards an extreme transcendentalism which was little different from Deism, just as remote and cold. Sūfī mystics approached a monism in which the differences be-tween God and man were abolished; man became God and religion was imperilled. But even these two extremes found it hard to exclude some mediators: the Prophet himself, the Imāms of the Shī'a, and countless saints. And the great mass of Islam, learned and lay, rich and poor, has clung to faith in the unique but com-pasionate God and in his sinless interceding Apostle.

'So in the worship of the Creator,' says Miss Padwick, 'this second figure emerges, assuming the functions of the Divine Logos, or of the Holy Spirit; called by names that else are reserved for God alone, a creature, yet isolated in the pre-creation glory

[1] C. Padwick, *Muslim Devotions*, pp. 152f.

from all other creatures.'[1] Muhammad is regarded as more than Logos, he is a personal Lord and friend, the mediator between God and man, in most Islamic faith.

Islam is so greatly different in its initial assumptions from Buddhism that it would be hard to conceive of two more opposed religions, yet in some ways they are strangely akin. Islam and Buddhism both started with human figures who had no pretensions to divinity. They did not claim to found new religions, so much as to restore eternal truth. They would both have rejected the notions of Avatars or Incarnation. Yet in the end both Gautama and Muhammad arrived not far from what is implied in those names, testifying to the human need for the Incarnation.

Similar processes of glorification may be observed in many religions, indeed perhaps this is an ingredient of all religion, expressing the need for a personification of the deity. Zoroaster holds a central place for the Parsis, Confucius was revered as 'co-equal with heaven and earth' for over two thousand years, and for orthodox Judaism Moses is 'the chief of the prophets' and 'peace be unto him'. In modern times religious fervour has centred round the persons of Lenin and Stalin, and even more round Mao Tse-tung, 'the never-setting red sun', whose guards cry 'eternal life to Chairman Mao', as in Ghana they said that Nkrumah would never die and as Biafran soldiers chanted to Ojukwu as saviour.

ADOPTIONISM

The glorification of the leader, which is so common a feature in other religions, no doubt took place in Christianity. But there are essential differences, and it is clear that the reasons for beatification are not the same and they are not the whole story. In Christian doctrine it is divine action that precedes and produces faith, so that the nature of Christ was not determined by men's reactions to him.

The Christian church began with men and women who were attached to Jesus, the teacher from Nazareth. At the earliest stage there would be no problem of his humanity, for he was known as a human being, though he was 'mighty in word and deed'. When

[1] *Muslim Devotions*, p. 256.

the disciples came to believe in Jesus as the promised Messiah, there would still be no doubt of his humanity, which was known to everybody in his lifetime and was plain in his death.

The Resurrection of Christ, and the descent of the Holy Spirit at Pentecost, revealed wider implications of faith to the disciples. According to the book of Acts, Peter speaking at Pentecost said that 'God has made him both Lord and Christ, this Jesus whom you crucified' (2, 36). This verse, it is often said, shows that the disciples believed that the human Jesus was now 'adopted' by God as Lord and Messiah, and so the first Christology of the church was Adoptionist. But it seems strange to make such a bold claim largely upon the evidence of one verse, or what is called 'the clearest example'.[1] It is true that a similar sentiment to that of Acts appears to be expressed by Paul when he said that after the cross God 'highly exalted' Jesus and 'gave him the name which is above every name' (Phil. 2, 9). But this is not Adoptionism, because Paul had already spoken of the pre-existence and self-emptying of Christ.

Others have said that the man Jesus was adopted into divinity at his baptism, where a voice from heaven said to him, 'Thou art my Son, in thee I am well pleased'. This was the older form of Adoptionism which seems to have been held by the Ebionites who said, according to Epiphanius, that 'Jesus was begotten of the seed of a man, and was chosen; and so by the choice (of God) he was called the Son of God from the Christ that came into him from above in the likeness of a dove. And they deny that he was begotten of God the Father, but say that he was created, as one of the archangels, yet greater, and that he is Lord of angels.'[2] Nowadays it would be asked whether this voice from heaven was heard by anybody else but Jesus, and if not how it could have shaped the faith of the first Christians. The claim that God adopted Jesus, at the baptism or Resurrection, introduces an unfortunate time element into discussion of his nature.

If the faith of the first Christians is considered, before the larger problem of the nature of Christ in itself, then there are plenty of signs that they looked upon Jesus as at least supernormal at a very

---

[1] J. Knox, *The Humanity and Divinity of Christ*, p. 7.
[2] *The Apocryphal New Testament*, p. 10.

early date, perhaps from their first acquaintance with him. The Gospels say that Jesus was hailed as the Holy One of God, the Son of God, the Son of the Most High God, the Messiah, the Son of David, to select only some of the titles used in Mark. All of these names have been frequently discussed, but at least it can be assumed that the first writers of the story of Jesus believed that men had held the reverential attitudes towards him that the titles imply.

What Jesus said about himself, and how far he encouraged such attitudes of reverence, is even more debated. His use of the title 'Son of Man' is one of the most discussed problems and has been called fundamental to modern formulations of Christology. Did he use it to indicate the Messiah? Was that himself or some coming figure? Would he become the Messiah at some future date? Did the usage of the term change or develop? How many passages are original, if any? Such matters have been debated with a destructive abandon that would be suspect in other literary fields, though a reaction against scepticism is apparent and it is held that the use of the name Son of Man by Jesus is fact rather than fiction, since it has no currency in the early Church. What is remarkable is the way in which the evangelists, writing later and with much variety, are careful to put the use of the term Son of Man into the mouth of Jesus alone, so that whether it indicated his Messianic views or not, it was his own choice.

Technical questions must be left to the experts, regretfully, for too much looking at the trees can hide the wood. But in the larger field of comparison with other religions, Christian doctrine is remarkable for its rapid development. Whether the early Christians thought that the man Jesus was 'adopted' by God or not, they seem to have come very soon to show attitudes of reverence and even worship towards him. Luke says that at the beginning of his ministry Peter fell at the feet of Jesus crying, 'Depart from me, for I am a sinful man, O Lord' (Luke 5, 8). The Fourth Gospel, admittedly late, declares that Thomas at the Ressurrection called Christ, 'My Lord and my God' (John 20, 28). And the earlier Acts of the Apostles show Stephen at his death invoking the glorified Jesus at the right hand of God (7, 59). It seems that early Christians held such attitudes to Christ to be proper expressions of faith, and they were Jews, monotheists, whose devotion had to be adjusted to the influence of Christ upon them.

Jesus was as clearly historical as Muhammad, but although devotion later grew up towards the Prophet traces of it in his lifetime are few. The reverence shown to Christ in the New Testament can be more fully paralleled with the devotion given to the Buddha. But although the Buddha was a man Buddhist scriptures are so late, developed and extensive, largely consisting of dialogues, that it is difficult to extract from them an early human picture. Even so, and this is a crucial difference, there is no claim that the Buddha came from God, and the concepts of Buddhahood are so different from Christian doctrines as to make true comparisons difficult.

The Buddha was finally 'adopted' to the most supernatural status although, in theory at least, any man can rise to similar Buddhahood. Muhammad is not an 'associate' of God, for 'association' is one of the most deadly sins to a Muslim, though in practice the role of Muhammad may seem to be not far away from that high position. But the Adoptionist theories of the Ebionites and some moderns fail to do justice to the theism in which the whole Biblical and Christian doctrine is set. Jesus did not become divine at the baptism or at the end of his life, as a preparation for his work or a consummation of it, but 'God was in Christ' from the beginning. No New Testament writer speaks of the work of Jesus in purely human terms, as simply his own achievement, though none doubts that he lived as a man on earth.

MUHAMMAD AND CHRIST

The modern stress upon the humanity of Jesus has brought reactions from members of other religions, notably Muslims. If Jesus was human, then Muhammad was even more human, so to speak, but in the best way. Christians have criticized Muhammad for his polygamy and his wars, but Muslims see in him the pattern of perfect humanity.

Jesus has always been honoured in Islam, even when Christians have been attacked, and it is said that the name of Jesus appears in nearly every Muslim religious work, or at least those of the Sūfī mystics. His sinlessness has never been doubted, for the Qur'ān itself said that he and his mother were protected from Satan (3, 31). The virginal birth and the miracles of Jesus are mentioned several times in the Qur'ān and have been accepted throughout Islamic history. Some modern Muslim writers find faults in Jesus; such as his rebuke to the Syro-Phenician woman, permission of the destruction of the pigs by Legion, cursing the fig tree, and cleansing the temple by force. But such attacks are rare and they are rejected by most Muslims to whom, as to Muhammad himself, Jesus is prophet and Messiah. When the name of Jesus is mentioned Muslims still say, 'Jesus, on whom be peace'.

A more sophisticated assessment of the relative roles of Muhammad and Christ is found in some fairly sympathetic writers, such as Seyyed Hossein Nasr. He says that it is difficult for a non-Muslim to understand the role of Muhammad as prototype of the religious life, especially if he is compared with Christ or the Buddha. For the earthly career of the Prophet seems too human, and engrossed in the troubles of social and political activity, to be a model for spiritual living.

But it is just here that Nasr sees the Prophet's appeal to ordinary men. For Christ and the Buddha, he says, gave a message that 'was meant primarily for saintly men', and they 'founded a community based on monastic life which later became the norm of a whole society'. Whether this is true of the Buddha or not, it must be strongly disputed that such a monastic ideal was ever taught or demonstrated by Christ, despite the actions of some of his later followers. But, Nasr continues, Muhammad should rather be compared with Rāma or Krishna, 'who although in a completely different traditional climate, were *avatāras* and at the same time kings and householders who participated in social life'.[1]

Our discussions earlier will have shown that this parallel with the legendary Avatars is not happy, and even less sound than a comparison with Jesus. But the question of the Prophet's social life serving as a model for ordinary men needs some consideration. Muhammad participated fully in social life; he was married several times, had a household, was a ruler and judge, a general and statesman. He underwent the hardships of ordinary life, as well as

[1] S. H. Nasr, *Ideals and Realities of Islam*, 1966, pp. 68f.

those necessitated by the special needs of his social and political activities. The value of political life directed by spiritual principles is evident in modern times, whereas the Christian ideal may seem too far removed into the spiritual realm, says Nasr, as when Christ said, 'My kingdom is not of this world'. But while many of the slanders made by non-Muslims against the Prophet's married life are baseless, his polygamy and wars may be an embarrassment. To justify the character of Muhammad his spiritual vocation and religious activities are even more important than his social and political life.

On the other hand, modern study of the Bible stresses the humanity of Jesus, his involvement in the material concerns of his day, and his devotion to the Kingdom of God, which would come 'on earth as it is in heaven'. That Jesus was not married does not appear so strange now as before knowledge became available about the Essene communities, on the shores of the Dead Sea and elsewhere; some of them practised celibacy, though Jesus lived in the world and not in a secluded community. And the place of women among the followers of Jesus shows the appeal that he had to both sexes, and his knowledge of their problems.

In another work Seyyed Hossein Nasr says that 'Christ plays a very important role in Islam, but this is not a distortion of the Christian conception of Christ. He is, independently of Christianity, a part of the Islamic religious view.' And he claims that the position of Christ in Islam is independent of 'any historical borrowing' from Christianity, for any similarities to Christian story 'come only from the common transcendent archetype'. This seems to be a reference to the Heavenly Book, the 'Mother' of the Qur'ān, by reference to which some writers explain the apparent borrowings of the Qur'ān from the Bible. But critical literary study would show that Islam could have had no knowledge of Christ apart from the sixth-century Christians and their scriptures, from which Muhammad derived all his knowledge of Christ.[1]

The place of Christ in Islam is often significant, and nearly always honourable, but it is even more formed by the thought of

[1] S. H. Nasr, 'Islam and the Encounter of Religions', in *The Islamic Quarterly*, 1966, p. 55.

Muhammad and the Islamic 'church' than was Christian doctrine by the church after the time of Jesus, because of the distance of Islam from the historical life of Jesus. Yet Muslims have often assumed that they knew Christ better than Christians did, because of the versions of the story of Jesus given in the Qur'ān and Traditions which vary from the Biblical picture. So Cantwell Smith says that he knows of no book by a Muslim which shows a 'feel' for the Christian position, nor any that takes its doctrines seriously. This means that not only do Muslims deny the central Christian doctrines about Christ, but they do not recognize that Christians take them seriously. By imagining that they know Christianity better than Christians do themselves, Muslims have been prevented from gaining an understanding of the faith by which Christians live.[1]

Muhammad was a great Prophet, and he needs to be recognized as such by Christians, and no longer defamed as so often in the past. The Qur'ān undoubtedly contains revelations of God, and Islamic history has many profound thinkers and real saints. But the Christian faith *in* Christ is different from the Islamic confession that Muhammad is the Apostle of God. For, despite many variations in devotional history, and attempts to get away from Deism, Islamic faith is *in* God, and not in Muhammad. A simple comparison of the processes of glorification of Muhammad and Christ tends to obscure this basic difference, in starting point and goal.

The Christian faith in Christ is also faith *in* God, and how these two aspects of faith can be reconciled depends upon the doctrine of the Trinity, which Muslims have always denied.

[1] W. C. Smith, *Islam in Modern History*, 104n.

19

Christianity and Other Religions

HISTORY AND FAITH

In comparisons that have been made in the preceding pages, between the Incarnation in Christ and the Avatars and Buddhas of India and the Far East, again and again it has been remarked that there are strong Docetic tendencies in Avatar and similar faiths. Their Saviours either did not certainly live as men on earth, or if they did the stories have become so overlaid with legend that it is difficult to get back to the original figure. But does this matter, and is not Christianity in a similar situation?

That there are Docetic and pluralistic trends in Hinduism and Buddhism may be admitted and even made into a virtue. The countless worshippers of Amida Buddha seem to be unconcerned by his mythical nature, and though the Japanese reformer Nichiren declared that Amida was a figment of the imagination yet the true Buddha to whom he sought to return was the glorified Śākyamuni sitting on a Vulture Peak in the Himalayas. Mahātma Gāndhi said both that his Krishna had 'nothing to do with any historic person', and that whether Christ and Avatars 'actually lived on earth does not affect the picture of them in men's minds'.[1]

In fact it does affect the picture, because in so far as the historical words and deeds of the Saviour can be established so much less can their contents be distorted by inferior imitators. That this is particularly important for Christianity is shown by the existence of four canonical Gospels, in all of which the church has believed that it can find the teaching and actions of Christ, behind any bias of the evangelists.

No doubt the mythical elements do not matter very much for

[1] See references above on page 104.

Krishna, but this marks a vital difference between his story and that of Christ. If there is any historicity in the Krishna saga he was a complex character, compounded of herdsman chief, romantic miraculous child and youth, conquering warrior, and finally divine teacher and lord. There can hardly be an imitation of Krishna, as a moral and religious example for daily life, in the first three of these aspects. The noblest side appears in the Bhagavad-Gītā, where he is simply the divine voice. Historical and critical study is never likely to establish that Krishna spoke these words at an identifiable time and place. They are, frankly, the inspired but free compositions of a very great religious poet, Vyāsa or whoever conceived them. Their connection with Krishna is simply that of encouragement to virtue and devotion to a supreme deity, and the Gītā only tentatively and occasionally links its precepts with any human life of the Avatar, a term which it never uses and the theme of which receives scanty treatment in its verses.

It is true that Christian scriptures and teachings have contained a good deal of miracle and myth, and however much attempts may be made nowadays to 'demythologize' tradition some kind of mythology will always be necessary. The use of spatial imagery is natural to theology; since the heavens are above us they will always be apt symbols for the transcendence of God. Modern efforts to get rid of a God 'up there' resort to speaking of him 'in the depths', which is just another spatial metaphor. And faith in the supremacy of Christ will always necessitate doctrine that may be called Christology.

But Christianity has been sensitive to the dangers of Docetism and, as was pointed out earlier, whereas Buddhism increased this tendency in the most orthodox circles, in Christianity it has been constantly resisted. No doubt Christian writers did not always make such a great emphasis upon historical accuracy in the past, but in modern times the growth of historical sciences has accelerated the need for discovering the factual basis of Christianity and efforts to bring 'the end of Docetism'. It is right that criticism should be stringent, because of distinctive elements in Christian faith which are obscured by Docetism.

Christians believe that the Gospels contain the words of Christ, as distinct from apocryphal gospels, and, however much these

words may have been varied or modified in the course of trans-
mission by the evangelists, moderate critics hold that there is a
considerable body of authentic teaching which the Gospel writers
have been at great pains to preserve. The effect of these teachings
upon the non-Christian world has been powerful in the present
century, not least upon Gāndhi who owed it to the church that it
had preserved the words of the historic Christ.

Not only the teaching, but the life and death of Christ are of
central importance to Christian faith, indispensable to its remaining
distinctively Christian. The words of Christ are invaluable, but his
person as the manifested love of God on earth, God in Christ, is
essential to faith. Further, the person of Christ has had a profound
effect upon the modern world beyond Christendom. Only the life
of Muhammad is as well documented, among religious leaders,
and there moral and religious comparisons need to be made.

For Christianity Christ is the living Word of God, as Muhammad is not strictly for Muslims, though we have seen that devotional demands have exalted him far above his own claims. But
Christianity is not just tied to a book as 'word' of God, with all the
dangers of fundamentalism and literary criticism which that
entails, and which Islam must face sooner or later. Christian faith
takes on cosmic dimensions when Jesus is considered in relation to
historic human life, but as sent by God for our salvation. The
doctrine of Christ inescapably involves a new doctrine of God.

Both of these doctrines need expression in modern terms, in
ways which are far beyond our present purpose. But a possible
development may be suggested between the evolutionary theories
of science and Incarnational belief. Teilhard de Chardin, who was
strongly opposed to a 'vague and meaningless pantheism', looked
towards a higher pantheism which comes to its climax in the
Incarnation. As we have seen earlier, an undifferentiated pantheism
has no room for Incarnation, but it is central to the 'modified
non-dualism' of Rāmānuja in which men are united to God but
not identical with him. Teilhard spoke of Christ as 'sprung up as
man among men', in order 'to direct and superanimate the general
ascent of consciousness into which he inserted himself'. He called
this 'a prodigious biological operation', in which Christ assumed
'the control and leadership of what we now call evolution'. And

the goal of everything is union with God, in which God shall be all in all, 'a superior form of "pantheism" without trace of the poison of adulteration or annihilation'.[1]

OTHER REVELATIONS

Christian faith holds to the supremacy of Christ, yet it must acknowledge the activity of God 'at sundry times and in divers manners'. In the past it was readily admitted that God spoke to the Old Testament prophets, and the great Greek philosophers were also 'baptized' into Christian thought. But can one speak of revelations of God to Hindus, Buddhists, Parsis and the rest? Why not?

R. C. Zaehner, in one of his important books on comparative religion, says that, 'of the revelations of God outside Israel, the most impressive is undoubtedly the progressive revelation in India which showed to man first that there is one principle which informs both the cosmos and the human soul, secondly that the human soul is immortal, and finally that there is a personal God who not only informs and directs all things but who also becomes incarnate'.[2]

To begin a consideration of the relationship of other religions to Christ it is easy to turn to Hinduism. The richness and lack of definition in this religion make it apparently adaptable to anything, and many Christian studies of world religions dwell on India and neglect the more obstinate but important facts of Islam. The Hindu personal gods, Avatars, and immortal souls can all be seen as finding fulfilment in Christianity. The superior age of Hinduism, which is often claimed for it with little firm historical evidence, as against Judaism for example, makes it equally easy to fit into a similar category with Israel, as a forerunner of Christ.

So the famous missionary J. N. Farquhar wrote of Christianity as 'the Crown of Hinduism', and he set a pattern for missionary thought which unfortunately too often assumed that if the Crown was known it was absolved from the study of Hinduism in its own right. But in what way does Christianity fulfil Hinduism?

[1] *The Phenomenon of Man*, E.T. 1959, pp. 293f.
[2] R. C. Zaehner, *At Sundry Times*, 1958, p. 183.

Do Christian rites fulfil Hindu rites, or Christian doctrines Hindu doctrines? Christian 'ideals of practice' may seem better to the Christian, but not to the Hindu. And to claim a richer experience, or better fulfilment of inner needs, is a statement incapable of proof.[1] No doubt some Hindus have found their ancestral religion unsatisfactory; some have renounced it, while others have tried to follow Christ still within it. What is envisaged for the rest, the three hundred million and more who remain Hindus? Is their religion to be destroyed, does missionary strategy aim at this, and is it right to do so?

Hinduism is so vast and diverse that in the main it has not troubled about such questions, for its octopus grip has embraced many religions and even made the Buddha into an Avatar. It has been seen that in the past Hindu teachers were often dogmatic, declaring that only the Vedas were inspired scripture, and that the scriptures of all other peoples were wrong. In modern times Hinduism is set up as a model of tolerance, as against the dogmatism and persecutions of Christianity, and the communal struggles and massacres between Hindus and Muslims are glossed over.

Yet the prevalent monism is just as dogmatic. On the one hand it is a confidence trick, which hides the fact that the vast majority of Hindus have always been theists. And on the other hand the modern pantheistic attempts to reduce all religion to monism are inaccurate and intolerant. Dr. Radhakrishnan, in his many works, never tires of asserting that all religious statements and revelations are relative, and the only thing that is finally valid is the inner experience of the Absolute. The monistic recipe is repeated in one of his latest books: 'Man becomes aware of his potential identity with the divine.'[2] So all religions are reduced to a common denominator, by setting up mystical experience as an absolute.

Buddhism is also pre-Christian and could be fitted into the category of preparation for Christianity, but with more difficulty. Hindus have accepted Christ as an Avatar, but not as a unique Incarnation. Theravāda Buddhists, while conceiving of other Buddhas past and to come, yet hold to one supreme Buddha in the

[1] E. J. Sharpe, *Not to Destroy but to Fulfil*, p. 290.
[2] *Religion in the Changing World*, 1967.

present world eon. Mahāyāna Buddhism has countless supernatural beings, but these would spoil the simplicity of the Christian faith. Buddhist writers seem to have even less 'feel' for the
Christian position than do Hindus, and 'one can look in vain for
any serious effort to fulfil the first condition of religious dialogue:
to listen to the other as such, and restrict in the greatest possible
measure one's own perspective'.[1] Buddhist propagandists who
object to Christian missions are often the most ardent missionaries
for Buddhism.

Islam is different but more difficult, for this great religion is
post-Christian and hard to fit into any preparatory scheme: John
of Damascus saw in Islam a Christian heresy, a misunderstanding
of Islam that has long been perpetuated. But Muslims have turned
the notion of progressive revelation to their own purposes, thereby
showing the danger of a purely evolutionary doctrine. They see
Christianity as a possible road to Islam, though unhappily
obscured by many errors. True Christianity was preached by
Jesus, they say, and the sincere Christian before the coming of
Muhammad was already a Muslim, 'submitted' to God. Muhammad was the Seal of the Prophets, repeating and confirming all
that went before, and correcting the errors of Jewish and Christian
interpretations of scripture. He ended the line of the prophets and
is the best of them all.

In modern Muslim eyes the obstacle to true dialogue lies with
Christians. Muslims recognize Jesus as a great prophet, and his
Gospel as a truly revealed Law, why cannot we recognize
Muhammad and the Qur'ān?[2] There is some force in the question,
and W. C. Smith in his essay on 'Is the Qur'ān the Word of God?'
points out that the problem of his essay has never been debated
seriously.[3] Accepted as axiomatic by Muslims, it has not even been
considered by Christians. Christian scholars have done a great
service by critical study of Islamic history and institutions in the
past century, but the theological implications have hardly been
touched. Yet the Muslim demand does not get to the root of the
problem. It assumes that Jesus can be fully understood within Mus-

---

[1] J. Cuttat, in *Mélanges de Lubac*.
[2] L. Gardet, *L'Islam*, 1967, p. 394.
[3] *Questions of Religious Truth*, 1967, pp. 39ff.

lim categories, and it rejects not only the theology of Paul but also the faith that lies behind all the Gospels.

Christian misunderstanding of other religions arises from similar failure. Too commonly it regards the religions as only subservient to Christianity, ultimately dispensable, and it does not pay tribute to their importance as revelations of God in their own right. This is shown by the use of the exclusive term 'non-Christian', which treats all other religions together without distinction, and it suggests that they are all false, compared with the only true Christianity. This description suggests that the religions are organizations and can be contrasted as such, though sometimes it is said that they are 'religions' while Christianity is not one. To which it can be retorted that the others also are not 'religions'. We have invented titles for them which they did not use previously, such as Hinduism, Buddhism, and so on. But to their followers they are monks of the 'way of Buddha', or 'devotees' of Krishna, or 'submitters' to Allah.[1]

If there are revelations in other religions, their followers cannot properly be called unbelievers, infidels or heathen. They are rather our brothers in faith. They may not have seen the revelation of God in Christ, or even as Muslims they may have rejected a distorted picture of Christ, yet Christ is present to true believers by grace.[2]

SALVATION IN OTHER RELIGIONS

There are more important questions still than the recognition that there is some kind of previous revelation of God in the different religious traditions. Other faiths can be regarded as preparations for the Gospel, and this is the general 'liberal' attitude towards them, if it stops short of complete egalitarianism or indifference. Scriptures of other faiths have been regarded as national Old Testaments, and selections from them have been used in Christian worship. But the problems remain: are these religions only quests which never find the goal, or do men find God there? Is there salvation outside the Church? Do Hindus find God in spite of

[1] W. C. Smith, *The Meaning and End of Religion*, 1962, pp. 61f.
[2] Bede Griffiths, *Christian Ashram*, 1966, p. 196.

Hinduism, or is it a valid channel of grace to men? And, if it is, how does this fit the traditional exclusiveness of Christianity?

The evidence of the New Testament is complex. The restriction of the mission of Jesus to the Jews was added by Matthew to the simpler version in Mark, in the story of the Syro-Phenician woman where a simple statement of priority is made into a threefold exclusion (Mark 7, 26f.; Matt. 15, 24f.). The Fourth Gospel says, 'No one comes to the Father but by me', but it does not define its terms, and it says elsewhere that 'other sheep I have which are not of this fold' (14, 6; 10, 16). According to Acts Peter declared that 'in no other name is there salvation' (4, 12), but commentators have debated the form of the name, it could not be only the Aramaic word Jesus, and another name of Christ is the eternal Word of God.[1]

The early Church was oppressed with persecution for three centuries, its numbers were decimated, and the faithful were compared to the few who were saved in Noah's Ark. An exclusiveness grew up which was expressed by the African martyr-bishop Cyprian in the words 'outside the Church there is no salvation'. The Church here seems to take the place of Christ, and although Cyprian's extreme rejection of the lapsed and heretics was repudiated later, yet his formula was often defended in succeeding centuries. Not only, or chiefly, other religions but other Christians were condemned, and at various periods it was maintained that everyone outside the Catholic Church was damned.

This extreme teaching is now repudiated by the Roman Catholic Church, to the extent that the Holy Office in 1952 declared that 'a person who stated that no one out of the Church could be saved was himself out of the Church and excommunicated'.[2] Indeed Roman Catholic theologians seem now to be much more concerned with the theological problems raised by the new knowledge of other religions than do many Protestant theologians.

A number of Roman Catholic discussions and decisions in recent times show a great broadening of attitude and understanding of the new problems. In the Declaration of the Second Vatican

[1] E. C. Dewick, *The Christian Attitude to Other Religions*, 1953, p. 92.
[2] H. Küng in *Christian Revelation and World Religions*, ed. J. Neuner, 1967, p. 33.

Ecumenical Council on *The Relation of the Church to Non-Christian Religions* it was stated that 'from ancient times down to the present day there is found in various peoples a certain recognition of that hidden power which is present in history and human affairs, and in fact sometimes an acknowledgement of a supreme Godhead, or even of a Father'. Tribute is paid to various religions in turn. 'In Hinduism men probe the mystery of God . . . they seek liberation . . . by deep meditation or loving and trustful recourse to God'. Buddhism also recognizes the inadequacy of this world and seeks liberation. Muslims are regarded 'with esteem' because they worship one God and venerate Jesus and Mary. 'The Catholic Church rejects nothing which is true and holy in these religions . . . which . . . often reflect the brightness of that Truth which is the light of all peoples.'

So much for general revelation in other religions. But what of salvation, is that present in them also? In introducing this decree to the Council Cardinal Bea remarked that it was the first time that the Church had laid down principles in such a solemn way. Of those who do not know Christ he said, 'they can be saved if they obey the command of their conscience'. And again he said that those who live according to a right conscience 'are united to Christ and his mystical body through implicit faith'. And in the Constitution on the Church the Vatican Council declared that those who are still ignorant of the Gospel, yet sincerely seek God by following the voice of their conscience 'can attain to eternal salvation'.[1]

Such declarations of the possible salvation of men in other religions is welcome, not as a novelty but as the official doctrine of the Church. They are supported by a teaching of 'implicit faith'. This has often been expounded, and attacked, as teaching that men of other faiths have implicit faith in the Church. But it is now recommended as meaning implicit faith in Christ. Faith is necessary for salvation, this faith is inspired by the grace of God, and it results in acts of goodness.[2]

[1] *Christian Revelation and World Religions*, pp. 7, 34.
[2] *ibid.*, p. 90. Karl Rahner uses the term 'anonymous Christians' for other believers, in his *Das Christentum und die nicht christlichen Religionen*. For a strong attack on his views see H. van Straelen, *Our Attitude towards Other Religions*, 1965.

To what extent then are other religions means of salvation? Do men respond to the divine initiative through their religions, or independently of them, or in spite of them? In reply to such questions it is affirmed that religions do not save men. Not even Christianity does that, for only God can save. So the question means, does God use other religions to show his salvation to all people, so that they are providential means of salvation? It cannot be denied that other religions have had good influences upon their adherents, for they are the mainspring of oriental cultures and profoundly affect most realms of life. Hence they are ministers of the grace of God to men and means by which his salvation comes to them.[1] The many noble and saintly lives that have appeared in all the great religions are evidence of this.

It has been suggested, by Karl Barth and the missionary apologist Hendrik Kraemer and others, that religions are only 'natural', the work of 'godless man'. They are the purely human means by which men try to make themselves divine. This is plainly untrue of Islam, and it is astonishing that Kraemer could not see it. But we have also remarked on the strength of the theistic religions of India, and the grace-faith religion of Mahāyāna Buddhism. Even Theravāda Buddhism is not self-salvation but dependence upon the supernatural Buddha and Dharma.

In fact men in no religions live in a purely 'natural' and godless world. Paul told the Athenians that God was not far from each one of them, 'that they should seek God, if haply they might feel after him and find him'. (Acts 17, 27) All religions are revelation, in the sense that God speaks to men through them. The revelations are different, and they are transmitted with varying fidelity. Some of them are pale and all are imperfect, but there is one true Light, 'which lighteth every man'.

The Avatar doctrines of Hinduism undoubtedly reveal belief in the divine interest and involvement in the world. The Gītā, the stories of Rāma and Krishna, the songs of the medieval mystics, the monotheism of Śaiva Siddhānta, all lead men to God. But there is also a dark side to Hinduism, haunted by demons, divided by caste prejudice, and marred by blood sacrifices such as those still practised by the followers of Kālī. So Hindus are not saved by

[1] *Christian Revelation and World Religions*, p. 13.

Hinduism, but they are saved by the grace of God who uses the best Hindu traditions to show his mercy and inspire faith and good living.

The world religions are not perfect, to be left alone without change or reform, and neither is Christianity. As our own age has seen many attempts to cleanse the churches, according to their needs, so it must see radical changes in the world religions, despite the obscurantism of some of their western followers. But these religions must not be regarded as essentially evil, in the manner in which some missionaries still treat them. They are not basically rival religious systems to Christianity. If they are not 'non-Christian', neither are they anti-Christian, in many of their truths and divine revelations. Muhammad was neither a heretic nor an opponent of Christianity, but a reverent admirer of Christ. It was a tragedy that the Church of his time had never adequately evangelized Arabia, so that even six centuries after Christ there was no translation of the Gospels into Arabic that Muhammad might have read or learnt. Similarly Hindu monism, though perhaps misguided, has undoubtedly been a long and earnest search for truth which aimed at unity with God.

The truths of other religions come from God, and are not just the products of natural morality or natural piety. They must be divine, if all truth comes from the divine Word. Objection is often made to this point of view by defenders of some kinds of traditional missionary activity. Teachers of 'comparative religion' are blamed for confusing the minds of missionaries, and undermining their purpose of converting the world to Christ in this generation. Better have done with all this syncretism, if not heresy or diabolical mischief, it is said, and denounce all other religions as wrong in favour of one brand or another of Christianity. This is not the place to formulate a theology of missions, which needs to be done again in every generation. But it must be protested that the problems are not of our own making. The other religions are there, they will not just go away if we ignore them.

The new knowledge that is available about other religions makes a new attitude towards them essential, which will be more appreciative than that of earlier more ignorant days. Too often missions were envisaged as a conquest, an imperial duty, and they were historically often linked with the colonialism of Britain,

France, Spain, Portugal, Holland and the rest. But the Church is sent to serve, like its Master, 'not to be ministered unto but to minister'. This applies to the relationships with other religions as with people; the task is 'to serve the present age'.

Much of what has been said is rather negative, admitting that there may be some truth and a few saved in world religions, rather grudgingly. But far more positive recognition of their virtues and values needs to be made. Christians can afford to be much more generous towards the good in other religions, as it appears to them; acknowledging the holiness of saints, the devotion of the simple, the truth-searching of philosophers, the noble examples of founders and apostles. The servant of God should listen to what God has said and is saying to men in other traditions, he should consider those religions as their historical ways to God, and he should try to discover how their values can be clarified and enriched to provide a fuller way.

THE UNKNOWN CHRIST

The catholicity of the Bhagavad-Gītā is one of its most attractive features, which has had continuous influence upon Indian religious history, and it can provide a pattern for Christian understanding today. The Gītā recognizes that a man may worship other gods, and follow this or that religious rule, but it is God who ordains both that his faith should be unswerving and that he should obtain his desires (7, 20f.). There are those who despise the embodied Lord, ignoring his unmanifested state, but all men of great soul worship him as the imperishable Deity or offer ritual acts and formulas, and even those who worship other beings worship God alone in reality (9, 11f.; 9, 23f.). Yet the Gītā does not hesitate to declare that the path of loving devotion is the highest and best. It is true that men can worship the unmanifested and indefinable divinity, yet this brings greater toil and the unmanifested goal is hard to attain. But those who worship the Lord in love, casting all their actions on to him, soon find him to be the Saviour from the round of transmigration (12, 22f.). Finally they are told to abandon all duties, to come to God alone for refuge, for they are 'greatly loved' by him (18, 64f.).

It is in a rather similar spirit that Fr. Raymond Panikkar, with his Indian background, seeks to discover *The Unknown Christ of Hinduism*. The encounter of Christianity and Hinduism, whether for study or mission, cannot take place if one religion ignores the other. Some Christians are intent upon destroying Hinduism and choose to be blind even to its noblest teachings, while some Hindus propose a co-existence which is a virtual passivity in which neither religion contributes anything to the other. Noting similarities of ideas and practices is not sufficient for a real encounter, for what are meeting are religions, faiths which influence the whole of life. To understand Hinduism one must know the appeal of Hinduism as a religion, just as it is said that Islam cannot be understood until one is tempted to become a Muslim. We have noted the failure of most Muslim and Buddhist writers to get the 'feel' of Christianity, because they regard it as a collection of doctrines rather than an appealing faith.

How then can Christianity and Hinduism meet? They meet in Christ, says Panikkar. First of all creation takes place in Christ, 'in him all things were created' (Col. 1, 16). Creation manifests God, it is a theophany; but with the Incarnation we see that it is a Christophany which reveals the nature of God as love. Yet Incarnation is more than an appearance, a manifestation, since the Word in Jesus was a real man, who lived and sweated and died. It is to this truly incarnate Jesus that Christianity would lead its sister religion, which is both mother and daughter as well!

If all things subsist in Christ, as the apostle says, then it is Christ and no other who inspires and hears prayers in all religions, and who leads men everywhere to salvation. This is the truth that the Gītā had adumbrated. Whatever truths there are in Hinduism come from Christ, and any devout prayer and worship are his. Such a view is consistent with early Christian teaching. Justin Martyr in the second century said that Christ was 'the Logos in which every race of men shared. Thus those who lived with the Logos are Christians even if they were counted godless'. And Augustine said that 'the reality, which we now call the Christian religion, was present among the early people, and up to the time of the coming of Christ in the flesh was never absent from the beginning of the human race'.

That Christ is present in Hinduism does not mean, however, that he is fully seen there. Indeed he is *The Unknown Christ*. Christ has still to be recognized by Hinduism. This is not to say that all of Hinduism should be destroyed, or that such should be the aim of the Christian mission: it is there to serve, and the service is transformation rather than destruction. But Hinduism is not static, nor is any other religion. It has changed many times in its long history, and its diversity is rich and bewildering. Many reforms are needed, they are recognized by Hindus, and they have been the aim of the many Samajes of modern times. The Christian churches in India, despite some successes, are a tiny minority, not more than two or three per cent of the population. But the indirect influence of Christian thought, the Unknown Christ making himself known, has been incalculable. The changes that are taking place should prepare the way for the recognition of Christ not only as hidden but as revealed and incarnate. Conversion is not necessarily changing into another religion, but it is changing into a new life, a life in Christ which is a new creation.

Death and resurrection are required of Hinduism, if it is to leave what is wrong or misleading and find the truth in Christ. But similar death and resurrection are required of Christianity, if it is to enter into true dialogue with the religions of Asia and Africa. The Christian task is not to destroy those religions but to reveal Christ, and make him the Known Christ. Hindus claim that their religion is eternal, *sanātana dharma*, and it is so as far as Christ is seen there, but Hinduism needs to find its fulness at the place where God is revealed in love and suffering and triumph.

THE INCARNATION

It is necessary to say that Christ is in all religions, because Christ shows the very nature of God as love, taking the initiative and seeking all men. 'God commends his love towards us, in that while we were yet sinners Christ died for us.' Christ died for Hindus, but appreciation of his Crucifixion has not yet come to them, if they have not realized the true meaning of his Incarnation.

To speak of the Unknown Christ is generous, but it must not be allowed to hide the meaning, importance and centrality of the real

Incarnation. The Avatars of Hinduism lead up to Christ and they are valuable preparations for him. More easily than Jews or Greeks, Indians can understand the coming of God in human form. Yet this very ease has great dangers, and the casual way in which many modern Hindus consider Christ as just another Avatar thereby deprives him of significance and challenge. The Avatars, after all, were a flashing kaleidoscope of theophanies, coming and going in the endless cycles of ages. They were never really men.

The Hebrew background has lasting importance, and even the Indian Church will never be able to dispense with the Old Testament, however much it uses other scriptures as well. For with the Hebrew insistence on the importance of the material world for spiritual things, its firm materialism, Jesus of Nazareth is fully a man, a human individual, dated and located. It is Jesus as a man that Hindus need to understand, and it does not matter if he is only a man to them at first. That was how he appeared to the first disciples, and it is better to follow Christ in his humanity than have a 'spiritual' faith in an ethereal being who is more foreign than the Avatars. Martin Luther, who is said to have taken the humanity of Jesus more seriously than any theologian since Irenaeus in the second century, declared that one must know Jesus as a man before one can confess him as Lord.

The doctrine of the Incarnation does not fit easily into all forms of Hinduism, and it has been seen how the fully monistic philosophers were uneasy with the Avatar portions of the Gītā. In modern times monism has become such a popular presentation of Hinduism, against the practice of the vast majority of Hindus, that one hardly dare say 'boo' to a monistic goose. Yet if the pantheists have the right to propagate their monotony, others may claim the freedom to set forth another teaching.

The doctrine of the Incarnation can be shown as the fulfilment of what God had already revealed to Hindus. It accords with personal theism, such as that which the Śvetāśvatara Upanishad proclaimed; 'the supreme Lord is intelligent, the possessor of qualities'. This Lord was shown as both transcendent and immanent, bestowing grace, distinguishable from his devotee, and inspiring loving devotion. Śaiva Siddhānta and the Īśvaragītā reinforce this theism, with personal appearances of the Lord and divine messages from him. The Bhagavad-Gītā transfers devotion to Krishna-Vishnu, who is higher than the neuter Brahman and appears in visible form on earth in Avatars. The stories of Rāma and the songs of the medieval mystics continue this theme with elaborations, some of which are more felicitous than others.

Against this theistic context the Incarnation in Jesus both has a preparation and appears as quite new. Clearly the links of the Incarnation with Buddhism and Islam are different, and they need to be worked out appropriately to each religion and culture. For Hinduism, the humanity of Jesus is especially important, though it should be distinguished from historicity. The historical sense has been weak in Hindu tradition, and to insist first of all upon a Christian understanding of history is to invite disappointment and and misunderstanding. True appreciation of history can begin with the man Christ Jesus, the Word 'made flesh'.

At the beginning of this book reference was made to Aldous Huxley's assertion that the doctrine of the incarnation of God is found in most religions. It should have been apparent long since that this is not so. The Sūfī mystics almost to a man rejected Incarnation and many wandered in the deserts of monism. Mahāyāna Buddhism knew nothing of the idea of God, though it found substitutes in Buddhas and Bodhisattvas. The closest approach to Christian belief is in the Avatar faith of Hinduism though it had little historicity and no real suffering. Huxley's further claim that because Christianity held to only one Avatar it had bloodier crusades than any other religion is a *non sequitur*. Steven Runciman, in his great history of the Crusades, has shown that the notion of a holy war was repugnant to most Christians for the first thousand years, and it still is to many Christians in the eastern and other churches. On the contrary, the eastern churches had suffered from the holy wars of Islam. Hinduism has not organized crusades, but the class oppressiveness of the Brahmins has been notorious, not to mention recurrent communal battles. Certainly Christianity believes in the uniqueness of Christ, but it has become clear again and again that faith in the uniqueness of the central object of devotion is a characteristic of most religions.

This book does not claim to present a complete and new interpretation of Christology, which would be far too great a task for one man. But if these are days when 'soundings' should be taken to prepare new charts for faith in the light of our wider knowledge, then it is hoped that it will contribute something towards that end. Christian doctrine is now placed in the context of all the religions of the world and the points of contact, comparison, resemblance and difference must be taken into consideration. This may help to show in what ways Christ completes previous revelations of God and how he opens a new and living way.

Jesus reveals God in Incarnation, God in action, God in the Perfect Man. He shows the very nature of God, in love and suffering. The Incarnation does not appear in all forms, but only in those which are consistent with humanity, life and death. Christ 'emptied himself' and lived and died on earth, and yet at the same time he is the eternal Word 'in whom all things consist'. As the Unknown Christ he inspired many forms in the world religions, and as the Known Christ he was incarnate.

The Word which was with God, whose life was the light of men, the true light lighting every man, who was in the world, came unto his own, became flesh and dwelt among us. Divine law and right (*dharma*) were manifested in Avatars and Buddhas, divine love and suffering were incarnate in Jesus Christ.

Bibliography of Texts

(a) HINDU

Griffith, R. T. H. (trs.), *The Rig Veda* (1897)
— *The Hymns of the Sāmaveda* (1893)
Macdonell, A. A. (texts and trs.), *A Vedic Reader* (1917)
Edgerton, F. (trs.), *The Beginnings of Indian Philosophy* (1965)
Zaehner, R. C. (trs.), *Hindu Scriptures* (1965)
Keith, A. B. (trs.), *The Veda of the Black Yajus School, Taittirīya Samhitā* (1914)
Eggeling, J. (trs.), *The Śatapatha Brāhmana* (1882–1900)
Bühler, G. (trs.), *The Laws of Manu* (1886)
Hume, R. E. (trs.), *The Thirteen Principal Upanishads* (1921)
Radhakrishnan, S. (text and trs.), *The Principal Upanishads* (1953)
Mahābhārata (text, Poona edn., 1927f.)
Roy, P. C. (trs.), *The Mahābhārata* (2nd edn. 1919–1935)
Bhagavad-Gītā (text and trs.), W. D. P. Hill (1928), F. Edgerton (1944), S. Radhakrishnan (1948), R. C. Zaehner (1969)
Thibaut, G. (trs.), *The Vedānta-sūtras, with the commentary by Śankarācārya* (1904)
Śāstri, A. M. (trs.), *The Bhagavad-Gītā with the commentary of Sri Śankarachāryā* (1897)
Thibaut, G. (trs.), *The Vedānta-sūtras, with the commentary of Rāmānuja* (1904)
Govindacharya, A. (trs.), *Śrī Bhagavad Gītā with Śrī Rāmānujā-chārya's Viśishtādvaita Commentary* (1898)
Buitenen, J. A. B. van (trs.), *Rāmānuja on the Bhagavadgītā* (1953)
Rao, S. S. (trs.), *Vedanta Sutras with the Commentary of Sri Madhwacharya* (2nd edn. 1936)

Bibliography of Texts

— *Bhagavad Gita translated according to Sri Madhwacharya's Bhashyas*
(1906)

Böhtlingk, O. (trs.), *Pānini's Grammatik* (1964)

Wilson, H. H. (trs.), *The Vishnu Purāna* (1870)

Burnouf, E. (text and trs.), *Bhāgavata Purāna* (1898)

Raghavan, V. (texts and trs.), *Srimad Bhagavata* (no date)

Shastri, H. P. (trs.), *The Ramayana of Valmiki* (1952)

Renou, L. (trs.), *Le Raghuvamça* (1928)

Hill, W. D. P. (trs.), *The Holy Lake of the Acts of Rāma* (1952)

Allchin, F. R. (trs.), *Tulsī Dās Kavitāvalī* (1964)

— *Tulsī Dās The Petition to Rām* (1966)

Keyt, G. (trs.), *Gīta Govinda* (1947)

Bhattacharya, D. (trs.), *Love Songs of Vidyāpati* (1963)

— *Love Songs of Chandidās* (1967)

Pradhān, V. G. (trs.), *Jnāneshvari* (1967)

Hooper, J. S. M. (trs.), *Hymns of the Ālvārs* (1929)

Behari, B. (trs.), *Bhakta Mira* (1961)

Ray, N. K. (trs.), *Sri Sri Chaitanya Charitamrita* (2nd edn. 1959)

Dumont, P. E. (text and trs.), *L'Īśvaragītā* (1933)

Matthews, G. (trs.), *Śiva-ñāna-bōdham* (1948)

Kingsbury, F. and Philips, G. E. (trs.), *Hymns of the Tamil Śaivite Saints* (1921)

Thompson, E. J. and Spencer, A. M. (trs.), *Bengali Religious Lyrics, Śākta* (1923)

Macnicol, N. (trs.), *Psalms of Marāṭhā Saints* (1919)

Keay, F. E., *Kabīr and his Followers* (1931)

Orr, W. G., *A Sixteenth-century Indian Mystic* (Dādū). (1947)

Singh, T. and others (trs.), *Selections from the Sacred Writings of the Sikhs* (1960)

Monier-Williams, M., *A Sanskrit-English Dictionary* (1899)

Bloomfield, M., *A Vedic Concordance* (1906)

Jacob, G. A., *A Concordance to the Principal Upanishads and Bhagavadgītā* (1891)

(b) BUDDHIST

Horner, I. B. (trs.), *The Book of the Discipline* (Vinaya Piṭaka), 1952

Rhys Davids, T. W. (trs.), *The Dialogues of the Buddha* (Dīgha Nikāya), 1899–1921

Horner, I. B. (trs.), *Middle Length Sayings* (Majjhima Nikāya) 1959

Woodward, F. L. and Hare, E. M. (trs.), *Gradual Sayings* (Aṅguttara Nikāya), 1936

Rhys Davids, C. A. F. and Woodward, F. L. (trs.), *Kindred Sayings* (Samyutta Nikāya), 1930

Radhakrishnan, S. (trs.), *The Dhammapada* (1950)

Hare, E. M., (trs.), *Woven Cadences* (Sutta Nipāta), 1945

Rhys Davids, C. A. F. (trs.), *Psalms of the Brethren* (Theragāthā) 1913

Aung, S. Z. and Rhys Davids, C. A. F. (trs.), *A Compendium of Philosophy* (Abhidhammattha Saṇgaha), 1910

— *Points of Controversy* (Kathā Vatthu), 1915

Law, B. C. (trs.), *Buddhavaṁsa* (1938)

Cowell, E. B. (trs.), *The Jātaka* (1895)

Horner, I. B. (trs.), *Milinda's Questions* (1964)

Jones, J. J. (trs.), *The Mahāvastu* (1949)

Mitra, R. (trs.), *Lalitavistara* (1881)

Kern, H. (trs.), *The Saddharma-Pundarīka* (1909)

Suzuki, D. T. (trs.), *The Lankavatara Sutra* (1932)

Müller, F. M. (trs.), *Sukhāvati-vyūha* (1894)

Barnett, L. D. (trs.), *The Path of Light* (Bodhi-charyāvatāra), 1909

Pe Maung Tin (trs.), *The Expositor* (Buddhaghosa's Atthasālinī), 1920

Conze, E. (trs.), *Buddhist Scriptures* (1959)

(c) JAIN

Jacobi, H. (trs.), *The Acārānga Sūtra* (1884)

— *The Kalpa Sūtra* (1884)

Ghoshal, S. C. (trs.), *Darva-samagaha* (1917)

Johnson, H. M. (trs.), *Trishastiśalākā-purushacaritra* (1931)

(d) ISLAMIC

Bell, R. (trs.), *The Qur'ān* (1937)

Arberry, A. J. (trs.), *The Koran Interpreted* (1955)

Bibliography of Texts

Guillaume, A. (trs.), *The Life of Muhammad* (1955)

Abdel-Kader, A. H., *The Life, Personality and Writings of al-Junayd* (1962)

Massignon, L. (trs.), *Le Dīwān d'al-Hallāj* (1955)

Chidiac, R. (trs.), *Réfutation excellente de la Divinité de Jésus Christ d'après les Evangiles* (1939)

Nicholson, R. A. (trs.), *The Mathnawī of Jalālu'ddīn Rūmī* (1960)

— *Rūmī, Poet and Mystic* (1950)

Watt, W. M. (trs.), *The Faith and Practice of al-Ghazālī*, 1953

Bibliography of Modern Writings

Abegg, E., *Der Messiasglaube in Indien und Iran*, 1928
Affifi, E. A., *The Mystical Philosophy of Muḥyid dīn ibnul 'Arabī*, 1939
Akhilananda, S., *Hindu View of Christ*, 1949
Andrews, C. F., *Mahatma Gandhi: his own story*, 1930
Arafat, W. N., 'The Elegies on the Prophet in their Historical Perspective', *Journal of the Royal Asiatic Society*, 1967
Archer, W. G., *The Loves of Krishna in Indian Painting and Poetry*, 1957
Aulén, G., *Christus Victor*, E.T. 1931
Baillie, D. M., *God was in Christ*, 1961 edn.
Barrett, C. K., *The Gospel according to St John*, 1956
Basham, A. L., *History and Doctrines of the Ājīvikas*, 1951
— *The Wonder that was India*, 1954
Benz, E., 'Indische Einflüsse auf die frühchristliche Theologie', in *Abhandlungen der Akademie der Wissenschaften*, 1951
Bhave, V., *Talks on the Gita*, 1960
Brunner, E., *The Mediator*, E.T. 1934
Chakkarai, V., *Jesus the Avatār*, 1930
Conze, E., *Buddhism, its Essence and Development*, 1951
— 'Recent Progress in Buddhist Studies', *The Middle Way*, 1959
— *Buddhist Thought in India*, 1962
Cragg, K., *The Call of the Minaret*, 1956
Daniélou, A., *Hindu Polytheism*, E.T. 1964
Dasgupta, S., *A History of Indian Philosophy*, 5 vols., 1922–55
Dayal, H., *The Bodhisattva Doctrine in Buddhist Sanskrit Literature*, 1932
Devanandan, P. D., *The Concept of Māyā*, 1954

Dewick, E. C., *The Christian Attitude to Other Religions*, 1953

Dibelius, M., *From Tradition to Gospel*, E.T. 1934

Dowson, J., *A Classical Dictionary of Hindu Mythology and Religion*, 8th edn., 1953

Farmer, H. H., *Revelation and Religion*, 1954

Farquhar, J. N., *Permanent Lessons of the Gītā*, 1912

— *The Crown of Hinduism*, 1913

— *Modern Religious Movements in India*, 1915

Foucher, A., *La Vie du Bouddha*, 1949; E.T. abridged, 1963

— *Les Vies antérieures du Bouddha*, 1955

Fuller, R. H., *The Foundations of New Testament Christology*, 1965

Garbe, R., *India and Christendom*, E.T. 1959 edn.

Gardet, L., *L'Islam*, 1967

Ghose, Aurobindo, *The Life Divine*, 1955 edn.

— *Essays on the Gita*, 1959 edn.

Glasenapp, H. von, *Der Hinduismus*, 1922

— *Der Jainismus*, 1925

— *Immortality and Salvation in Indian Religions*, E.T. 1963

Gonda, J., *Aspects of Early Viṣṇuism*, 1954

— *Die Religionen Indiens*, i, 1960; ii, 1963

Griffiths, Bede, *Christian Ashram*, 1966

Guérinot, A., *La religion Djaïna*, 1926

Gupta, M. N., *The Gospel of Śrī Rāmakrishna*, 1907

Hussein, M. K., *City of Wrong*, E.T. 1959

Huxley, A., *The Perennial Philosophy*, 1946

Isherwood, C., *Ramakrishna and his Disciples*, 1965

Jaini, J., *Outlines of Jainism*, 1940

James, M. R., *The Apocryphal New Testament*, 1924

Kennedy, M. T., *The Chaitanya Movement*, 1925

King, W. L., *Buddhism and Christianity*, 1963

Knox, J., *The Humanity and Divinity of Christ*, 1967

Koestler, A., *The Lotus and the Robot*, 1960

Lamotte, E., *Histoire du Bouddhisme Indien*, 1958

Landau, R., *The Philosophy of Ibn 'Arabī*, 1959

Lang, D. M., *The Wisdom of Balahvar*, 1957

Ling, T. O., *Buddhism and the Mythology of Evil*, 1962

Lubac, H. de, *Aspects of Buddhism*, E.T. 1953

Macauliffe, M. A., *The Sikh Religion*, 1909

McLeod, W. H., *Gurū Nānak and the Sikh Religion*, 1968

Massignon, *Essai sur les Origines du Lexique technique de la Mystique Musulmane*, 1954

Moule, C. F. D., *The Phenomenon of the New Testament*, 1967

Müller, F. M., *Rāmakrishna his Life and Sayings*, 1951 edn.

Murty, K. S., *Revelation and Reason in Advaita Vedānta*, 1959

Nasr, S. H., *Ideals and Realities of Islam*, 1966

— 'Islam and the Encounter of Religions', *The Islamic Quarterly*, 1966

Neuner, J., ed., *Christian Revelation and World Religions*, 1967

Nicholson, R. A., *The Idea of Personality in Sūfism*, 1923

Nikhilananda, S., *Holy Mother*, 1963

Otto, R., *India's Religion of Grace and Christianity compared and contrasted*, E.T. 1930

— *The Original Gītā*, E.T. 1939

Padwick, C. E., *Muslim Devotions*, 1961

Panikkar, R., *The Unknown Christ of Hinduism*, 1964

Parrinder, E. G., *Upanishads, Gītā and Bible*, 1962

— 'Śrī Aurobindo on Incarnation and the Love of God', *Numen*, 1964

— *Jesus in the Qur'ān*, 1965

— *The Significance of the Bhagavad-Gītā for Christian Theology*, 1968

Pittenger, W. N., ed., *Christ for us Today*, 1968

Radhakrishnan, S., *An Idealist View of Life*, 1929

— *Indian Philosophy*, 1940 edn.

— *Eastern Religions and Western Thought*, 1949

Schimmel, A., 'The Veneration of the Prophet Muḥammad, as reflected in Sindhi poetry', in *The Saviour God*, 1963

Schubring, W ., *The Doctrine of the Jainas*, E.T. 1962

Sharpe, E. J., *Not to Destroy but to Fulfil*, 1965

Shehadi, F., *Ghazālī's Unique Unknowable God*, 1964

Smart, N., *Reasons and Faiths*, 1958

— *A Dialogue of Religions*, 1960

Smith, D. H., *Chinese Religions*, 1968

Smith, W. C., *Islam in Modern History*, 1957

— *The Meaning and End of Religion*, 1964 edn.

— *Questions of Religious Truth*, 1967

Sparks, I. A., 'Buddha and Christ; a Functional Analysis', in *Numen*, 1966

Stevenson, S., *The Heart of Jainism*, 1915

Straelen, H. van, *Our Attitude towards other Religions*, 1965

Streeter, B. H., *The Buddha and the Christ*, 1932

Suzuki, D. T., *Mysticism, Christian and Buddhist*, 1957

Tagore, R., *Gitanjali*, 1931 edn.

Tagore, S. and Devi, I, trs., *The Autobiography of Maharshi Devendranath Tagore*, 1915

Teilhard de Chardin, P., *The Phenomenon of Man*, E.T. 1959

Tejasananda, S., *The Ramakrishna Movement*, 1956

Thapar, R., *Aśoka and the Decline of the Mauryas*, 1961

Thomas, E. J., *The Life of Buddha*, 1949 edn.

— *The History of Buddhist Thought*, 1951 edn.

Tillich, P., *Systematic Theology*, 1953 edn.

Watt, W. M., *Muhammad Prophet and Statesman*, 1961

— *Islamic Philosophy and Theology*, 1962

Wensinck, A. J., *The Muslim Creed*, 1965 edn.

Wilms, F. E., *Al-Ghazālīs Schrift wider die Gottheit Jesu*, 1966

Zacharias, Fr., *Avatars and Incarnation; Dreams and Reality*, 1942

Zaehner, R. C., *Mysticism Sacred and Profane*, 1957

— *At Sundry Times*, 1958

— *Hindu and Muslim Mysticism*, 1960

— *The Convergent Spirit*, 1963

Zimmer, H., *Philosophies of India*, 1951

— *Myths and Symbols in Indian Art and Civilization*, 1946

Gibb, H. A. R. and Kramers, J. H., *Shorter Encyclopaedia of Islam*, 1953 edn.

Lewis, B., Pellat, C., and Schacht, J., *Encyclopaedia of Islam*, New Edition, 1960ff.

Index

Index

Index

Index

Index

Incarnation, 14, 103, 120, 221f., 223f., 278; of Krishna, 165, 224; of Moses, 224, 256; of Muhammad, 204, 224
Unknown Christ, 250, 275ff., 279
Upanishads, 17f., 42f., 99, 101, 234, 277
Ur-Gītā, 32, 119

Vallabha, 82, 105
Vālmīki, 63, 66, 123
Varāha Purāna, 72n.
Varuna, 15f.
Vasubandhu, 133
Vasudeva, father of Krishna, 21, 29, 51, 76, 121, 126, 186f.
Vāsudeva, name of Krishna, 28f., 34, 38f., 52, 55, 132f., 187f.
Vatican Council, Second, 270f.
Vāyu, Avatar of, 59
Vedānta, 17, 50f., 54f., 99, 233f.
Vedntāa Sūtra, 50ff., 280
Vedas, 15f.
vibhūti, manifestation, 39
Vidyāpati, 79, 82, 101
Vinaya Pitaka, 131, 134, 137
Vinaya-patrikā, 69
Vinoba Bhave, 105
Vipassi, former Buddha, 152ff., 163
virginal birth, 134, 168, 183, 211, 242, 160
Vishnu, god of Avatars, 16, 19, 21, 23ff., 87f.; in animal myths, 23ff.; in Buddhism, 133, 171; rarely named in Gītā, 32f.; in Jainism, 187f.;

Krishna as Avatar, 32ff.; Rāma as Avatar, ch. 5; his three strides, 16, 25, 80
Vishnu Purāna, 23, 72f., 81, 121, 182
Vishnu-swāmīs, 82
Vivekānanda, 107f., 230f., 233f.
Vrindāban, *see* Brindāban
vyūha, manifestation, 55, 60, 86, 179

Wahhābī, 254
Watt, W. M., 193n., 287
Weber, A., 117n.
Wensinck, A. J., 287
Wilms, F. E., 193n., 287
Wilson, H. H., 76n., 281
Woodward, F. L., 247n., 282
Word, *see* Logos

Yakkhas, 131
Yaśodā, Krishna's foster-mother, 73, 81, 184
Yaśodharā, Buddha's wife, 171, 184
Yoga, 18, 35f., 55, 62, 113
Yoga Sūtra, 53
yoni, 91
Yudhishthira, 21, 23, 124
yuga, age, 22, 38, 56

Zacharias, Fr., 287
Zaehner, R. C., 35n., 52f., 62n., 126n., 199n., 266, 287
Zen, 175
Zimmer, H., 20, 24n., 182, 183f., 223, 225f., 287
Zoroastrianism, 26, 161n., 256